THE MINNESOTA RESPONSE

Tom

Best wishes

George

About Foreword Writer

Michael V. Martin, Chancellor of Louisiana State University, previously was president of New Mexico State University, vice president for agriculture and natural resources at the University of Florida, and dean of the College of Agricultural, Food and Environmental Sciences at the University of Minnesota. In 2007, he received the Justin Smith Morrill Memorial Award, named after the author of the federal act establishing land-grant universities.

About the Authors

George Morse is a professor emeritus of Applied Economics, University of Minnesota. From 2002 to 2007, Dr. Morse served as associate dean and director, University of Minnesota Extension. He provided statewide leadership for Extension program staff and for some of the teams that restructured Minnesota Extension in 2004.

Jeanne Markell is the Ralph H. Tabor Fellow with the National Association of Counties in Washington, D.C., during 2008 and 2009. Previously, she was associate dean and director for external relations for University of Minnesota Extension and part of the team that developed the new Minnesota model.

Phil O'Brien is a financial analyst with the University of Iowa. From 2000 to 2005, he was director for finance for the University of Minnesota Extension. He holds an M.A. in economics (Univ. of Illinois at Chicago) and an M.A. in public policy analysis (University of Wisconsin-Madison).

Adeel Ahmed is a regional extension educator in community economics, University of Minnesota Extension, and is located in St. Cloud, Minnesota. He earned an M.S. from the Hubert H. Humphrey Institute for Public Policy at the University of Minnesota.

Thomas K. Klein is associate director of the Minnesota Council on Economic Education. Earlier, he worked for University of Minnesota Extension for nine years as chief financial officer, director of the resource development unit, and director of marketing. He earned an MBA from the University of Minnesota.

Larry Coyle is an Extension Professor and distance education specialist with University of Minnesota Extension. As CIO of Minnesota Extension from 2004-2006, he led the Minnesota's implementation of the regional center technology plan. He holds an M.S. degree in Instructional Systems Technology from Indiana University.

The Minnesota Response:
Cooperative Extension's Money and Mission Crisis

Edited by George W. Morse

Contributing Authors
George W. Morse
Jeanne E. Markell
Philip O'Brien
Adeel Ahmed
Thomas K. Klein
Larry D. Coyle

iUniverse Publisher
Bloomington

THE MINNESOTA RESPONSE

Cooperative Extension's Money and Mission Crisis

Copyright © 2009 by George W. Morse

iUniverse books may be ordered through booksellers or by contacting:

iUniverse

1663 Liberty Drive

Bloomington, IN 47403

www.iuniverse.com

1-800-Authors (1-800-288-4677)

ISBN: 978-1-4401-5541-3 (pbk)

ISBN: 978-1-4401-5542-0 (ebk)

ISBN: 978-1-4401-5543-7 (hc)

Printed in the United States of America

iUniverse rev. date: 9/23/2009

For Elizabeth Morse

Contents

List of Tables

Foreword

For nearly a century land-grant universities through the cooperative extension service, have delivered valuable, practical educational programs to citizens in their communities. Many, myself included, believe that the Extension Service, created under the Smith-Lever Act of 1914, is one of the most profound institutional innovations in the history of American higher education.

Throughout its history Extension in every state and every county, has connected the people to their university. County Extension offices were created to provide ready access to Extension faculty and educational materials.

While production agriculture has been a primary focus of Extension, many other segments of the economy and society have benefitted. Since its inception, Extension has continued to serve as a connection between all citizens and their land grant university. The point is that Extension has continually sought to transform itself to be both relevant and viable.

Today, in many states, the Extension Service is under severe economic pressure from decreases in all three funding sources, federal, state, and county. Certainly, Minnesota's Extension Service has not been spared pressures and challenges of tight budgets. Land-grant universities and state legislatures are struggling to reframe the breadth, depth, and access to Extension programs in light of challenging economic resolute.

At the same time, economics has begun to force change in extension. The relationship between extension and its clientele is changing.

At one time extension specialist and extension agents were the exclusive source of research based information and advice to farmers and rural citizens. Urban oriented programs were rare and minor. The private sector offered little in terms of research or advice to agriculture. Now programs, like master gardeners and nutrition education, serve urban citizens and many urban areas (including Minnesota's Twin Cities) encompass multiple counties.

Moreover, the extension needs of traditional agricultural clientele have changed as well. Private sector consulting services are now readily available and most successful farmers bring advanced education to their enterprises. Thus, the old county agent delivery system has become less relevant and less effective.

George Morse and colleagues report on a significant restructuring of Extension in Minnesota. While not without controversy, Minnesota acted boldly in positioning Extension to meet the programmatic needs of clientele while coping with new fiscal realities. The University of Minnesota's Extension Service has moved from a county-based delivery model to a combination of regional offices with regional and statewide field educators as well as county offices.

Any change of this magnitude is both controversial and complicated. Morse and company provide a well-articulated explanation of the rationale, process, and outcome of the Minnesota restructuring. This book is instructive and useful for at least three reasons. First, it demonstrates that an Extension Service can recreate itself to cut costs while protecting program quality.

Second, this book offers a useful road map to regionalization of Extension for other states that may wish to consider adopting the Minnesota model.

And finally, Morse and company offer a thoughtful assessment of outcomes and performance of the Minnesota model now that it has been functioning.

As land-grant universities seek to rebuild programs based on "best practices," this book contributes valuable, experienced-based insights into the choices available as Extension programs continue to evolve and respond. The Minnesota model as presented here should prove informative to many others.

Michael V. Martin

Chancellor

Louisiana State University

Preface

This book is about the Minnesota Extension 2004 response to the money and mission crisis that is facing many state Cooperative Extension Services. It is aimed primarily at people outside the state of Minnesota who are curious about whether this unique model is working. While many Minnesota Extension stakeholders will find the book interesting, some will find it old news.

We started this book because we received so many questions from colleagues and Extension stakeholders in other states about the changes in Minnesota. Initially, the questions expressed deep concern that Minnesota had gone off the deep end. More recently, people are asking if the Minnesota model is working and if it would work in their state. Even though the new regional/county model appears to be working well in Minnesota, we understand the circumstances in each state are different. You will have to decide whether this model, or parts of it, would be useful and feasible in your state.

The Cooperative Extension System (or simply Extension) has a serious money and mission crisis. Nationally, the purchasing power of Extension funding from its three major public sources has fallen rapidly in recent decades. At the same time, many argue that Extension needs to reach out to new underserved audiences, develop new programs for existing audiences, and improve the effectiveness and quality of many of its programs. In almost every state, Extension is being squeezed by increasing expectations and falling purchasing power.

Faced with lower budgets, some Extension administrators argue that new communication and political methods should be used to secure more resources. This strategy is risky because if more resources are not secured, then there is less programming. If there is less programming, the public value of Extension declines, resulting in less public support. This approach might start a downward spiral.

Minnesota Extension, when faced with a 13 percent budget cut in 2004, was unwilling to accept a diminished future and adopted regionalization and specialization in order to find new ways to do business or ways to "do more with less."

Part I of the book documents the nature of the mission and money crisis in Extension nationally and explores the claim by economists that specialization increases productivity. In other words, specialization allows you to do more with fewer resources rather than having to work harder.

Part II of the book describes the seven major policies that define the Minnesota model. Although we call it the Minnesota regional/ county model throughout the book, this is but one aspect of the complete set of policies. In addition to regionalization, there are changes in the funding of regional and county positions, the degree of focus and specialization, and the supervision of field staff by state specialists, the development of statewide programs and business plans, new scholarship and promotion expectations, and new roles for regional directors.

Part III of the book explores whether the Minnesota model is working. What is the evidence on how the Minnesota regional/ county model has changed program quality, scholarship by educators, access to Extension, and public support? Two sets of survey results plus other data are used to explore these questions.

Every state has different jargon and terminology for Extension positions. The terms, Regional Extension Educator, program specialists, Extension field specialists, and Extension Educator in (name of the area of expertise) have all been used to describe very similar positions. Minnesota Extension changed the titles for some positions and structures in 2008. In this book, the original terms are used since the survey of field staff used these. For those interested in the new terms, see Appendix B. There is also a glossary for those unfamiliar with Extension jargon.

All of the authors of this book are either former senior administrators who helped design the Minnesota model or current staff. In Part II, these roles were valuable in helping us detail the nature of the model and the original rationale for it. In Part III, these roles had the potential of introducing considerable bias. For two reasons, I believe we have avoided this bias. First, as a professor for

28 years, I am more interested in contributing to the social science literature than simply selling the model. In this spirit, we point out both positive results and our mistakes. Obviously, we would focus only on the positive if this were simply a public relations effort. Second, in Part III, rather than offer only anecdotal data, we also present some systematic evidence on the impacts. On the other hand, we point out issues where we lacked sufficient data to draw firm conclusions and we suggest several areas of additional research.

It is both too early and too late for this book to come out. As a researcher, I would have liked to do some additional research on the impacts before publishing the book. In addition, some of these impacts will only be known in another 4 or 5 years. Yet, others are upset that we did not have the book out a year or two ago. Partially to accommodate this group, I chose to publish the book through a print on demand publisher because the time line was much shorter than traditional academic publishing houses. There are some potential tradeoffs in status and professional reward in doing this. However, as a professor emeritus, I am not too worried about the next promotion and I trust that if the book is valuable, it will be widely used. If not, trees will be saved!

This book is only the beginning of the research needed to explore the long-term impacts and viability of the Minnesota model and alternative types of regionalization and specialization. Maybe, if Extension learns to "do more with less," the public will see such a good return on their investment that they will invest more in the Cooperative Extension Service.

George Morse
Professor Emeritus
Applied Economics
University of Minnesota

Acknowledgements

This book was a team project. Many more individuals contributed to the development of the Minnesota regional/county model. A brief description of their leadership roles are outlined in Appendix C: Leadership for the Minnesota Model.

First, I want to thank my five co-authors, Jeanne Markell, Phil O'Brien, Adeel Ahmed, Thomas Klein, and Larry Coyle, for their contributions to this book. Without their contributions and their encouragement, this book would not have been done. Likewise, I thank University of Minnesota Extension Deans Charles Casey (2001 to 2005) and Beverly Durgan (2005 to present) who supported my research on this book while I was the Associate Dean/Director for Minnesota Extension.

Many of my Minnesota colleagues provided valuable data and information which was used in the book, including: Neil Anderson, Thomas Bartholomay, Dale Blyth, Scott Chazdon, Gregory Cuomo, Michael Darger, Sherri Gahring, Tim Ha, Gary Hachfeld, Jo Anne Hardy, Joyce Hoelting, Laura Kalambokidis, Louise Letnes, Mary Marczak, Diana Martinson, Leslee Mason, Kent Olson, Patricia Olson, Renee Pardello, Ryan Pesch, Bruce Schwartau, Richard Senese, William Gaines Smith, Thomas Stinson, and David Werner.

Several colleagues read parts of the book or read the staff papers on which some chapters are based and provided valuable feedback and suggestions, including: Dale Blyth, Michael Boehlje, Scott Chazdon, Vernon Eidman, Beth Emshoff, Joyce Hoelting, Laura Kalambokidis, Mary Marczak, Diana Martinson, Leslee Mason, George McDowell, Kent Olson, Lee Raeth, Scott Reed, Richard Senese, Toni Smith, and Robert Stine. Mary Hoff, Susan Fey, and Elizabeth Morse assisted with copyediting.

Finally, I thank my wife, Elizabeth, for her encouragement and patience as I worked on this book.

While all of these suggestions were very helpful, I, and my co-authors, remain responsible for any remaining errors.

George W. Morse, Editor

PART I

THE CRISIS AND A SOLUTION

Chapter 1

Extension's Money and Mission Crisis

George Morse

Extension programs brace for cuts, decreased funds.

Kantele Franko
Associated Press
March 16, 2009

Creativity and imagination are needed to ...be an agent of change through extension education, where the needs will continue to grow faster than funds.

R. J. Hildreth and Walter Armbruster
1981

The Cooperative Extension System (Extension) has been one of the most successful outreach institutions in the United States for nearly 100 years (See Appendix A for a brief history). The success of the Extension in agriculture and rural areas has led to rising expectations for delivering programs on other issues and in urban areas. Yet,

Extension is feeling pressure from declines in participation as a percentage of the total population and from diminishing and uncertain budgets.

In 2009, the Associated Press reported many states are facing funding cuts. The recommended cuts in state funding range from 16 to 50 percent. There is a "money and mission crisis" in many states. While 2009 is an especially difficult year, the financial pressures have pursued Extension for years (Hildreth and Armbruster 1981).

This chapter reviews the history of the decline in participation, employment, and funding in Extension, which are fueling the current financial crisis. Next, the new demands being faced by Extension are discussed. The primary conclusion from this review is that Extension faces very difficult times ahead, being asked at every front to expand its reach and quality, but to do so on fewer resources -- to "do more with less." This book suggests it is possible for Extension to meet this challenge, countering critics who argue Extension may no longer be viable, or an institution whose time has come and gone.

The Money Crisis

Extension budgets, adjusted for inflation, have been declining for years. Base funding from the federal partner remained nearly constant in nominal terms and falling in real purchasing power from 1996 to 2004 (JTF, 2006). While federal funding has increased in nominal terms from 1996 to 2004, the increases have been from competitive grants and dedicated funds. More importantly, the total federal funds had 20 percent lower purchasing power in 2004 than in 1996. The long-term fiscal pressures on the federal government will make it difficult for the federal share to increase.

The Joint Task Force (2006) blames most of the depressed financial situation on the declining share of federal funding, called Smith-Lever funds. They write:

As a result of flat funding levels in the Smith-Lever program, reductions have occurred in more than 85 percent of state

4

programs. These reductions have resulted in significant program reorganizations in more than half the states and territories that responded to the survey. In many cases, these reorganizations have led to staff cuts and, in some states, to program elimination (JTF 2006).

The state share has been expanding, but the increasing volatility of state funds is putting more pressure on this source. Counties are likewise facing rising fiscal pressures and already provide relatively little funding for local positions in some states. In 2009, the financial problems in a number of states and counties might result in major cuts to Extension.

Extension's primary expenditures are for people: county agents, area agents, campus faculty, support staff, and administrators. The total number of full-time equivalents in Extension nationally grew until 1982 (Ahearn, Yee, and Bottom 2003; USDA 2008).

Since 1982, there has been an 18 percent loss in county agents and a 29 percent loss in area agents, both in full-time equivalents (FTEs). In contrast, there was a 44 percent gain in state specialist FTEs over this period. The number of administrators and supervisors has grown by 74 percent. While there are interesting questions about the changes in the mix of positions, these are left for future analysis. For now the two major observations are: (1) the number of FTEs is higher than one might expect with the declining or shrinking budgets, especially considering the salary changes over time, and (2) the number of educators is either flat or falling even as expectations are increasing.

While the funding cuts expected in 2009 are very severe in some states, financial cuts are not new to Extension. Over the last two decades, there have been continuing financial pressures and recurring crises for state Extension services. Yet, at the same time, many Extension stakeholders, both new and existing, expect more from Extension.

The Mission Crisis

In part, due to the past successes of Extension, there are rising expectations for Extension to improve the quality of its programs, to deal with new types of issues, and to reach new audiences. To meet these rising expectations, either Extension needs more staff or must become more efficient in using existing staff.

Higher Quality Programs

Public services have been exploring ways to increase the quality of their programs since the early 1990s, when the total quality management (TQM) started to be used in the public sector (Krone 1991; Hyde 1992; Poister and Henry 1994; Poister and Harris 1996). More recently, there have been many suggestions on ways for public agencies to become more efficient and entrepreneurial (Osborne and Gaebler 1992; Osborne and Hutchinson 2004; Collins 2005). In Extension, the growing concern for quality comes from the public's increased expectations of quality in the private sector being transferred to the public sector, greater competition from private sector outreach programs and the Internet, and more highly educated audiences.

Osborne and Gaebler (1992) remind us that the quality of public sector services has not always been highly regarded. They point to epithets: "It's close enough for government work" and "I'm from the government, and I'm here to help." Yet expectations are changing. Sensenbrenner (1991) illustrates this graphically with the following example:

> "People are making comparisons," says one quality expert. "They call American Express on Monday and get a credit card in the mail by the end of the week, but it takes six weeks to get a lousy driver's license renewed. You might not think the motor vehicle division competes with American Express, but it does in the mind of the customer." (Sensenbrenner 1991)

Extension leaders recognize the need for Extension to invest in improved quality, more diverse audiences, and greater participation. The Extension Committee on Organization and Policy has initiated major efforts on measuring and improving quality (Excellence in Extension Task Force 2006) and new programming initiatives and audiences (Cooperative Extension Section 2007). The Task Force developed a twenty-cell matrix to describe excellence, with two different conceptual frameworks. Based on this, the task force identified sixty-one criteria as measures of excellence (See Chapter 10).

These criteria are important and relevant measures of quality. However, many are nearly impossible to achieve in a highly decentralized system in which each county extension committee sets priorities, allowing few economies of scale. As evidence of this difficulty, note that as of June 2009 – four years after the report -- there were still no publicly available national data on even the primary criteria.

Hoag (2005) suggests a need for program teams to focus more tightly on public goods and their competitive advantages; to follow good business practices; to target audiences; to document results; and to build political support.

McGrath, Conway, and Johnson (2007) explored whether Collins's (2005) hedgehog principle fits Extension. The basic questions Collins asks are:

1. What are we passionate about? What are we called to do?
2. What can (or cannot) we be the very best at in the world?
3. How do we effectively attach our work to its economic drivers?

Since the focus here is the quality of programs, the answer to question two is most interesting. McGrath, Conway, and Johnson (2007) write:

> Extension is the best organization in the world at scholarly engagement and the application of knowledge in service to

society. Integration and application of knowledge is what we do. Scholarly engagement is how we get the job done.

Quality, like beauty, is often in the eye of the beholder. We each have our own opinions about quality service when we go to a restaurant, and tip the server accordingly. While Chapter 10 explores quality measurements in more detail, one proxy for quality is the degree of participation in programs. Increased participation in Extension programs is likely with heightened audience perception of value for their investment of time and funds. However, as detailed later in this chapter, it appears that participation in Extension programs as a percentage of the total population is falling rapidly.

High-quality programs require heavy front-end investments, as detailed in Chapters 7, 8, and 9. This includes audience identification, needs assessment, distance education, applied research, curriculum development and testing, materials development, and marketing. Rarely do individual county extension educators have the luxury of spending the time necessary to develop each of these components.

New Issues and Audiences

There is an active debate on whether Extension should shift the allocation of its staff away from agriculture to other areas. From 1977 to 2007, Extension returned its focus to agriculture and family development with heavy cuts in youth programs and community development. Agriculture and natural resources staff grew slightly in total FTEs and grew from 41 percent to 45 percent of all FTEs in 1992. The home economics and nutrition program grew from 22 percent to 26 percent of the total FTEs, probably due to the growth in the food stamp nutrition education program. Nearly three-quarters of the reductions came from 4-H youth work, with one-quarter from community resource development. Youth work declined from 29 percent to 23 percent while community resource development dropped from 8 percent to 6 percent (Ahearn, Yee, and Bottom 2003). In 2007, the percentage of FTEs in agriculture and natural resources had increased to 46 percent (Hewitt 2008).

McDowell (2004), Bull, Cote, Warner, and McKinnie (2004), and Hoag (2005) argue that Extension's survival depends on addressing new societal problems and reaching new audiences. Since Extension's initiation in 1914, the percentage of the population engaged in farming has fallen from 30 percent to under 2 percent. The U.S. population is also much more urbanized. To some, this suggests that Extension should devote much more of its staff time to urban problems and populations (Borich 2001, Kotval 2003). In addition, rapid growth in Hispanic and other ethnic groups suggests the need for programs that are culturally adapted to their needs (Alves 1993; Meyer 1999; Farner, S., Rhoads, Cutz, and Farner 2005).

Roling (1988), Seevers, Graham, Gamon, and Conklin (1997), Ison and Russell (2000), McDowell (2001), Wolf and Zilberman (2001), and Leeuwis (2004) all make suggestions on ways Extension can improve its quality and increase its access. While all of these ideas are excellent and many might be necessary in order for Extension to stay competitive with the many other private and public providers of outreach education, the suggested approaches add burdens to an already highly stretched Extension field staff. It is not possible for field staff to participate in all of these efforts in major ways as their numbers become smaller. Even given the near-missionary zeal of most Extension field staff members, it is only possible for them accomplish so much with the same delivery model and fewer staff members. Even in states that have not lost field staff recently, field staff members face tremendous time pressures. For these ideas to be tackled, field staff members need the economies of scale of statewide teams and individual specialization.

Extension Program Participation

Program participation is one proxy for program quality. Participation in programs is likely to increase when target audiences perceive high program quality and value relative to their investments.

Trends in Extension Participation

Trends in public participation for Extension are very difficult to evaluate for a variety of reasons. First, the federal funding agency, Cooperative Service Research, Education and Extension Service (CSREES), stopped requiring states to report participants by program area in 1990. The federal Office of Management and Budget recently asked CSREES to require this, but data are not yet available. Second, it is very difficult to make comparisons between programs, between states, or over time. Unlike credit hours and continuing education units, there are no standards to define extension participant units. For example, a master gardener must complete 50 hours of coursework and donate 50 hours of volunteer time the following year. How do you compare this with a one-hour program?

A second approach to measuring participation would be to ask members of the public if they have participated in Extension programs. In 1995, 85 percent of a national random sample of adults had heard of Extension either by name (45%) or by one of its key programs (Warner, Christenson, Dillman, and Salant 1996). In the 1995 sample, 24 percent more were aware of 4-H (69 percent) than the organizational name of Cooperative Extension Service (45 percent). This was the case for every area of work except community development. This suggests that many are likely to support individual programs but not the overall Extension program simply because the programs are not branded to Extension. Despite these high levels of awareness of Extension and its programs, the percentage of the U. S. population participating fell considerably. As shown in Table 1.1, the percentage of respondents who indicated someone in their family had used Extension at some point remained constant at 26 percent from 1982 to 1995. However, only 8 percent of the 1995 respondents or their family members used Extension in the previous year, compared to 12 percent for the 1982 respondents. Since the U.S. population grew from 231.6 million in 1982 to 262 million in 1995, this means actual participation fell from 27.8 million in 1982 to 21 million in 1995.

Unfortunately, use of Extension was lowest among several demographic groups that are growing - urban people, non-farmers, and minorities. In addition, it was low among young people, which might simply reflect age-specific interests or signal a trend for the future.

In reviewing the results in Table 1.1, keep in mind that 75% of the respondents were from urban areas, an accurate reflection of the national population, but possibly not an accurate reflection of Extension target audiences and users. The authors reported that, "every farm resident in the 1995 sample was aware of Extension" (Warner, Christenson, Dillman and Salant 1996).

Table 1.1:
Use of Extension Programs

	1982	1995
Ever Used	26%	26%
Past Year's Use	12%	8%

Source: Warner, Christenson, Dillman, and Salant. 1996.

Hypotheses on Declining Participation

There are many hypotheses offered for these declines. Some of the most common ones are:

1. Extension is one of the nation's best kept secrets;
2. The educational programs offered are no longer relevant to society;
3. The private value of Extension programs is not well understood; and
4. Extension field educators are no longer seen as credible sources of information and education.

Best-kept secret. It is common to hear Extension administrators claim the reason for these declines is that the public does not know about Extension. Frequently, it is worded, "Extension is one of the best kept secrets." Yet, between 85 and 87 percent of the total population recognized either the Extension name or the name of one Extension program (Warner, Christenson, Dillman, and Salant 1996). The "best kept secret" argument does not hold.

Extension programs no longer relevant. Another reason for the declining participation is that Extension's educational programs are no longer relevant to the needs of society. McDowell (2001) argues that Extension has too many educational resources in agriculture compared to other issue areas. The percentage of educational staff in agriculture and natural resources was 46 percent in 2007, a little higher than in 1977 (Ahearn, Yee, and Bottom 2003; Hewitt 2008). This focus comes when total employment related to agriculture has fallen from nearly 30 percent when Extension started in 1914 to 2 percent today.

Private value of extension programs not understood. People participate in programs when they see a positive net benefit for doing so (McDowell 1985). If there is little evidence that the programs achieve the desired outcomes and impacts, and if there is a lot of competition for people's time or many other opportunities for the same programs, participation would decline. Very few Extension programs have been carefully evaluated and peer reviewed.

Extension field educators no longer credible. In order for Extension to have either private or public value in agriculture (or any other field), its field staff must be seen as credible sources of high-quality information. Some have suggested that the declines in Extension are due to the inability of field educators to maintain their credibility because of local demands to cover a wide array of topics, the knowledge explosion, the increased educational levels of audiences, and greater access to the Internet and other resources. For example, research in the 1980s found that commercial farmers in Indiana, Illinois, and Iowa rarely consulted with county agents on major decisions (Ford and Babb 1989). This was followed by a number of other studies that found Extension was at the middle or lower in rankings as the most important source of information (Batte, Jones, and Schnitkey 1990; Batte, Schnitkey, and Jones 1990; Schnitkey, Batte, Jones, and Botomogno 1992; Ortmann, Patrick, Musser and Doster 1993; Patrick and Ullerich 1996; Gloy, Akridge, and Whipker 2000; Tucker and Napier 2002). Thompson and Gwynn (1989) report that a dean at a large north-central school said, "We found that regular county extension agents can no longer cope with the high technological nature and specialized nature of farm problems."

Much of this research is open to interpretation. Schnitkey, Batte, Jones, and Botomogno (1992) conclude, "Overall, Extension ranks highly as an information source." However, their data show that "CES received 11 % of the first, second, and third rankings for production decisions, compared to 6% for marketing and financial decisions." The authors contend this understates the influence of Extension because many private-sector consultants and media use Extension materials. However, the bulk of this written material comes from either campus faculty or specialized field staff and not generalized county agents.

Many chemical and/or seed companies and agricultural products supply cooperatives have increased their emphasis on outreach (Ortmann, Patrick, Musser and Doster 1993; Roseler, Chase, and McLaughlin 1994; King and Rollins 1995; Alston D. and Reding 1998).

Doing More with Less

Nearly every state extension service faces higher expectations for improved program quality with existing programs and audiences, and expectations to address new societal problems and new audiences. Yet at the same time, Extension faces increasingly tighter resources. This challenge of growing expectations and shrinking resources is Extension's "mission and money" crisis. It has even been suggested that Extension is on the brink of extinction (King, D. and Boehlje 2000) and that Extension is an idea whose time has come – and gone (McDowell 2004).

Naturally, one reaction to this dilemma is simply to set priorities tightly and cut back on the programs offered to fit the resources provided by the public. As one Extension Director said, "Don't tell them you can do more for less because our people are working as hard as they possibly can." Unfortunately, if there are no new resources forthcoming, this approach results in a shrinking Extension and hence lower public value. The lower public value results in lower public support and a continual downward spiral. A second approach is to mount an aggressive public awareness program of extension's public value and hope to see more resources. While there are new public relations tactics, there are many obstacles to the public relations approach, especially with large and growing federal deficits. A third possibility is the focus of this book: finding new ways of doing business that make it feasible to do more with less.

Across the country, Extension will need to do more with less. Public expectations for Extension are increasing, with pressures to serve more people, to reach new audiences, and to develop greater depth in the quality of their training. Yet, they will often need to do this with fewer resources, especially in the short run. States that do not learn to do more with less are likely to receive even fewer public resources and spiral downward even faster.

This book tells the story of how Minnesota tried a new approach to specialized regionalization in 2004 and what has happened since. Did Minnesota find a practical solution to Extension's mission and money crisis or did Minnesota make a mistake? What is the evidence so far? What is still unknown? The purpose of this book is not to sell the Minnesota model to other states. However, states that are exploring new regional options can use this book not only to evaluate the Minnesota experience but also to frame questions for other states with regional systems.

The larger goal of the book is to spark research on the consequences of alternative types of regionalization and specialization with Extension field staff. If this research is started now, it could be very helpful in the money and mission crises of the next decade.

Chapter 2

Regional Specialization: A Solution?

George Morse

Cooperative Extension should operate on
a multi-county or regional basis.

College of Agriculture Deans
Thompson and Gwynn 1989

As Extension resources decline, does true specialization of Extension educators result in greater access for the public, in closer campus faculty collaboration, in higher program quality, in greater public value and public support? Alternatively, does greater specialization and regionalization of Extension educators diminish some or all of these? In short, will specialization of Extension educators allow Extension to do more with less or will it weaken Extension?

Specialization (i.e., division of labor) was first suggested as a means of handling the "do more with less" dilemma by Adam Smith in 1776. After a brief introduction to the theory of specialization, major trends related to Extension field specialization are examined. The next two sections delve into a series of hypotheses on the advantages and disadvantages of field staff specialization. The focus is on specialization among the Extension staff located around the state rather than the campus faculty members (both tenure-track faculty members in academic departments and non-tenured faculty members), who are already very specialized.

Why Specialization?

Doing More with Less

In 1776, Adam Smith demonstrated that specialization (or division of labor) was the primary way of "doing more with less," or increasing productivity. The basic concept is that a group of individuals can produce more total output if they work as a team with each person working on the aspect of the work in which he or she has a comparative advantage. How does this apply to Extension?

Nearly all outreach programs require needs assessment, background research, curriculum development, marketing, teaching, and evaluation. One option would be for each individual field staff person to attempt to do all of these components by him or herself. With specialization, one or two members of a statewide team would tackle one component rather than each person being completely self-sufficient. Even if one member of a team can do all aspects of the program better, a team effort will still achieve more than a solo effort. The team advantage comes from the comparative advantage principle (Morse and Klein 2006).

Comparative advantage can best be understood by first considering the concept of absolute advantage. To illustrate this, consider a team of two people, Bob and Judy, who have two tasks to do and have to complete them in a way that meets the exact same quality standards. Judy can do both tasks in less time than Bob can, so she holds an absolute advantage over Bob. However, Bob has a comparative advantage in one of the two tasks.

A few numbers will help clarify the comparative advantage concept. Judy does Task 1 in 20 hours while Bob takes 80 hours to do exactly the same thing, or four times longer. On Task 2, Judy also is faster, doing it in 10 hours compared to 20 for Bob, or twice as fast. Hence, Judy has an absolute advantage over Bob on both Task 1 and Task 2. However, relatively speaking, Judy is even more efficient than Bob on Task 1 (which she does four times as fast) than she is on Task 2 (which she only does twice as fast). This leads us to say that Judy has a comparative advantage in Task 1 while Bob has a comparative advantage in Task 2.

Now consider comparative advantage between yourself and an assistant. Estimate the time it would take each of you to do each task and do it to the same standards. You will see that you often give the assistant tasks which you can do better but in which the assistant has a comparative advantage. This leaves more time for you to focus on the task on which you have a comparative advantage.

The above analysis is a static one and ignores the learning that occurs as people implement tasks. Naturally, as people specialize and repeat the same or related tasks in different settings, they learn subtle new skills in dealing with this task. This simply reinforces the existing comparative advantages. If Judy focuses on Task 1, she will become even more efficient, maybe learning to do Task 1 in only 15 hours. This increases her comparative advantage in Task 1 even though she maintains an absolute advantage in both tasks. Likewise, as Bob focuses on Task 2 he may learn to do it in 15 hours rather than 20 hours, increasing his comparative advantage in Task 2. As a team, Bob and Judy now have 10 additional hours, which they can use to celebrate their successes or to achieve even more.

The concept of comparative advantage explains the advantages of specialization. Specialization is related to regionalization in Extension simply because individuals who specialize in a given area of expertise need a larger market than one county. Furthermore, if educators are located in a county office, the public expects them to cover a much wider set of topics than is feasible for a specialized field educator.

The "Cut to Zero" Fallacy

In almost every presentation about specialization and its potential to do more with less, someone asks, "If we are successful in doing more for less, why won't funding agencies keep cutting us to get even more productivity? Why won't they eventually cut us to zero in the hopes of infinite productivity?"

The reasoning in the above question has the fallacy of assuming that the cuts are what generate the increased productivity. The cuts do not occur because productivity has improved. The cuts occur because there are inadequate public resources to fund all the desired public projects. While the cuts in resources do not enhance productivity, they force the organization to search for new ways of doing things that improves productivity. Economists would whip out some chalk and draw a production function for the old system and then another one for the new system to show that at every level of inputs, the new system generates greater outputs. While the author was itching to do this here, the example of production agriculture will be used.

Over the past 100 years, Extension has helped farmers find many new systems for producing food and fiber. Innovations such as tractors, hybrid seed, non-till, and many more have allowed farmers to produce greater output per unit of labor. That is, the farmers were doing more with less. Extension has been the leading agent of change in helping farmers to do this.

While there probably will be continual pressures to reduce public funding, those suggesting the "cut to zero" fallacy should be reminded that to increase productivity, new systems must be found. It is not possible to ask Extension educators to work harder because nearly all already are putting in extra time and effort. Theoretically, it is possible to invent an endless number of new organizational models or subsystems. However, each new system needs to be tested to see if it increases productivity. Simply assuming that it is always possible to cut resources and find a new model is folly.

Trends Affecting Specialization

Since Extension started in 1914, many changes have influenced how programs can be delivered. These include the following: (1) Extension audiences; (2) the roles of state specialists; (3) the number of private outreach efforts; and (4) communications and travel.

Changes in Extension Audiences

Extension audiences have changed in three important ways. First, educational achievement levels have increased; in some programs, an audience might have both Ph.D.s and high school dropouts in attendance. Second, the national economy has changed considerably, with on-farm employment being much lower today than when Extension started in 1914. Third, the country is become more ethnically and racially diverse.

Education levels. Educational levels have increased substantially since Extension started in 1914. In 1914, less than 10 percent of 17-year-olds graduated from high school (Miao and Haney 2004). In 1960, only 41 percent of high school students graduated compared to 85 percent in 2005; the college graduation rate changed over the same period from 7.7 percent of those over 25 years old to 28 percent (U.S. Census 2008). The educational level of farmers increased rapidly from 1964 to 2006 and now is almost the same as for the general population. In 1964, nearly two-thirds of farmers did not have high school degrees and only 4 percent of farmers had college degrees. In 2006, nearly two-thirds had completed high school and some college, and 25 percent had completed college (Ahearn and Parker 2009). As the educational levels of Extension participants increase, it has become increasingly difficult for generalist extension educators to keep current with the knowledge relevant to all their potential audiences.

National economy. Nearly 30 percent of the U.S. population worked on farms in 1900, compared to less than 2 percent in 2006. Further, many farm families now gain a major portion of their income from off-farm sources. Slightly more farm operators report their major occupation as an off-farm job than report farming or ranching. Farm spouses are more than twice as likely to report off-farm jobs as their major occupation (Ahearn and Parker 2009). As a result, over the past ten years, off-farm income has accounted for 80 percent of the total farm household income. Many farms could not continue in operation without a strong nonfarm rural economy. The nonfarm rural economy in now integrated into the global economy (Fernandez-Cornejo 2007). Due to these changes, even farm families are seeking programs on many non-agricultural topics.

Ethnic and racial diversity. One-third of U.S. residents have a "minority" heritage; Hispanics accounted for nearly half of U.S. population growth from July 1, 2004, to July 1, 2005 (U.S. Census 2004). The nation's population is diversifying so much that the concept of minority groups might eventually be outdated. Yet, Extension still struggles to serve many minority groups (Iverson 2008). When educators are hired at the county level, it is more difficult to attract minority educators to move into rural areas having little diversity.

Changes in Roles of State Specialists

The roles of state specialists have changed since the 1950s, creating gaps between the state specialists and the Extension Educators in the field. State specialists are usually faculty located on the university campus. Some of the state specialists are tenure-track faculty members who also have campus teaching and research responsibilities. These tenure-track state specialists are usually members of academic departments. Other state specialists have full-time Extension appointments and typically are in non-tenure track positions. Some of these non-tenure track specialists are members of academic departments and some of them work directly for Extension.

Rogers (1995) lists eight characteristics of Extension he felt lead to its success. Three of these related to the integration of applied research with extension and the close ties between campus faculty members and Extension field staff. However, since the early days of Extension, there have been major changes in these conditions. Rogers (1995) cited three elements, which are less true today than in earlier years:

1. A research system oriented to utilization, due to the rewards for researchers, research funding policies, and the personal ideologies of agricultural researchers

2. A spannable social distance across each interface between components in the technology transfer system, in which the social distance (heterophily) reflects levels of professionalism, formal education, technical expertise and specialization (e.g., when the heterophily gap between agricultural scientists and county extension agents became too great, state extension specialists were created as spanners or linkage agents)

3. Linkages among Extension's components, as provided by a shared conception of the total system, use of a common language by members of the system and a common sense of mission (Rogers 1995).

Each of these conditions has changed since originally identified by Rogers. While the changes have made both the county-based and county cluster based Extension delivery system less effective than it was when these were true, the changes also suggests that the system needs to adapt to the new realities.

Research system oriented to publishing. During the last 30 years, the competition between universities has increased and there is more pressure for faculty members to publish in peer-reviewed journals. As a result, departments reward faculty members for the number and quality of their peer reviewed publications rather than the research's utility to outreach education. While most faculty members are very interested in their research being used in practical, meaningful ways, they must "publish or perish." Faculty members with strong extension abilities who do not get tenure lose their jobs and Extension has to start over with a new faculty member or sometimes loses the position. Increasingly, faculty members in the land-grant colleges are competing directly with faculty members in Ivy League universities for grants to support their research. As a result, the research system is less and less oriented to utilization.

Loss of state specialist spanners. In addition to the publication and funding incentives, the knowledge explosion has increased incentives for campus faculty members to specialize. The amount of knowledge available for use in outreach education doubles frequently, with estimates ranging from every six months to each decade (Harding and Vining 1997). For example, the number of ecological journals has increased from just eight in 1920 to more than 80 in the 2000 (Bergstrom, C. and Bergstrom, T. 2006). This makes it very difficult for faculty members who are generalists to stay current. Hence state extension specialists, who were once hired as "spanners" between researchers, have themselves become more specialized. State specialists hired with a M.S. degree for this spanner role in the 1950s and 1960s started to retire in the 1980s. Academic departments responded by hiring Ph.D.s as state specialists. Since the new Ph.D. state specialists typically have joint extension, research, and teaching appointments, they tend to focus their area of specialization much more tightly than the M.S. state specialists they replaced. This has led to a greater gap between the state specialists and field extension educators. In some states, this resulted in two state Extension Services, one on campus, and one in the field. Since it is very unlikely that the academic departments can afford to hire M.S. level individuals as spanners and PhDs cannot achieve tenure without focusing, there is a need for some other position in Extension to play this role.

Linkages broken. With the loss of M.S. level state specialists, gaps developed between Extension field and campus operations. Campus faculty members increasingly looked to communities of interest and target audiences for feedback on important problems, while field staff looked to geographic communities, such as county extension committees, for feedback on needs. Campus faculty members tended to develop programs that were tightly integrated with their research programs and the expressed needs of a focused statewide audience while field staff members were highly reactive in their programming, delivering many different programs in a limited geographic area. Given the funding sources and incentives, both campus and field staff members were being logical but this resulted in broken linkages between the two groups.

Changes in Private-Sector Outreach

During the past 25 years, private agricultural input firms have started to bundle their commodities with outreach education. A number of researchers have found that farmers are starting to get more information from these private sources than from Extension (Ford and Babb 1989; Ortmann, Patrick, Musser and Doster 1993; Roseler, Chase and McLaughlin 1994; King and Rollins 1995; Alston and Reding 1998).

Changes in Communication and Travel

When Extension started in the early 1900s, travel was difficult. There was no interstate highway system and commuting was local. Telephones were not common in rural areas and long distance service was unreliable and expensive. The Internet and e-mail had not been invented. Changes in travel and communications have opened new avenues for program delivery.

Travel time. In some parts of the nation, counties were set up to be just large enough that a person could travel by horse and buggy from the outer boundaries to the county seat and return in one day. Naturally, with interstate highways and modern automobiles, the range that can be covered in a day is much greater than the original county. For example, in 2000 nearly 34 million people commuted to work in a county other than the one they live in, an increase of 85 percent over 1960. Nearly half of those entering the workforce from 1990 to 2000 left their own county to go to work, with the average time for all commutes being more than 25 minutes. These changes in transportation make it easier and cheaper for audiences (or Extension staff) to travel across county lines for programming -- just as they do for commuting to work, shopping, and entertainment. This makes specialization more feasible than it was in the early 1900s.

Communication. By 2007, 55 percent of all farmers had Internet access and 75 percent of farms with sales and government payments of $250,000 or more had internet access (National Agricultural Statistical Service 2007). Compare this to the lack of telephone service in many rural areas in 1914. This means that farmers have access to educational information generated by Extension programs in other states as well as by other public or private parties. For example, farmers are using the Internet to seek information much more frequently from non–U.S. Department of Agriculture (USDA) sources (56 percent) than from USDA sources (33 percent) (Mishra and Park 2005).

To attract users to either a Web site or a workshop, the quality of the information or educational program must improve. This typically means that those providing the information need to focus so they can invest heavily in the curriculum and materials, can practice the presentation with different groups, can learn from different groups, and can establish a reputation for excellence. While at first this shift in communication would seem to favor generalists who simply know how to use the Internet well, this is not the case. Using the Internet well requires a strong background in an academic discipline. Further, many teaching opportunities require immediate responses and do not permit time for doing research. These trends suggest that field staff need to specialize more.

Advantages of Extension Educator Specialization

How does the theory of specialization apply to Extension field staff? The focus on specialization for Extension field staff rather than on the campus faculty members is because the latter already are highly specialized. Throughout the book, our discussion will focus on the regionalization and specialization of Extension field staff doing educational programming.

Specialization of Extension field staff might increase productivity by:

1. allowing the recruitment and development of higher quality field staff and state specialists;
2. leading to greater collaboration between Extension educators in the field and campus state specialists;
3. leading to higher quality of programs with a given level of resources;
4. increasing the geographic access throughout the state; and
5. resulting in greater opportunities to secure resources.

Higher Quality Workforce

Greater field staff specialization is expected to make it easier to do the following:

1. recruit high quality people for Regional Extension Educator (REE) positions;
2. recruit and retain high quality people for campus state specialists positions;
3. develop incentives for field staff to build their human capital; and
4. provide opportunities for field staff to build their experience and to learn from their audiences.

Hiring high quality extension educators. If the field staff position requires generalist duties, it is difficult to hire specialized individuals. If the job not only requires a master's degree in a specific area of expertise but also involves work in this area, faculty members at other universities will circulate job announcements to students.

25

Faculty members seldom help in the recruitment for generalist's positions or ones falsely labeled as specialized.

Hiring high quality state specialists. If the Extension educators are more specialized and able to collaborate professionally with campus state specialists, this makes the state specialist positions more attractive. For decades, state specialist positions have been considered second-class in some academic departments. This stemmed from a history of M.S. level positions in these roles and from state specialists who worked closely with non-specialized educators.

Investments in human capital. Traditional county agents must respond to a wide range of local questions. If a county agent (or educator) is specialized in livestock and is the only agricultural agent in a county, he or she will be expected to answer questions on all aspects of agriculture, including residential horticulture. It is common for a local person to say something like, "Well, I know that livestock is your specialty and not insects on roses, but I'm sure you know more about them than I do." Alternatively, they may say, "I know your specialty is livestock, but could you check with someone at the university and get back to me on my problem with my roses?" When one-fourth of the county agent's salary comes from the county and these questions come from a county commissioner or someone who knows the commissioner, it is very difficult to respond with a version of "I don't do windows -- or rose bugs." This diversity of demand draws time away from a focused area and reduces the incentives of county agents to invest deeply in their human capital in any one area or specialty.

A further problem is that campus faculty members often lack incentives to develop in-depth training programs for generalist field staff. Often the field staff lack basic training in their area of expertise and have low rates of follow-up. Often finding training dates that do not conflict with other training sessions is difficult.

Learning from participants. Most teachers find that no matter how much they prepare, they seldom do a perfect job teaching a class or running an outreach workshop. The second workshop goes better than the first workshop, the third goes better than the second does, and so on. In Extension, audiences in different parts of the state have different questions and different work and life experiences. As they offer suggestions and ask new questions, Extension staff members learn more about their topic. Thus, a state specialist working in 40 communities on the same program learns more from the audiences than a county agent working with one or two counties.

The above theory suggests what to expect in terms of human capital because of specialization. However, is the theory correct for Extension? Initial results on this are reported in Chapter 5, 10 and 11.

Campus Faculty and Field Teamwork

Greater specialization among the field staff is expected to lead to greater collaboration with campus state specialists. In many states, there are two Extension Services: one on campus, delivered by state specialists; and one in the field, delivered by county agents. Sometimes, even in the same area of expertise, each is not fully aware of what the other is doing. When this dual Extension exists, the field staff portion often is not well grounded in the latest scholarship and research. Campus state specialists in states that lack specialized Extension educators often find it difficult to work with field staff. The non-specialized educators lack background knowledge on the issues and often do not have credibility with the leaders of the target audience.

In 1999, a panel of four Minnesota Extension state specialists describing their programs was asked: "What would happen to your program if the field staff simply did not exist? How much would it diminish what you are able to achieve in your program?" All four said that it would not make a big difference in their ability to deliver. As one specialist put it, "I would love to have some Extension educators with a specialty in our area of work. If we did, we could do so much more. Unfortunately, there are none that have this specialty, so we deliver our program directly."

The ideal system is campus faculty members providing the research backup and working on teams with field staff to develop practical outreach curriculum. This is more likely if field staff are specialized enough to provide some return on the time invested by faculty members. If not, campus faculty members work directly with the audiences. In the early 1990s, this is exactly what had happened in many areas of outreach in Minnesota, de facto creating two Extension Services.

Does this theory about specialization apply to Extension Educators? On the other hand, is this just dreaming? Results related to this are found primarily in Part III.

Higher Quality Programs

Because of greater field staff specialization, it will be more feasible to:

1. invest in curriculum development and evaluation; and
2. facilitate multidisciplinary or issue programming.

Quality program investments. Investments in curriculum development, in order to become the best in the business, take a lot of time (McGrath, Conway, and Johnson 2007). Outstanding programs adapt as needed to their audience's current concerns, use both evaluations to improve their programs, and draw on new skills from in-service training to enhance delivery. None of this is possible if the county agent is constantly required to shift focus and work with different issues or completely different types of groups.

High-quality program evaluation requires replication of programs in order to have sufficient observations to learn what really works. When educators work only in one or a few counties, it is difficult for them to secure the number of replications necessary to justify the time to design a high-quality evaluation tool. These economies of scale are also important in curriculum development.

Multidisciplinary or issue programming. Very seldom do problems of individuals or communities fall only into one discipline. They are not economic, sociological, or technical problems. Rather, they are problems (or issues, as many prefer to say) that have economic, sociological, and technical aspects. To adequately help individuals or communities deal with these issues or problems, the most effective educational programs incorporate the relevant disciplines. Laughlin and Schmidt (1995) suggest that regional offices would encourage collegial interaction. State specialists in different disciplines are often located in different buildings, whereas Regional Extension Educators in different areas of expertise office together. It has been suggested that as REEs from different areas of expertise and disciplines share ideas about their individual programs, they might find that they are dealing with different aspects of the same issue or with the same target audience and have some opportunities for collaboration. Potentially, this will spill over to partnerships between academic departments to work on these issues in both extension and research.

Greater Access to Extension Programming

As specialization of field staff increases, access to Extension programming increases because of the following:

1. REEs can build greater social capital and credibility with influence leaders in their community of interest or target audience;
2. market research can focus on the needs of specific communities of interest; and
3. statewide teams can deliver a tested curriculum in any part of the state.

Social capital. Social capital always has been important to Extension. In the early days of Extension, social capital was earned simply by the county agent living and working in the community. Even in smaller communities, this is not as feasible today as it was due to the vertical integration of many organizations. Now, field educators need to develop solid reputations and trust with leadership of specific communities of interest. While it is feasible to build social capital with the leadership and membership of targeted audiences over large regions, this only works if educators are specialized and focused.

Needs assessment. Needs assessment gives Extension users a high degree of control over the priorities for Extension programs, which is essential for strong outreach programs (Rogers 1995). Successful needs assessment is difficult because it must identify issues that are just emerging for which the public demand will be high in six to nine months. This forecast of future demand allows time to develop the curriculum, test teaching methods, prepare materials, find sponsors, market the program, arrange logistics, and design pre-and post evaluations. The better a field staff member knows the audience and its leaders, the more effective this needs assessment can be. A close relationship with the target audience allows both informal and formal needs assessment to be more effective. However, an in-depth relationship with a community of interest or target audience requires that the educator know people in this group throughout the state. This is not possible without some degree of specialization and focus.

Statewide teams. It is very difficult to establish statewide program teams in the traditional county agent model. First, agents must be responsive to local needs within their county, or least within their cluster of counties, before undertaking any statewide efforts. Sometimes both the county and the statewide efforts come together in a timely fashion, but often they do not. Second, a statewide team of seven agents, each from a different district, generally has seven different supervisors or district directors. This increases the transactions costs because choices have to be made about allocation of time. A team of seven educators often has eight "bosses"—one district director each and a program leader. To develop new initiatives or policy requires concurrence first among the eight bosses before the seven-team members have clear signals. Educators who are specialized and who report to the same supervisor have an easier time working on statewide teams that include both other field staff and campus specialists.

The results relevant to these hypothesized benefits are reported in Chapter 12 on impacts on access. Chapter 8 outlines in detail the nature of needs assessment in a regional/county system.

Greater Public Support for Extension

Greater specialization of field staff is hypothesized to lead to greater public support and funding. It is assumed the public funding for Extension is in exchange for public value to non-participants as well as the private value to participants. This means the greater the access to and participation in programming and the effectiveness of the programs in generating changes in private and public value, the greater the public funding and support for Extension. External relations efforts can be tremendously important in helping the public, particularly funders who are not directly involved, understand the public value.

Others have suggested that greater specialization will lead to sufficient improvements in the effectiveness of Extension programs that commodity groups and other interest groups will provide grants and contracts to Extension to fund Extension educators over multiple years. Some even expect that specialization might lead to these groups providing more funding for specialized educators than counties have provided in the past.

Yet, many Extension stakeholders have assumed that state and county funding is tied directly to having most extension educators located in county offices. They are concerned that a specialized regional system will break the ties to counties and result in rapidly diminishing county support. They fear that the diminished county support will signal lack of public interest in Extension to state legislators and result in diminishing state funding or even reductions in federal funding. Minnesota's experiences with each of these types of public support over the five years of the new system are reported in Chapter 13.

Disadvantages of Specialization

Naturally, there are potential disadvantages of increased field specialization. Just as evidence is needed about the hypothesized advantages, the hypothesized disadvantages need to be identified and empirically tested. The major questions and hypotheses about disadvantages of increased field staff specialization are as follows:

1. regional educators might be out of touch with the local values;
2. access to Extension programs might diminish;
3. flexibility to respond to new problems might be lost;
4. the work might be too focused and not cut across areas of expertise; and
5. travel and workload might increase.

Out of Touch with Local Values and Norms

Warner and Christenson (1984) point out that support for Extension depends on it being in touch with local values, and the direct participation of the public in planning and developing programs. They write, "Extension has a strong local identity. Agency personnel are local residents. They live and work in the county. And while Extension agents are respected for their technical expertise, they are also treated as friends and neighbors" (Warner and Christenson 1984).

A major fear of moving to a regional system is that there will be a loss of political support, especially during times of major statewide financial crisis. The fear is that, when political support is needed, REEs will not be able to secure it in the same way county agents could. The loss of local support is suggested as a disadvantage by Laughlin and Schmidt (1995). While they list potential pros and cons, no empirical evidence is included. Chapter 13 discusses the impacts of the specialized regional model on public support.

Diminished Access

Some stakeholders are concerned that regionalization might diminish access to people in counties without a regional center, especially smaller, more remote counties (Laughlin and Schmidt 1995). Will REEs, seeking to maximize the number of people they can reach and minimize their costs of delivery, write off a very small county? Alternatively, does access actually increase, as specialized regional educators are located around the state? Chapter 12 discusses the impacts on access of the specialized regional model.

Loss of Flexibility

Some educators are concerned that specialization and active participation in a statewide program team will reduce their individual flexibility to change their activities as easily as they could as independent county agents. The need for statewide teams to deliver programs suggests this is true. Once a team has agreed upon the nature of its program and program deliveries, each team member has a responsibility to implement her portion of the program. This reduces her individual flexibility. The premise, however, is that the teamwork will increase the team's capacity enough to allow a more rapid response to new problems. Chapter 5 reports on regional educators and campus faculty's perceptions of the changes in focus.

Lack of Multidisciplinary Input

Will specialization by field staff result in less multi-disciplinary programming, with each area of expertise working in its own silo? Will increased collaboration by teams within an area of expertise crowd out working across areas of expertise? Alternatively, will the areas of expertise collaborate on issues? Patrick Borich, Dean and Director of the Minnesota Extension Service in the 1980s, points this out in a 1988 Journal of Extension article.

The clientele we're hired to help also face changes that are so rapid and of such magnitude that they feel uncertain about the future. A potential danger in staff specialization is that clients are left on their own to integrate specialized advice. Specialists have traditionally been poor integrators. Extension has an obligation to approach problems holistically from the perspective of clients and find solutions that integrate multiple knowledge bases. This will require genuine interdisciplinary, cross-program team efforts, not individuals acting alone out of their own specialized knowledge base (Borich, P. 1988).

Chapter 5 has results related to this question.

Increased Travel and Workload

There is little doubt that travel time will be greater for REEs, since some have a much larger number of counties to cover and many cover the entire state. Will increased efficiencies from specialization balance this additional travel, or will the amount of time spent on the road increase so much that it diminishes the amount of programming time available or overloads employees?

Chapter 5 has results related to changes in travel and workload. Research on the balance between the advantages and disadvantages of regionalization and specialization is reported for Minnesota in Part III.

History of Extension Field Specialization

First, the calls for specialization by Extension leaders are reviewed. Then, the experience in seven states at attempting specialization and regionalization are examined.

Calls for Specialization of Field Staff

Chapter 1 reports Rogers' (1995) contention that the first county agent in the country was from New York. Rasmussen (1989) suggests the first one was from Texas. Rasmussen writes that in 1903, before the start of federal support for Extension, Seaman A. Knapp obtained private funds to hire field educators to set up demonstration farms. These field educators worked over districts of 10 to 20 counties. The first county agent, W. C. Stallings, was hired in Smith County, Texas, to work on the boll weevil threat. He was so successful and the threat was so great that "businessmen offered to pay most of the expense involved in employing an agent to work full time with the farmers in the one county, which led to the use of the term 'county agent'" (Rasmussen 1989). Soon the county agent became the primary means of delivering educational programs.

Regardless of the location of the first county agent, most Extension administrators and county staff believe that the county is the primary unit of Extension. As Rasmussen (1989) wrote: "Many state Extension directors say that it is essential to have Extension represented one way or another in every county if the Cooperative Extension program is to continue to enjoy local support."

However, many Extension leaders have recommended increased regionalization and specialization of field staff. These recommendations come from directors of Extension, deans of colleges of agriculture, and Extension's highest policy group, Extension Committee on Policy (ECOP). Here is a sampling of these recommendations.

In 1981, the American Agricultural Economics Association annual meeting devoted a session to extension program delivery. R. J. Hildreth and Walter Armbruster (1981) argued that Extension must find new ways to increasing productivity, i.e. the efficiency of their program delivery. They suggest several types of increased specialization, including greater use of regional and national specialists. Further, they suggest specialization by field educators as follows:

Another way of achieving cost efficient specialization might be to have local or area agents who have particular interest and expertise act as a state or even regional specialist (Hildreth and Armbruster 1981).

In 1987, the ECOP-sponsored Futures Task Force recommended that in each county, one or more Extension staff positions be continued at the local level but be backed up by regional educators with more technical expertise. Another Extension leader wrote:

It is unrealistic to expect county-level personnel to serve as technical experts dealing with the entire range of needs of today's clientele. Rather the staff of the future should concentrate on accomplishing the mission of Extension, have increased multicounty responsibilities, and cooperate with state specialists in conducting local educational programs and providing the opportunity to apply research (Rasmussen 1989).

A 1989 *Journal of Extension* article reported on suggestions from agricultural deans on ways Extension could provide better service to farmers. The two most common responses were as follows: (1) "the need for more specialists and fewer generalists to upgrade subject-matter competency" and (2) "Cooperative Extension should operate on a multi-county or regional basis" (Thompson and Gwynn 1989).

In 1991, Extension directors indicated they expected to see "a shift from the single county office to multicounty agent or office" (Agnew 1991). While expecting more of these regional or multicounty agents, the directors also felt these arrangements should "evolve locally rather than be imposed by the state" (Seevers, Graham, Gamon, and Conklin 1997). Michigan and Wisconsin attempted to encourage specialization and regionalization in this fashion, encouraging local bartering of services by the county extension directors.

Many other individuals have called for increased specialization and regionalization over the past twenty years (K. L. Smith 1991). Laughlin and Schmidt (1995) outline the pros and cons of regional offices as a means of increased efficiency. However, their 1,600-word article is a list of pros and cons of regional offices developed by participants of a workshop, without any accompanying empirical evidence of their validity.

State Efforts at Specialization

At least eight states (Alabama, Illinois, Iowa, Michigan, Minnesota, Nebraska, Ohio, and Wyoming) have adopted alternative types of specialization and regionalization of field staff. The models they used, however, are very different. A few states have specialized teams of multicounty educators for a given issue or target audience, but do not have this type of specialization for all areas of expertise and issues. Other states have used clustering, or county clusters, in which educators within a small set of counties specialize but continue to be housed within a county office and paid for by their host county. Each of these will now be reviewed by the year they adopted a regional system.

Minnesota's county cluster model (1987-2003). Minnesota adopted the county cluster model in 1987 as a means of providing greater expertise for local programs than could be found in a single county. The educators self-selected their own specializations, were housed in county offices, and were paid about 25 percent by the county. They were expected to work about 75 percent in their home county with 25 percent in the cluster. The twenty clusters had between three and seven counties and from nine to fifty agents. Before picking their specialization, educators discussed the needs within their cluster and considered their current expertise.

In almost every case in which there was a clear need, the educators arranged for someone to be "specialized" in that area, regardless of background. As a result, a number of educators who specialized in community development reported that they selected this program area because no one else wanted to and they saw a need. None of the educators who selected community development had academic training or professional experience in community economics and only two of them had experience in leadership development. However, every cluster was expected to have people in agriculture, 4-H, and family development.

Hutchins (1992) described the benefits and costs of this approach based on interviews with 15 county agents from 15 counties. The agents reported the following benefits: (1) specialization, (2) higher quality of programs, (3) more opportunity to deliver materials multiple times, and (4) greater collegial support. They also reported the following costs: (1) continuing generalist responsibilities, and (2) increased time demands on the agents.

In 1989, when the author asked county educators about their county cluster roles, a typical response was "Yes, I do cluster work, but I don't tell anyone in my home county because they are worried that we spend too much time on cluster work." This meant that the home county expected 100 percent of the individual's time and the cluster work became something beyond 100 percent. This makes the cluster work a volunteer effort rather than a job responsibility.

Iowa's field specialist model. Iowa was one of the original states to try regionalization, with some early efforts taking place in the 1970s. In the early 1990s, it shifted to something similar to the Minnesota county cluster model with a few major differences. Rather than being called county agents, field staff members are called "field specialists." Similar to Minnesota's cluster work, field specialists are housed in county offices rather than in area centers or regional offices. In addition, field specialists are supervised and evaluated jointly by the program leader in their area of expertise and by a district director. Just as this book is going to press, Iowa adopted a new system, as described later.

Ohio State's multi-county agents and clusters. Bartholomew and Smith (1990) documented the stresses of the 23 multicounty agents in Ohio in 1989. This article helps clarify the differences between field specialists and agents with multiple counties to cover. In the multicounty approach, the focus is on county-level audiences rather than on communities of interest that cover multiple counties or even the entire state. As a result, the Ohio agents reported the need to keep multiple sets of mailing lists, attend multiple county advisory meetings, and so on. While Ohio's multicounty agents would recommend a multi-county assignment to experienced educators, they did not feel inexperienced ones could handle them.

Another article on cluster work in three Ohio counties was very positive (Cropper and Merkowitz 1998). One of the benefits listed for the cluster work is increased specialization of educators; however, it provides no empirical evidence on either this or the other benefits.

Nebraska's multicounty extension programming units. After an experiment in five regions of the state from 1986 to 1989, Nebraska adopted twenty-one multicounty regions called Extension Programming Units (EPUs). Each EPU included an average of about four counties, ranging from two to ten counties. The model adopted appears to be very similar to the Minnesota county cluster model described earlier. Two years after the full implementation, field staff members were generally positive about the change (Rockwell, Furgason, Jacobson, Schmidt, and Tooker 1993).

Illinois's center based/multicounty model. Starting in 1992, Illinois restructured into seven regions (now five). Illinois has thirteen regional centers that provide programming across the state. The educators' programming is not confined to their region. In addition, all of the counties have an office where counties can hire as many staff as they can afford. This is very much like the Minnesota model adopted in 2004. However, a major difference is that all professional staff members at the center and the county level are supervised by the five regional directors. No *Journal of Extension* articles could be found that document the impact of the Illinois experience.

Michigan State's self-selected areas of expertise model. Starting in about 1995, Michigan State University Extension organized eighteen areas of expertise (AOE) as self-selected work teams (Leholm, Hamm, Suvedi, Gray, and Poston, 1999; Leholm and Vlasin 2006). These include both campus state specialists and field staff who elected to be a part of an AOE. In some cases, individuals in an AOE worked over more than one county in trades with neighboring counties. The county extension directors worked each of these trades out with the field staff involved. The evaluation of members of the field staff in an AOE was done jointly by county extension directors and by regional directors.

Wyoming's multicounty programming. Wyoming adopted the multicounty strategy in 2002. It appears that the model was very similar to the Minnesota county cluster model. Schafer (2006) reports Wyoming livestock producers did not perceive a difference in single-county or multicounty programming.

Minnesota's regional/county model (2004). Minnesota's regional/county model is described in the balance of the book. Some of the major differences are in the supervision of the field staff, the location of their offices, the nature of needs assessment, the nature of the program planning, and the nature of the promotion system.

Alabama's regional model. In mid-2004, Alabama adopted a regional model with some features like that of Minnesota's new model. A number of Extension Educators were named as Regional Extension Educators who worked in multiple counties and who were paid entirely with state and federal funds. However, three major differences exist. First, the regional educators have a very complex reporting system. They report to the county extension coordinators who report to the district directors who report to the Associate Director of Programs rather than reporting to campus specialists as in Minnesota. Second, the regional educators are housed in county offices rather than in regional ones. Third, the geographic area covered by regional educators in Alabama is determined centrally rather than by program teams and program areas.

Specialization Requires Regionalization

Is regionalization necessary for specialization? Theory suggests regionalization is necessary but not sufficient for Extension educators to be as highly specialized as the campus state specialists in the 1960s. First, there is unlikely to be sufficient demand to employ fully a specialized educator in one county or a cluster of counties. This is the case even when there is an urgent need for the depth of knowledge by a segment of the population. Second, the educators lose the opportunity to learn from a wide variety of audiences if they can only teach in one or a few counties. Third, educators housed in a county office cannot refuse to provide some assistance on topics outside their area of expertise, particularly when the public sees the request as fitting within the educators' responsibility. Fourth, an educator in a county office cannot commit to statewide programming efforts that might conflict with local demands, even if the local demands are outside the educator's area of expertise. Doing so, the educator would risk losing local public support. All of these suggest regionalization is necessary for specialization.

As outlined in Chapters 5 through 9, regionalization is not sufficient for the regional educators to be highly specialized. To be specialized, the regional educators must be carefully selected, supervised by state specialists, have clear statewide program teams and business plans, incorporate scholarship and evaluation into their programs, and understand and articulate the public value of their programs. Equally important, the specialized regional educators need to be complimented by generalists or program coordinators in the counties. This is particularly true for 4-H youth development, nutrition education and agriculture due to the long traditions in these program areas.

Conclusions

Theory suggests that specialization will increase the outcomes and impacts of Extension programs. National Extension leaders have called for increased field staff specialization for many years.

Yet, there remains great fear that increased specialization and the resultant regionalization will result in the loss of public support.

Early attempts at specialization and regionalization were largely moves to have agents cover multiple counties without major changes in the way that they work. This was often called the county cluster delivery model. The focus was on conducting needs assessment and programming county by county with some cross-county efforts. Networking and social capital building had to be done county by county rather than shifting to communities of interest. Supervision continued to be by district directors, who often saw their primary responsibility as keeping county commissioners satisfied enough to fund local positions.

Extension educator reactions to early attempts at specialization and regionalization have been mixed. While most educators liked the opportunities to specialize, many found their generalized role in their home county continued and hence their workloads increased.

Most states, adopting some form of regionalization, claimed that the multicounty type of delivery leads to specialization. As of June 2009, there was no literature available that defines the dimensions of this specialization or tests the type of hypotheses outlined earlier. Many state specialists felt the term "extension field specialist" was often an oxymoron, since the educators were part time in their area of expertise and self-selected into their "specialization" (Morse and Ahmed 2007). Unfortunately, there has been no research comparing the characteristics, methods of work, and achievements of the "specialists" under the county cluster model or the several types of multicounty models with "specialists" under a regional model that shifted control from the county to the state.

Minnesota's new system of regional delivery is completely different from the county cluster model used earlier in Minnesota and most states. It is very different from the multicounty model used in some other states. Since many of the Minnesota Extension Educators have worked under both the new Minnesota regional model and the prior county cluster model, Minnesota provides a good location for studying the differences.

Chapters 3 to 9 describe the Minnesota regional/county delivery model and its supporting parts. Chapters 10 to 13 report data on the differences created by moving from the Minnesota county cluster model and the Minnesota regional/county model. The final chapter explores common questions from other states.

The aim of this book is not to advocate the Minnesota model but to spark a new line of institutional research that examines alternative ways in which Extension can "do more with less." Without this research, Extension is likely to end up "doing less with less." If Extension can learn to "do more with less" maybe the public will realized what a great investment Extension is and invest more rather than less over time.

PART II

THE MINNESOTA RESPONSE

Chapter 3

Minnesota's Regional/County Model

George Morse and Philip O'Brien

You never want a serious crisis to go to waste....
It's an opportunity to do things you could not do before.

Rahm Emanuel on Rahm's Doctrine

On December 4, 2002, Thomas Stinson, the Minnesota state economist, announced that the state faced a $4.5 billion deficit for the next fiscal year, or 13 percent of the state's biennium budget. Shortly after, Governor Pawlenty announced he would balance the budget entirely by cutting expenditures. The University of Minnesota Extension's Dean and Director Charles Casey knew this would mean cutting Extension positions for a second year in a row. Even though it was impossible to predict the exact nature of the coming budget cut, the previous cuts suggested it would be between 10 and 15 percent.

Almost weekly, an ad hoc team comprised of Associate Dean and Director George Morse, Assistant Director for External Relations

Jeanne Markell, Assistant Director for Finance Philip O'Brien, and Director of Communications Aimee Viniard-Weideman met to prepare options for Dean Casey and his Council to consider.

However, by January 12, 2003 the ad hoc team was very demoralized. Extension had to give non-renewals to its staff by June 11, 2003, only 150 days away, including weekends. They knew they had to have a plan well before June so they could handle non-renewals in a systematic fashion. The size of the pending cuts would simply not allow Extension to tighten its belt without cutting positions.

Complicating this even more was the fiscal relationship between Extension and counties. As in many states, the counties funded a significant portion of each local Extension educator and 100 percent of the clerical staff, so the county funding was an important factor. The fiscal year for counties was January 1 to December 31 while Extension's was July 1 to June 30. Counties did not have to make final decisions on their Extension budget until December 31, 2003, which was over six months after Extension had to make personnel decisions.

The possibility that some counties would not fund Extension was high because of their own cuts from the state. The bottom line was that Extension needed to make a decision on lay-offs (technically, they were non-renewals) by June 11, 2003 without knowing whether counties were going to be able to fund county positions.

Questions, Questions, Questions

During December 2002, the administrative team explored many options for handling the funding cuts. The size of funding reductions required something different, especially since the year before there had been a five percent overall cut.

While there was considerable interest in specialization and regionalization by several team members, others were very concerned about the connections to the counties. They feared that if counties reacted too negatively, this could even reduce our state funding. This was particularly important since Extension had difficult legislative hearings in the prior session about its 2002 restructuring.

The more the administrative team discussed options, the more questions surfaced. The team groped with answers to the following questions:

1. How can we maintain a critical mass of field educators in a given area of expertise if we do not know which counties will continue to fund Extension?

2. What type of educational programming should we provide to people in counties that do not provide any funding?

3. Can we find a system that will give counties greater choice and clarity regarding what they want to fund locally?

4. Can we find a system that will encourage greater scholarship on the part of the field staff, enhance the quality of our programs, and create closer campus faculty-field staff relationships?

5. Can we find a system that will create stronger connections to target audiences and communities of interest?

6. Can we find a system that does not require restructuring every time there is a state or federal budget crisis?

7. Can we find a system that is acceptable politically to the field staff, Extension stakeholders, and legislators?

Each of these questions underwent a lot of discussion. For a while, the more clearly the team understood what would be desirable, the less feasible it seemed that any one system could do all of this. Here is the discussion related to these questions.

Critical Mass in Area of Expertise

The first question Extension struggled with was "How can we maintain a critical mass of field educators in a given area of expertise if we do not know which counties will continue to fund Extension?"

Under the system used prior to 2004, each county educator was funded by federal, state, and county funds with about 25 percent being county funds. In hiring new educators, Extension administrators worked with the county to determine the focus of the job (4-H, agriculture, community development, natural resources, and family development). Then the Extension Human Resource Office posted a position announcement and did the initial screening. Often a search committee interviewed the top five or six candidates and screened the pool down to two. The final two candidates were taken to the county for interviews and the county Extension committee had the final decision. This process, because it involved the county agent and county funding, made the county think of these agents as "their" educators.

At times of severe budget cuts, this system of hiring gave Extension very little influence over the portfolio of Extension educators in the state. To understand this, picture the following scenario:

1. Extension feels it is essential to maintain a team of nine livestock field specialists;
2. Six of the nine educators in livestock are in counties which announce they can no longer fund any Extension positions; and
3. Extension administration identifies six other funded positions in neighboring counties that rank lower in importance.

Given the traditional hiring system, consider the reactions of the neighboring counties who are funding the six positions, which Extension has identified as lower priority. In most cases, these neighboring counties would not want to shift their funding to a livestock position to accommodate Extension. The local stakeholders for the existing non-livestock educators would make these changes in assignments nearly impossible. If Extension insisted on non-renewal of the non-livestock educators, the odds of losing county funding for all of these positions would be high. Thus, Extension's ability to adjust its portfolio of positions was very limited under a traditional county or county cluster model.

The bottom line is that given these arrangements with counties, Extension could not make strategic plans about the type of work they would do. Without determining the program priorities, after getting public input, it was impossible to develop high quality statewide programs and have them closely tied to research at the university.

To navigate this minefield takes intensive and time-consuming discussion and negotiation between Extension, the stakeholders, the county commissioners, and the county Extension committees. Imagine doing those negotiations over 87 counties in three months; the odds of having a balanced team under the current county system were slim to none.

Educational Programs for Non-Paying Counties

The second question facing Extension was "What type of educational programming should we provide to people in counties that do not provide any funding?"

Extension is not a mandated service for counties. Most of the other services delivered at the county level are mandated by the state and the county is the direct provider of these services. Hence, cutbacks in state aid to counties impacts them twice, once as they lost funds and again as the public perceived reductions in state services. Since the public perceived these state services as county ones, these were seen as cuts from the county government. This put Extension in a very vulnerable spot with respect to continued county funding. In 2003, counties spent about $16 million on Extension, with the majority of it spent on office space, secretaries, and travel but about $4 million paid directly to the University of Minnesota Extension for county educator positions. What should Extension do if a county cut back or did not spend anything on Extension?

There were many suggestions. Some suggested that we simply stop programming in counties that stopped funding Extension. They argued that you could not get into a university football game without paying for the ticket. However, this begged the question of what to do if people from that county signed up for a program or called an educator in a neighboring county. It also ignored the fact that people in that county pay state and federal taxes and had a right to expect something from Extension. Those using the football ticket analogy argued that people still had to buy tickets even if they paid their state and federal taxes. However, this change would have been a major cultural shift for the Extension stakeholders and could have made it politically unfeasible.

Others suggested asking people who signed up for an Extension program what county they were from and then politely pointing out that the county has not provided funding. Actually, this was done in another state when a county refused to fund an agricultural position. Yet, this seemed to have practical, equitable, and political drawbacks. In the practical side, it would have been difficult to administer evenly. Further, if Extension was trying to encourage stakeholders in non-paying counties to again fund positions, it would want them to sample Extension programs and recognize the benefits. Considering equity, people in counties not funding Extension still have paid their state and federal taxes. State and federal taxes cover about 75 percent of the cost of the county educators. Hence, it would be unfair to deny them all services. Politically, Extension expected that many stakeholders and county commissioners would be unhappy with this and go to their legislators. Since the legislators could not provide more money in 2004, it is difficult to imagine what the outcome would have been; potentially, it may have meant deeper cuts for Extension.

Greater Choice and Clarity for Counties in Local Positions

The third difficult question that Minnesota Extension faced was: "Can we find a system that will give counties greater choice and clarity regarding what they want to fund locally?"

In Minnesota prior to 2004, as in most other states, counties had a choice in the type of educators in their county. However, the decision was not completely up to the county. Typically, Extension leaders decide on the type of position they wanted and then negotiate this with the county Extension advisory committee and the county commissioners. This process tended to favor the status quo, replacing a retiring county agent in a given area of expertise with another one in the same area of expertise. The established stakeholders in the original area of expertise were simply better organized to express a preference for this than the many other possible sets of stakeholders. As Mancur Olson (1971) has shown, a small group of well-organized stakeholders often gets their way in the political arena.

When Extension adopted the county cluster approach in 1987, educators were expected to work at least 25 percent in the five or six counties outside their home county. Some county commissioners and stakeholders wanted educators to spend full-time in their county. Various reporting systems were employed to show counties the benefits of the in-flow of educators from other counties, as well as from sharing their educators with other counties; however, this data was not convincing to some local stakeholders. Some commissioners were certain that they contributed more to the cluster than they received. As a result, many educators focused mostly on their host counties.

Another concern in some counties was that the educators were too qualified and paid too much. Extension felt it was important that educators have a master's degree so they could work more closely with campus faculty and deliver higher quality programs. Further, Extension felt that educators should receive the same pay for the same qualifications regardless of which county they worked in. Yet, some rural counties felt these Extension policies led to salaries that were too high for their county. The Extension rebuttal was that they did not want to disadvantage rural counties in their ability to attract quality candidates. The challenge was to find a system that gave counties greater clarity in what they got and greater choice in the type of people the county funded.

Closer Campus Connections, Scholarship, and Quality Programs

The fourth major question faced by Extension was "Can we find a system that will encourage greater scholarship on the part of the field staff, enhance the quality of our programs, and create closer campus faculty-field staff relationships?"

Since Extension had to make major changes, could Extension find a system that would reinvigorate closer connections between Extension educators and campus faculty? After all, the ties to research are what give Extension its comparative advantage in outreach over other outreach programs sponsored by community college, technical colleges, and the private sector (McGrath, Conway, and Johnson 2007). However, over time the ties between campus and field staff had eroded until there were two Extension Services in Minnesota – one by field staff and the other by state specialists from campus. The state specialists tended to focus on communities of interest and develop in-depth curriculum, which often were used statewide, regionally, and nationally. With some notable exceptions, the extension educators operated on a very responsive short-term basis. As a result, county-based educators often were not able to invest as heavily as they would have liked in program development, marketing, and evaluation. Many field staff did not have an opportunity to keep up-to-date with the scholarship in their area of expertise and very few had a chance to share their experiences with their peers via some form of scholarship.

Stronger Connections with Communities of Interest

The fifth one was "Can we find a system that will create stronger connections to target audiences and communities of interest?" The essence of Extension's mission requires it to focus on local people. However, the concept of "local" has started to take on new meanings in a global economy and internet world. Now almost every commodity group or interest group has a regional, state, and national organization that is looking after its interests, including its educational interests. Extension's close ties to counties have had tremendous benefits, but they have limited Extension's ability to work on educational program development and delivery with these state, regional and national organizations. The time required for doing work on statewide or national issues is more than county-based staff can contribute. While state specialists have worked with these issues, the incentives for field educators to work with state specialists were relatively limited. Could we find a system that would allow closer relationships between Extension program teams that include state specialists, field educators, and communities of interest?

Restructuring Not Required Frequently

After a series of restructurings and two major ones in two years, the sixth question was, "Can we find a system that does not require restructuring every time there is a state or federal budget crisis?"

Restructuring is defined here as "the redefinition of the roles and responsibilities of many or all of the field staff in major ways." Restructuring does not include the changes in focus within areas of expertise done in response to feedback from the target audience. Nor does it refer to changes within one or two support units within Extension. Rather, it reflects system-wide changes.

Minnesota had been through a series of painful restructurings due to budget cuts in the past twenty years. It is likely that state and federal budgets will continue to fluctuate over many years. When this happens, will it be necessary for Extension to restructure each time there is a severe dip? Naturally, severe budget cuts are likely to result in staff layoffs. However, would it be possible to find a system that would not require almost every person in the organization to change their job responsibilities as has been the case in the last several restructurings? In addition, would it be possible to find a system that would not require Extension administration to negotiate with 87 counties whenever some reductions have to be made?

A Politically Acceptable Option

A final very crucial question was, "Can we find a system that is acceptable politically to the field staff, Extension stakeholders, and legislators?"

Ultimately, this was a paramount criterion. If we could not find a solution that was acceptable to field staff, county Extension stakeholders and the legislature, it was unlikely to be adopted. "Acceptable" does not mean that everyone had to cheer at its adoption but that at least a majority was willing to go along with the change. Without this, a system that met all of the above criteria was doomed.

New Minnesota Regional/County Model

By January 12, 2003, more than a month after Extension heard the alarming news about the $4.5 billion state budget deficit, our administrative team had identified most of the above questions. Despite hours of discussion, the team was going in circles. Finally, the author, recalling a recent article by Michael Martin (2002) encouraging agricultural economics faculty to assist university administration, realized this was a public finance question and asked Vernon Eidman, the department head of Applied Economics at the University of Minnesota to help Extension with some ideas.

Club Theory Suggests Regional/County Model

On February 12, 2003, Dr. Eidman spoke to the twenty-two people in the Dean Casey's Council and outlined club theory and how it might apply to our case (Buchanan 1985, Eidman 1995). The basic premise is that people join a club and pay a base fee. For that base fee, they get basic services. For additional fees, they get additional services. This is the same business model used by sports' clubs and cable TV.

Dr. Eidman suggested Extension create regional offices for regional educators and ask counties to pay a base fee for which they would receive basic services. Those that wanted to pay more would receive services that are more detailed.

Before the Extension Council decided to use this as a basic approach, George Morse did a force field analysis on the proposed model with the members of the Dean's Council. The advantage of the force field analysis was that it allowed the team to consider the pros and cons without having to state an opinion about the overall desirability of the proposal. First, the basic concept was laid out. Then each person was asked to evaluate the pros and cons of the concept and then to suggest any modifications which might correct the disadvantages. At this early stage in considering the "club theory" model, the team was not asked if they liked the concept overall or if they would vote to approve it.

During those force field discussions, the members of the Extension Council revised the proposal a bit. First, it was assumed that every county paid the base fee already by virtue of their citizens paying state and federal taxes. This meant that Extension would provide the basic services to every county from the regional educators, using state and federal funds to cover the costs of regional educators and their programs. No county funds would be required for these regional educators.

A county without a regional office would have the same access to programming as one with it, assuming the same population and needs. Extension defined very explicitly what counties would get from the regional system in 4-H and what they would get with increasing levels of investment in local 4-H coordinators and support staff. Extension eventually called the new system simply a regional model or a regional/county model.

Minnesota's Regional/County Model

In this book, the term "Minnesota model," or the "Minnesota regional/county model" are used for this new delivery approach. Some suggested the model be called a "mixed regional/county model" because of the importance of these two features and since early on, we often used these terms internally. Others argued the model was much more than the regional/county model and was a hybrid of ideas from other states, economics, and business and should be called simply a "hybrid" model. The terms "Minnesota model" and "Minnesota regional/county model" are used interchangeable in this book to describe a delivery system with the following features:

1. Regional offices are set up to support as many regional Extension educators (REEs) as can be covered by state and federal funds.
2. Counties are free to purchase as many local positions as they wish.
3. The REEs would be much more specialized.
4. Both REEs and county educators are University of Minnesota employees.
5. REEs are asked to join program teams with campus faculty and develop statewide program business plans.
6. The promotion criteria for REEs require much greater scholarship, program leadership and outreach teaching.
7. Regional directors manage the regional offices and external relations with counties.

Regional/County vs. County Cluster Models

The contrast between the major features of the University of Minnesota Extension before and after the restructuring are shown in Table 3.1 and described below.

Office Locations

Before the 2004 restructuring, all of Minnesota Extension's 589 field staff members were located in 87 county offices. This included 251 Extension educators, 99 nutrition education assistants, 19 4-H program coordinators, 175 support staff, and 45 field administrators. After the restructuring, 130 regional extension educators (REEs) were housed in eighteen regional offices. The 130 REEs reflected the total number that Extension could afford using only state and federal funds. Each regional office also had a regional director and several support staff. The regional offices were not designed as walk in centers or places to do the majority of the educational programs. Rather the regional offices were primarily places for REEs to do preparation.

Table 3.1:
Minnesota's County Cluster vs. Regional/County Model

Feature	County Cluster Model (before 2004)	Regional/County Model (2004 and after)
Office Location and Funding	Extension Educators (EEs) were located in 87 county offices and funded 25% by counties.	REEs are housed in one of 18 regional offices with all funding from state and federal sources.
County Positions	All positions were located in counties.	Eighty-six (of 87) counties funded local positions.
Specialization and Focus	Each educator self-selected area of expertise and worked in 1 to 3 counties.	Program leaders assign REE to an area of expertise. REEs cover larger geographic areas.
Supervision	Field staff is supervised by district directors.	Field educators are supervised by campus/faculty state specialists.
Program Teams and Business Plans	Educators are sometimes in statewide program teams.	Educators required to be on a statewide program team and develop a program business plan.
Promotion	Promotion not required Length of service a factor.	Promotion focuses on scholarship, leadership, and teaching. Promotion required.
Regional Directors	County Directors located in 45 (of 87) counties.	Regional Directors manage regional offices and do external relations.

Funding

Prior to the reorganization, extension educators were funded by a combination of federal, state, and county funds. Counties paid about 25% of the salaries and some other expenses for about 40% of the total cost of an educator. The rest was paid by state and federal funds. In total, counties put $4 million into Extension's budget of $55 million in 2003. In addition, counties paid another $11 million for office rental, travel, and support staff. Regardless of the structure in 2004, counties were likely to cut Extension funding due to the cuts in state aid.

After the restructuring, Extension used state and federal funds to operate 18 regional centers and to cover the salary and expenses of 130 regional extension educators and 71 support staff and administrators.

County Positions

After the 2004 restructuring, the majority of Minnesota Extension's educational positions (61% of FTEs) remain in counties (See Table 6.2 in Chapter 6). Unlike the old system in which counties paid about 25 percent of the salary on every position and all of the support staff salaries, in the 2004 system, Minnesota Extension paid the full costs for the REEs while counties paid the full cost for the local positions. Counties could purchase any type of position, provided the program teams (composed of state specialists and REEs) could back them up with relevant research and programming materials. To help counties explore their options, each program area developed a menu of possibilities for local positions. As we expected, almost all of the counties purchased program coordinators for 4-H clubs and most of major farming counties purchased agricultural positions. In agriculture, many counties shared one person with another county. Details of the county's important role are provided in Chapter 6.

Specialized Regional Extension Educators (REEs)

In order to increase program quality and to encourage closer ties to campus, the REEs were organized into 18 Areas of Expertise. Unlike the self-selected specializations prior to 2001, the educators after 2004 were selected by the program leaders to have specific experience, training, and focus. Rather than being hired as an agricultural educator, the REE was hired to specialize in one of five areas of expertise in agriculture: Agri-business Management, Crops, Food Safety, Horticulture, or Livestock. Some were hired to be specialists in sub-fields with their area of expertise, for example, dairy or beef specialists within the Livestock area of expertise. Chapter 5 outlines the nature of specialization of educators before and after the changes, and Chapters 10 to 13 outline the impacts of this increases specialization.

REEs Supervised by Campus Faculty

With two exceptions, REEs are supervised by state specialists on campus. In contrast, before 2004, the REEs were supervised by District Directors who had responsibility for all 18 areas of expertise. The hope was that the new supervisory model would create much closer ties between field staff and campus faculty in the academic disciplines.

In the case of new hires, capacity area leaders defined the positions, appointed the search committees, and made the final hiring decision. In almost every case, someone from the target audience and county commissioners were a part of the search committee. Previously the final decisions had been made by counties. It was also a major difference from the last restructuring when educators self-selected the areas in which they wished to specialize. The new approach was adopted on the assumption that it would allow the capacity area leaders to build statewide teams in which different REEs had different specialty skills within their general area of expertise. While every attempt was made to honor the wishes of the educators, the determining factor was the strength of the team for serving the public.

The two exceptions to campus-based state specialists as supervisor are: (1) 4-H club REEs and (2) county-based agricultural positions. More detail is provided on supervision in Chapter 5.

Program Teams and Business Plans

As soon as the new system started in January 2004, each REE was asked to join at least one statewide program team, consisting of both REEs from across the state and campus faculty. These teams were then asked to develop a program business plan that clearly identified their team, their target audience, the needs of the target audience, and other key components of a successful program. Defining these target audiences helped to shift the focus away from geographically defined audiences to communities of interest that were regional or statewide. In addition, these plans summarized recent needs assessment work, outlined the educational objectives of the program, and defined how they would approach delivery and evaluation of the program. The nature of these plans and their use is outlined in Chapter 7, "Program Business Plans."

Promotion of REEs

Minnesota Extension has a system of rank for field educators parallel to that of University professors (Assistant Professor, Associate Professor, and Professor) but which does not include tenure. Prior to restructuring, the District Directors coordinated the promotion review process for REEs at the district level. In 2006, both the process and the criteria changed in major ways. The Capacity Area Leaders were in charge of the new promotion process for all the educators in their capacity area. The new criteria gives much higher emphasis to scholarship, program leadership, and outreach teaching while still including the traditional criteria of program management, engagement, and service. While tenure is not granted, REEs are required to achieve Associate Professor status by their sixth year or face termination. Chapter 9 provides more detail on the new promotion process.

Regional Directors

One of the roles of the regional directors (RDs) focused on external relations with counties. Another of their major roles is to help counties evaluate whether to purchase a local county position and to provide oversight to the county staff in their region. The RDs also manage the regional support staff, equipment, supplies, and building maintenance. Unlike district directors in most states, they do not supervise the REEs. The RDs role will be outlined in more detail in Chapter 4 on external relations and Chapter 6 on the counties.

Benefits of the Minnesota Model

The Minnesota regional/county model has potential benefits for all of Extension's stakeholders, including county governments, program participants, campus faculty, Extension educators, Extension administration, University administration, and taxpayers who are not participants. The nature of these will be briefly explored now, but covered in more detail in the rest of the book.

External Stakeholders

Benefits for counties. County governments benefit from the greater clarity and choice from the Minnesota model. Under the new model, the local educators, which are funded by a county, work only in that county. Hence, counties have complete control over the type of positions they purchase locally.

For some counties, the possibility of reducing what they spend on Extension is a major benefit. While counties that support local positions receive higher levels of local attention, all of the programs are available to their county residents even if they did have to cut the support for Extension. One of the local stakeholders' concerns was that counties that did not hire a local 4-H program coordinator would not be allowed to have a 4-H Clubs. These clubs are allowed but they receive lower levels of support than when there is a local program coordinator.

Benefits to program participants. Program participants benefit from the Minnesota regional/county model when the program quality and access increases. If the participants perceive the benefits to them exceed the value of their time and financial costs, participation will increase. The initial evidence that the benefits to program participants is increasing is presented in Part III.

Benefits to taxpayers. Taxpayers who are not participants in Extension programs are important stakeholders because a large percentage of the funding for Extension comes from public funding. As described in Chapter 7 and 10, the public value of Extension programs depends on the expected impacts of the program, the program's educational effectiveness, and the number of participants. If the Minnesota model increases program quality and access, it will increase public value.

Internal Stakeholders

Benefits to campus faculty. Campus faculty with Extension appointments benefit when they can collaborate closely with the field Extension educators. The educators can deliver programs more widely, assist in adapting programs to unique audiences, provide feedback on programming, and contribute to research and teaching programs. The Minnesota regional/county model encourages greater statewide leadership by regional educators and encourages more scholarship as described in Chapters 9, 10, and 11.

Benefits to extension educators. Extension educators benefit from the new regional/county model if it provides them with more opportunities than in the past. Chapters 5, 10, and 11 report that most regional educators perceive this to be the case.

Benefits to extension administration. The Minnesota model gives Extension administration greater flexibility in funding and staffing options. When there are fiscal crises at the state or county level, the Extension administration no longer needs to negotiate with 87 counties in order to make adjustments. If it becomes necessary to scale back one or more areas of expertise due to severe budget cuts, this can be done in a way that delivers the greatest service possible without a system wide reorganization.

The Minnesota model opens the possibility of funding from entities other than counties, helping Extension diversify its funding. These fiscal benefits are described in Chapter 13.

Benefits to university administration. The central administration at the university benefits when Extension is highly valued by the public. On the other hand, when Extension has to restructure often, this creates negative publicity for the university as well as for Extension. Sometimes the negative public reactions spill over into the wider university budgets. The Minnesota regional/county model should reduce the frequency of system wide restructuring.

Risks of the Minnesota Model

The Minnesota regional/county model also has potential risk for both external and internal stakeholders.

External Stakeholders

Risks for counties. While the new model calls for providing programming to people from all counties, counties with small populations and located further from trade centers might find fewer programs being conducted within their borders. Program teams have incentives to reach the maximum number of people. This might encourage teams to focus on trade centers rather than small, remote counties.

Risks to program participants. If Extension was unable to help the REEs transition from generalist roles to specialist roles, program participants risks not seeing the benefits of specialization. If REEs attempted to do their work in the same manner as in the county-cluster system while covering ever-larger geographic areas, the effectiveness of their programs is likely to suffer.

Risks to taxpayers. Public value to taxpayers only occurs if the educational programs in Extension are effective in helping participants achieve new outcomes (Kalambokidis 2004). A risk to taxpayers is that the new system might diminish the program effectiveness of REEs, resulting in a decline in their public value.

Internal Stakeholders

Risks to campus faculty. There appears to be little direct risk to campus faculty of the regional/county model. However, if the transition to this new model was so unpopular that state funding fell, this could reduce the number of state specialist positions.

Risks to extension educators. If new REEs were not promoted from Extension Assistant Professor to Extension Associate Professor within six years, they would receive non-renewal notices. If current REEs with senior rank did not receive a favorable review confirming their rank within seven years, they had to forego raises until they passed this review.

Risks to extension administration. If the majority of REEs were unable to demonstrate new benefits of specialization to the communities of interest, Extension would have a difficult time sustaining long-term political support. Alternatively, if too many counties were unable to fund any local 4-H positions, this would weaken public support. This could lead to reductions in state funding and loss of regional and/or state positions.

Risks to university administration. Minnesota Extension had offices in every county prior to the 2004 restructuring. If many counties no longer had offices, the University would lose its most well known connection to communities. Further, if the new system proved to be a failure, this could have major political costs to both Extension administration and the University administration.

The Design Process for New Model

Not all of the elements of the new Minnesota model were decided at one time. Using club theory to separate out the roles of REEs and county educators was the first major decision. After numerous meetings from January to March 2003, members of the Dean's Council completed a force field analysis on the basic idea. This process helped the team explore ideas on a controversial topic in a fashion that did not require them to reveal their conclusions. This allowed individuals to change their minds if they developed new insights.

A daylong retreat of Dean Casey's Council was held on April 16, 2003, to make the final decision. The revised proposal was presented and then a roll call vote taken. Dean Casey asked for a 75 percent vote of the entire 22-person group as well as 75 percent from the five Associate Deans of Capacity Areas and 75 percent from the eight District Directors. Each person was asked to indicate a yes or no and the reason for his or her vote. The vote to adopt the new system was unanimous.

At this stage, the discussions did not include field staff or state specialists. Many state Extension administrators and staff are likely to feel that a much more participatory process would have been desirable. For example, when Alabama moved to a regional system, there was a two-year process of involving staff prior to the changes (Washington and Fowler 2005). While this would have been ideal, there are three differences from the Alabama situation. First, Minnesota had less than five months to develop and implement the new system. Second, the reductions were deeper in Minnesota than in Alabama. Third, given the turmoil of the previous 18 months from the 2002 restructuring, an open-ended discussion about even further cuts with no framework would have resulted in almost a complete demoralization of Extension field staff. Already, travel expenses in 2002 demonstrated that programming slowed down considerably during the recently implemented restructuring. A vision was necessary before inviting feedback on the ways to implement any changes. As outlined in Chapter 4, the key stakeholders were then informed of this broad policy direction and asked for suggestions and help in designing the details.

In June 2003, Minnesota Extension hired an external human resource consultant to study what type of supervision structure was best for the new regional specialization model. The consultant recommended that the supervision be shifted from the District Directors to the Capacity Area Leaders. Since the program teams were working statewide, this streamlined the supervision greatly. Rather than each program team having nine different supervisors, they had one area program leader who in turn reported to the capacity area leader. The earlier system also made it difficult to have supervisors who had direct experience and training in the same area of expertise as the REEs.

The changes in the promotion system started two years after the initial regional offices. While a study of potential changes in promotion had been started in the fall of 2002, this study was put on hold during the shift to the regional system. In retrospect, the delay was fortunate because the promotion system ultimately adopted would not have worked prior to 2004.

Program teams were required to complete program business plans within the first six months of the new regional system, starting in 2004. In 2005, the teams were required to develop and implement any two aspects of their business plans that the team felt offered the most potential. One aspect had to be related to their educational mission and the other to the program's financial sustainability. Hence, this effort was known as the "Mission and Money" project. In 2006, the program teams were required to develop a one page executive summary to be shared internally with Regional Directors, other Extension administrators, and between teams.

Efforts to identify the source of public value for each program started in the fall of 2002, before the Minnesota Regional/County system was adopted. However, it was intensified after the new system was in place and each of the programs had a public value statement in their 2006 executive summaries.

Summary and Future Research

Summary

When Minnesota Extension faced a major financial problem in 2003, it explored ways to strengthen its educational mission and its financial sustainability. Regionalization and specialization were seen as the means to enhance program quality and to enhance access to specialists throughout the state. An economic theory, called club theory, suggested a means of developing the Minnesota regional/county model in order to give counties greater choice in the types of positions they supported and clarity in what they received for their investment.

The Minnesota regional/county model depends on a series of policies in addition to regionalization. These include changes in office locations, funding, county positions, specialization, supervision, program teams, program business plans, public value definition, evaluation, promotions, and regional directors. Each of these varies in major ways from the county cluster delivery model used in Minnesota from 1987 to 2004.

Potentially, the Minnesota regional/county model has benefits for each of Extension's stakeholders, including county governments, program participants, and other taxpayers who are not participants, campus faculty, Extension educators, Extension administrators, and University administrators. Likewise, the model had risks for each of these stakeholders.

Future Research

This book presents rudimentary research findings on how the

Minnesota regional/county model works and its impacts on educator and campus faculty collaboration, program quality, access, and public support. Yet, many unanswered questions remain. Some of these will be discussed in each of the future chapters. Here are three questions related to the overall model that need future research.

1. How will the Minnesota regional/county model change over time?

2. What are the long-term impacts of the Minnesota regional/ county model on faculty collaboration, program quality, access, and public support?

3. How do different types of regional models compare?

Most of the states that have regional models use a county cluster approach similar to what Minnesota used from 1987 to 2004. Yet, there is considerable variation between these states. A multi-state research project to examine the consequences of alternative policies could help all states explore the best type of regionalization and specialization, including none at all, for their context.

Chapter 4

External Relations

Jeanne Markell

*If communications is not your top priority,
all of your other priorities are at risk.*

Bob Aronson 2003

The success of Minnesota Extension's reorganization to a regional/
county delivery system depended as much on perception of its
potential effectiveness as it did on fundamental soundness. Not only
must change bring a better "yes," but also key authorizers had to
be convinced that the ends justified the means of change. Early and
consistent attention to the attitudes and beliefs of stakeholders was
of utmost importance to the administrative leaders of the changes
effort. This chapter describes elements critical to the design and
execution of an external relations strategy that took this idea from
aspiration to actuality.

The Case for an External Relations Strategy

The overarching task for Extension leaders was to build a better mousetrap. The new model had to better connect Minnesota's needs with its land grant university. The team focused on vision, principles, policies, and procedures to achieve better outcomes for the people of the state. The new system also had to be a better model within a changing academic culture: a new university president and board of regents were demanding that Extension demonstrate greater accountability and fiscal sustainability in the new century of public higher education. The regional/county model system must produce higher quality, more relevant and further reaching program impacts than the status quo. In addition, Extension must find a new financial model to insure future stability with less dependence on public funding. These were huge orders, and because the proof was somewhere in the future, stakeholders would have to be convinced to invest in a blueprint of quite dramatic, even risky changes.

No other states had tried exactly what Minnesota proposed. As outlined in Chapters 3 to 9, Minnesota enacted an interrelated set of organizational changes to move Minnesota from a county cluster model to a regional/county delivery model. The overall complexity of the restructuring made it difficult to keep the conversation from being driven by emotional, nostalgic notions of how Extension structure should look. From the beginning, leaders sensed that those whose support was needed were inclined to focus more on the pain than the gain of change. Extension's historic relationship with its public was a key factor in anticipating the challenge of undergoing such striking change in a reasonably short timeframe. Since its creation at the turn of the century, the national Cooperative Extension Service prided itself on being "locally owned" by its stakeholders in each state. As such, state and county elected officials and the public (particularly those from areas that are more rural) typically view Extension as "their part" of Minnesota's land grant university. Legislators and commissioners not only shared in the funding of the enterprise, they were also engaged in operational matters such as advising programming, staffing, and budgets. Co-owner mentality of this nature fosters valuable brand loyalty and grassroots advocacy. When stakeholders see themselves as true partners rather than just customers, the result is a kind of hands-on involvement that strengthens the political base. This relationship can also help Extension listen to its customers and stay relevant.

The downside to this high level of affinity comes in the multiple layers of differing, and sometimes conflicting, self-interests on the part of stakeholders, making it more difficult for Extension leaders to change a course of direction, make needed decisions, and execute changes. This dynamic forced the Minnesota team to resist temptation to stay too "internal," and pay attention instead to the external. Typically, this is not a place where Extension wanted to be, as evidenced by the experiences of other states that have approached change efforts. A review over the past two decades of *Journal of Extension (JOE)* articles about Extension transformation shows a heavy tilt toward more attention to obstacles *inside* the organization. Most references in the literature to external influence on Extension change are in relation to "program" changes and not the kind of broader system change that Minnesota undertook in the 2001-2005 period. One exception is a 2005 Alabama Extension study that examined both internal and external resistance to major system change (Washington and Fowler 2005). Alabama leaders, like those in Minnesota, recognized that it was not enough to design a better mousetrap—without creating a favorable public perception, a better model would never see the light of day.

Roles and Responsibilities to Make it Happen

Extension, like many parts of the academic environment, seeks to be known more for its products than for its processes. Since the business of Extension is to provide informal education to address community needs, it is appropriate for the majority of the budget to go toward programs and program staff. System support such as communications, marketing, and external relations tends to be an incidental part of most budgets, often understaffed and poorly utilized in proactive ways. Fortunately, Minnesota's Extension leadership recognized the need to adequately support and empower its External Relations effort during this period of change, beginning with three core beliefs:

1. *The Extension Dean/Director must be a visible and accessible leader;*

2. *Everyone in the organization has an External Relations role, and each must be clarified, supported and held accountable; and*

3. *Internal resources should be supplemented with strategically chosen, outsourced communications consultants as needed.*

These three beliefs guided external relations responsibilities across Extension as explained below.

Extension Dean/Director - visible and accessible

The first core belief on roles was that the Extension Dean/Director must be a visible and accessible leader. The Extension Dean/ Director is the chief academic officer in the eyes of the university, but what matters most to the people of the state is that he or she manages "their Extension" enterprise in a fashion they deem appropriate. Stakeholders, especially elected officials, want direct and frequent contact and accountability from the leader of Extension. The magnitude of the two successive restructuring in 2002 and 2004 increased this expectation considerably. Thus, the first tenet of the External Relations strategy was to keep the Dean/Director, Dr. Charles Casey, front and center. Building external confidence in the plan depended on a credible, approachable, and well-prepared top leader who would work effectively to sell the plan to even the most ardent skeptics. The Dean/Director must not be shielded from the media or protected from public scrutiny. Next, in order to support this lead Dean/Director work, nearly every person in the Extension systems had a part to play in helping the plan survive.

Everyone Has External Relations Role

The second core belief, which guided external relations, was that everyone in the organization has an External Relations role, and each role must be clarified, supported, and held accountable.

Associate Dean/Director of External Relations. Given its importance to a successful outcome, the External Relations execution had to be vested in a cabinet level position, reporting directly to the Dean/Director. Fortunately, that position already existed in Minnesota's Extension administration. The Associate Dean for External Relations (the author) had oversight for strategy development, message management, staff delegation and support, and assessment of stakeholder response. She was part of all senior level decision-making and consultation and represented the team on external relations matters within the central university, as well as inside and beyond the Extension systems. An important footnote here is that Extension, like any other college unit, was expected by the university's central administration to work in tandem with University Relations on all external relations and communications strategies. The Associate Dean was expected to make sure this accountability and collaboration existed at every step of the way. This effort was too big to go it alone without the university relations support.

Communications Director. The Communications Director, Aimee Viniard-Weideman, had been with the organization for a number of years, holding increasing levels of responsibility for media, internal communications, and public relations. Her skills and expertise, including her contacts with communications professionals who could be helpful to Extension were valuable assets to the leadership team. The Communications Director was the point person for media contacts, staff training, and production of support and communication materials used in this "campaign for change." The Associate Dean and the Communications Director played tag-team during the most demanding times when the Dean /Director needed back up and support.

Administrators in field positions. Extension staff members responsible for administration of the field level were viewed as the front line managers for communicating changes and for soliciting input from the public throughout the state. Over the course of the planning and implementation cycle, the titles and scope of these positions changed from County Extension Director (one CED in each county) to Extension Regional Director (RDs). The RDs managed the 18 newly formed regional offices and had oversight over 3-6 counties each. CEDs and RDs were responsible for communicating Extension's public value to legislators, county commissioners, and local advisory committees. However, unlike the CEDs and the District Directors, the RDs had no supervisory role for the REEs as explained in Chapter 5. These mid-level managers were selected for their skill in relationship building, public relations, and organizational marketing. Throughout the various stages of the change effort, campus-based leadership depended on this network both to carry the plan for change at the local level (where they had frequently built significant social capital) and to listen carefully to local reception of the proposed changes and bring that input back to campus.

One challenge in doing this was that in the transition from county cluster model to the Minnesota regional/county model, there was a period of uncertainty about the job security and/or design of most field based staff. This ambiguity added a unique pressure on staff. Immediate supervisors of CEDs (District Directors), and then RDs (Directors of Field Operations), played an important role in coaching and supporting staff through these difficult months. Extension's External Relations and Communications department, lead by the Associate Dean and the Director of Communications, also worked closely with the field administrators guiding their efforts and providing training and skill development, media, government and public relations. Regional Directors, once in place at their centers, became the critical link between Extension, administration and their communities. They arranged and hosted listening sessions, program showcases, and media events to help the Dean/Director tell the story about positive change. An important factor to note is that all message management flowed out of the Dean/Director's office and this need for consistency was reinforced at all levels of the system. This was, of course, impossible to enforce completely, given the long history of decentralization in Extension.

Program faculty/staff. Administrative staff carried the lead on relationship building and communications with our county commissioners, legislators, and other key stakeholders, always with the understanding that the Dean's office and central administration of the university would be the central point for decisions about messages and strategies.

Those professional staff that created and delivered Extension's programs had a critical part to play as well. County and regional educators were expected to know and support the change plan elements and to contribute whenever possible to the public's appreciation of the plan. However, the most important expectation for this employee group was to provide excellence in programming and to communicate this to their primary audiences. Nothing would sell the plan more than evidence from campus and field program professionals that the proposed changes meant better program outcomes. It was important to minimize as much as possible the disruption that typically comes during a time of organizational change. It was critical that the public experience seamlessness from Extension in carrying out its mission and making a difference with programs. In the third year, the program teams were also asked to develop individual program public value statements as explained in Chapter 7.

Since the external relations and programming could have been mutually supporting, at cross-purposes or simply irrelevant to each other, the Associate Dean/Director for External Relations (Jeanne Markell) and the Associate Dean/Director for Programs (George Morse) coordinated their work on an almost daily basis. Since the Regional Directors reported, through the Directors of Field Operation, to Jeanne Markell and the Regional Extension Educators and county educators reported, through their Area Program Leaders and Associate Deans for the Capacity Areas, to George Morse, they were able to address potential conflicts between these two groups.

Support staff and support positions. Extension is a quite decentralized organization with a geographic spread from border to border in the state. Clerical and support staff in offices throughout Minnesota were key players in the external relations efforts. These local positions are often the first contact with extension for the public. Thus, the support staff was given training and support as members of the external relations team. The Director of Communications provided tools and coaching which was augmented on a day-to-day basis with support from CEDs and RDs.

Strategically Chosen Outsourced Expertise

The third core belief, which guided the external relations strategy, was that internal resources should be supplemented with strategically chosen outsourced expertise. Just prior to its reorganization, Extension had significantly reduced the centralized communications department as part of a university retrenchment and as a cost/ efficiency initiative. The culture of outsourcing for certain services was emerging in the system. This paved the way to move quickly to hire the type of expertise needed on communications when it became clear that Extension needed help preparing for the high stakes elements of the public pushback on the changes. Leadership wisely delegated this decision to the External Relations team who sought out one of the most highly respected, yet affordable, communication strategy firms in town. The decision to engage these services was clear upon hearing the leading philosophy of the firm's leader: "If communication is not your top priority, all of your other priorities are at risk. The greatest communication challenge you face is to make your point in a manner that persuades an audience to enthusiastically embrace your ideas and feel good about you" (Aronson 2003). The contract with the consultant added to Extension's capacity and skills to: (1) identify and develop key messages; (2) ensure message consistency; (3) develop presentations and written communications; and (4) increase success with crisis management. Finally, and most significantly, this consultant shared Extension's goal that a short term contract engender long term external relations skills: not only would the services of a consultant pay off with a better External relations effort now, but by working collaboratively with in house staff, the consultant would help build the skills of our internal team for the future.

Stakeholders: Who They Were and Why They Mattered

In early decades, Extension could rely on a more monolithic stakeholder base, one that could be steadfastly depended upon for support year after year. As both society and Extension have become more diverse, mapping stakeholders and their support has become complex. Extension professionals now must be more attentive to their many stakeholder groups, each of which has its own distinctions and special interests.

In 1996, a team of multi-state Extension professionals from four states studied stakeholder perceptions and discovered "that support for different aspects of the Extension program is found among different individuals" (Warner, Christenson, Dillman, and Salant 1996). Minnesota's leadership team knew the importance of stratifying key stakeholders and of determining the approaches needed to listen to their concerns and win their support.

Creating Public Value

A significant influence on the Minnesota external relations strategy was the book *Creating Public Value* (1995) by Harvard professor Mark Moore. Dr Moore, Founding Chairman of the Kennedy School's Committee on Executive Programs, advised the Extension leadership team in the fall of 2002 and he addressed the entire Extension organization at its all staff program summit. Moore's work aids leaders of public sector enterprises to know how they can best engage communities in supporting and legitimizing needed change, by placing the emphasis on an understanding of what creates public value. Working with Moore provided the Extension administration with a useful common language with which to move forward with external relations and indeed other parts of the change endeavor.

While Moore's public value concepts provided an overall framework for building public support, it did not provide specific guidelines for program teams to use in defining the public value of their individual programs. Dr. Laura Kalambokidis, Extension Economist in Public Finance, developed a training program for program teams to use in identifying and articulating the source of their public value. Public value is the value to program non-participants because of behavioral changes by program participants (Kalambokidis 2004). For example, when Extension teaches lake homeowners to plant buffer zones, build storm gardens and other means of improving lake quality, everyone who uses the lake benefits, not just the lake homeowners.

For the next several years, the "Public Value" framework would be integrated in staff development training and, eventually, even done with external supporters of Extension. This new vocabulary about "Extension Public Value" would become part of the lexicon to discuss return on investment to stakeholders both inside of and beyond the university.

The broader framework developed by Moore can be explained by picturing a "strategic triangle," of three distinct but connected concepts. The points on the triangle are Capacity, Public Value, and Legitimacy/Authority. Each part of the triangle had meaning to Extension leaders as they worked on the changes.

Capacity. The part of the framework Moore calls *Capacity* was a lens into the feasibility of the change plan. It reminded leaders that in spite of anything else, people wanted to know that the new model would "work" effectively.

Public value. The *Public Value* circle helped formulate two key messages. Early messages focused on "why" the structural changes were being made. A new delivery model was about more than structural change; it gave hope for stronger programs with more impact on the lives of Minnesotans. Later messages were about the public value of individual programs as outlined earlier. While the External Relations leadership handled the organizational messages on restructuring, the program leadership handled the individual program public value statements.

Legitimacy/authority. The third circle of the triangle, *Legitimacy/ Authority*, was the responsibility of the external relations strategy. Without legitimacy extended by those who authorize Extension as a public service, there would be no changes. Who needs to support us (allies) in doing this work? This guided the development of the following list of key audiences in several categories.

Key Audiences for External Relations

The key audiences for external relations efforts fall in three categories: (1) authorizers; (2) other funders and partners; and (3) program partners and participants. The authorizers include the following public sources of funds:

1. Congress,
2. state legislators,
3. county commissioners
4. United States Department of Agriculture, and
5. university regents.

Other funders and partners include:

1. grantors,
2. fiscal sponsors,
3. donors,
4. fee paying clientele, and
5. advisory and support networks.

Program partners and participants include:

1. collaborative organization, agencies, institutions in developing and delivering programs;

2. long standing communities of interest and geographic communities who are users of programs and services;

3. new communities of interest who are current audiences;

4. potential communities of interest who are future audiences; and

5. friends of Extension (former staff, retirees, and program alumni).

Why did each of these audiences matter in the external relations strategy?

Authorizers. In 1998-99, the foreshadowing years of Extension's sea changes in Minnesota, the Public Strategies Group (PSG) helped Extension think through its future and its financial sustainability. It was a significant time to think more carefully about how to keep authorizers supporting Extension's work. The key message from PSG co-founder, Peter Hutchinson, would be more fully developed nearly a decade later in his book on better government. In *The Price of Government: Getting the Results We Need in an Age of Permanent Fiscal Crisis,* Hutchinson repeats his advice to Extension: Authorizers (federal, state, county and university funders) are inclined to fund public sector activity that delivers what citizens want at a price they are willing to support (Osborne and Hutchinson 2004). Hutchinson and PSG convinced Extension to put the emphasis on outcomes vs. inputs and on return for investment vs. the cost of doing business. This is why the authorizers were the highest-priority audience in the external relations strategic plan. Resting on past laurels would no longer be an option.

Other funders and partners. The very same force that motivates authorizers to invest public dollars in Extension drives grantors, donors, and sponsors. Accountability to this segment of the stakeholder list was not a new expectation for Extension, though the climate of the planned reorganizing ratcheted up those expectations. Individuals and groups who pledged these extramural funds demanded assurance that the projects, services, and, in some cases, specific staff would not be jeopardized in a new delivery system. Some of these relationships involved longstanding Extension partners who feared their special interests might not fare well in the shuffle. The Dean/Director and other administrators devoted time and effort with these audiences; still, they could not always guarantee that Extension's new way of doing business would be compatible with the issues of everyone involved.

Program partners and participants. Significant changes to the delivery system throughout the state were also a concern to many of those who were frequent users of Extension's services. Traditional clientele were skeptical of the proposal to house fewer staff in county offices. Some criticized Extension for moving educators to regional centers, suggesting this was a move away from its original mission. The opposite was true. The changes were done to protect the original mission, using new methods. Newer clientele and program partners also needed assurance that the changes would be positive for meeting their needs. Finally, though they were the silent stakeholder segment, it was important for Extension to consider the "yet-to-be-reached" audiences in the design of its messages about moving to a regional, more specialized, and focused delivery system.

Once the above audiences were mapped, goals were set to move those in the "resister" column to the "accepter" column and, ultimately, to move "accepters" to "advocates." The following statement from a county commissioner is an example of the gain in seeing a resister move into the advocate column:

> *"None of us likes to see great things weakened or whittled away. In the case of the University of Minnesota Extension Service, I don't see that happening. I see a 100 –year-old institution continuing to make changes that reflect what Minnesotans really need."* (Richard Larson, County Commissioner, Kandiyohi County Minnesota in a letter to the editor of his local newspaper)

Managing External Relations through Internal Relations

This chapter discusses the external relations strategy that helped the restructuring gain acceptance. The audiences defined above were the centerpiece of that strategy, but an equally important *means* to that end was the task of a well-executed internal relations plan. The single greatest obstacle to the transition of external resisters into accepters and then advocates was that of staff morale. Numerous factors contributed to staff dissention. In some instances, individuals were fearful of losing their jobs or having their locations changed. Some were fearful that they would not be able to operate successfully in the much more specialized roles of regional educator. Some distrusted or disagreed with the motives for change. Others, though in agreement that the current model was not working, were not satisfied that the proposed changes and/or timelines were politically viable. It was essential for leadership to address all of these forms of staff resistance and try to understand and respond to opposition. This was the right approach simply out of justice and sensitivity to employee needs, but it was also critical to managing the potential of an external relations fiasco if employees took their issues outside the system.

For all those reasons, leaders were deliberate and mindful of managing up, down and across the organization in terms of attitudes about change. A number of studies have been conducted by state Extension systems relative to employee attitudes on change. A 2001 framework defined by Ann C. Schauber of Oregon Extension is particularly relevant to employees' attitudes during reorganization. Schauber (2001) described an employee's attitude toward diversity as belonging to one of three postures: *Supportive, Uncertain,* and *Defensive.* Such taxonomies are helpful to change leaders as they decide where and how to expend their energies. The Dean/Director met frequently with employee leadership groups and individuals, stressing the need for cohesiveness and for working on behalf of the greater good of the organization. This journey was not without setbacks. Some employees who either disapproved of the plan or feared for their personal futures used their connections with local legislators to fuel the fire of resistance. Some resented being expected to carry the consistent key messages and being asked to advocate on behalf of a plan they did not support. Extension's organizational value of employee autonomy backfired in some instances, as a ticket for individuals to try to turn the tide of the proposed reorganization. This resulted in a less-than-desirable flurry of misinformation and myths circulating while the legislature was in session and while the Dean/Director was attempting to define the assets and strengths of the new regional delivery system. Valuable time was lost whenever leadership found itself on defense rather than offense. One intervention by the external relations team was to empower regional directors to help shore up "attitude adjustment" among peers. They were provided with training, tools, and support to influence their colleagues to play a more positive role. Anointing Regional Directors as "field level external relations captains" was a key part of managing the impact of internal relations on external relations.

Media Relations: A Means to an End

The media was not a primary audience in the strategy, but a very critical secondary one. Print and electronic media outlets were identified as important means to the end of getting priority audience groups to understand and applaud the change effort. A plan of action was developed including message content, targets, messengers, and timelines.

The plan was developed in consultation with the U of M central administration external affairs office. This collaboration, though necessary and appropriate, was not always easy. Requirements to get sign-off and consensus on messages and methodologies sometimes delayed getting the message out, but it must be recognized that most of the mistakes made in media relations resulted from a lack of advanced preparations. In the 2002 restructuring, Extension found itself on the reactive, rather than the proactive, side of media coverage all too often. In the 2002 restructuring, the challenge for administration was to keep details of the change plan from becoming public too soon, before appropriate vetting had occurred with key authorizers. As some of these details leaked out, it became difficult to manage the message and avoid the harms of the rumor mill.

Media management became easier in the 2004 restructuring, with a more successful and proactive media plan and the ability to better "own the message." Extension staff and key external supporters helped build those connections with local newspapers, TV, radio and other print media, periodicals, newsletters, etc. Extension occasionally found itself in a reactive mode when editors or opinion writers printed stories based on myths or speculation. In such cases, staff would weigh the merits of public response. Unless it was obviously necessary to dispute gross inaccuracies, the posture taken was to avoid fighting the battle in the press. On the advice of the external media consultant, leaders worked to keep their sights set on one central message: for the plan to be given a chance. A number of principles guided the media relations portion of the external relations effort:

1. The Dean/Director would be the chief spokesperson for the media;

2. External Relations would provide tools and training to support both staff and friends of extension who have contact with media;

3. Every media opportunity was a chance to build public support for the changes through identified key messages;

4. All media releases, news stories, and press conferences would be directed at the level of the Dean/Director and/or the University's central offices;

5. Media contacts and press calls would be coordinated through the Director of Communications;

6. Press and media activity were to be, to the extent possible, an organized, forward looking tactics, rather than a tool for debate or defensive response to critics; and

7. Media coverage would be tracked weekly, tabulated, and circulated within the organization to take stock of the positive/negative swing of media coverage.

Looking back at the history of these two restructurings (starting in the late '90's through the first year of implementation in 2005), it is interesting to note how media relations and indeed all of external relations might be done differently today. Blogs and social networking technologies burgeoned since this time, causing planners to adapt and adjust to how these methods might both help and hamper message management. Renowned business and technology columnist Dan Gillmor tells the story of this emerging phenomenon, and sheds light on the increasing influence of technology on internal as well as external communications and media relations (Gillmor 2006).

Timelines, Transparency, Tactics, and Tools

This chapter has so far discussed the rationale for an External Relations strategy, the audience, and the roles and responsibilities of various players in the system. The remainder of this chapter will describe timelines, tactics, and tools that helped it succeed.

Timeline: Two Phases of the Change Effort

The timeframe for planning and rolling out the Minnesota Extension's two successive reorganizations was 2001-2005. These "reorganizations" were more than shifts to regional centers, as described in Chapters 3 to 9. The first reorganization was announced in December 2001 and implemented in July 2002. The second reorganization was announced in April 2003 and the regional centers opened on January 1, 2004. This second restructuring expanded those shifts in a way that put the changes more squarely on the public's radar. Namely, this would change the "face" of Extension, with the creation of 18 regional centers where many staff would be re-located. The second restructuring also included a bold plan to reconstruct Extension's historic county funding partnership (Chapter 3).

Consultation and Decision Making

The term "transparency" has taken on a kind of de rigueur in contemporary change management theory, being viewed as a contributor to a two-way function/channel to facilitate open communication between an organization and the public. A scan of the environment in which these two reorganizations played out exposed a good deal about the issue of transparency, given Extension's decentralized culture of very consultative decision-making. Plus, the nature of intense public sense of "right to know" about the inner workings of the enterprise meant leaders were constantly weighing pros and cons of public vetting before making sensitive decisions. In some instances, timing was a crucial factor (legislative calendar, hiring contracts and office leases) and erring on the side of public consultation had the cost of time. For other decisions, legal or contractual limitations left administrators with no say in how publicly a decision would be made (staffing decisions, etc). One of the greatest challenges to transparency was the sheer complexity of Extension's funding model prior to 2004. For example, an area of expertise team with nine regional educators had at least ten different funding partners. Each had funding from the Extension, based on state and federal funds, and each had funding from their home county. This made changes in the portfolio of areas of expertise so complicated that it almost happened by chance.

Legislators and other authorizers wanted to see the fine print of several layers and sources of Extension's funding, not an easy thing to communicate publicly. Extension struggled to tell its story of seeking change, in a clear and concise manner, disclosing as much fact and information as possible without cluttering up the key messages of change. The need to engage the public had to be balanced with the consequences of changing at too slow a speed. Deadlines, like the launch date for new regional offices, were needed to keep the system moving out of the neutral zone. Change management consultant William Bridges warns:

> One of the hardest times for leaders to stay the course is during the 'neutral zone' of the change process. This is the

in-between state, when the old way of doing things, the old identity or the old life is gone, but the new one hasn't yet become operational. It is a chaotic time, one when people are tempted to go back to the past or bail out of the change effort completely (Bridges 1992).

In this environment, it was not easy for the Dean/Director to determine what was "enough" consultation/deliberation before making needed decisions. A number of very volatile decisions were required to move ahead according to the timeline. Where should the regional centers be located? What programs should be discontinued or consolidated? The stakes were too high for one more plan to set on an administration shelf, so external relations had to be finessed to maximize the public input while minimizing the gridlock that often comes with an open decision making process. Leaders needed an effective strategy for not just putting out fires and responding to criticism, but to stay on the offense and avoid letting others frame the debate. The heart of that strategy was message management.

Key Messages and Message Management

Extension has thrived for nearly a century with the luxury of riding on its laurels and past reputation for public service. A consequence of this is little experience with marketing and brand management. Most who work for Extension assume that their good work speaks for them and the organization. Extension has little history with the kind of communication "campaign" that this restructuring demanded. As has been outlined, the leadership agreed that strategic communication should be directed from the top. This did not sit well with some staff. Some felt manipulated and restricted with directives about using consistent messages in their conversations about the changes. This situation called for added effort on the part of the external relations team in educating the system on what it meant to have an intentional, organized communications strategy. The external consultant was helpful in that training effort and in the deliberation of what key messages to use. The goal was to have three broad messages that would transcend the detail of proposed changes (staffing, structure, finance), and would get the audience to think about the benefits of Extension rather than the features. These are the three key messages around which the case for change was built:

1. *Extension makes a difference in Minnesota.* The University of Minnesota Extension Service connects community needs and University resources to address critical issues in Minnesota.

2. *Extension makes University research and knowledge practical and useful to the people of Minnesota.* Extension translates complex science and university discovery into education and information that makes sense in everyday life.

3. *Extension makes a difference in people's lives.* Extension's educational programs and services help improve quality of life and wellbeing.

Each message was to be supported with simple, short, clear proof points, and transitions to the need for Extension to change. Staff members were trained on how to communicate using these three messages, inserting examples and stories from their unique perspectives in the organization. Six things in particular were emphasized:

1. Make proof points clear, short and simple;
2. Use very specific and personal examples as proof points;
3. Keep the focus on Extension's benefits, not features;
4. Make sure the communication is clear, concise and convincing;
5. Keep the communication directed to the audience; and
6. Stay focused on the goal: to get support for the change plan.

Everyone in the system, from the Dean/Director to support staff, was expected to know and use the key messages, and training and support materials were provided regularly. The external consultant and the communications team conducted media and communication training workshops so people could practice the messaging and prepare for the public's questions and concerns. Staff and Extension advocates were given tools: fact sheets, briefing statements, and talking points at every step along the way.

Tracking, Accessing, and Adjusting

An implementation team, including members of the external relations staff, was appointed to track how things were going and to look for ways reaching the goal of getting the regional centers running by January 1, 2004. Some examples follow.

Problems with obvious solutions. One that comes to mind regards 4-H, one of Extension's most visible programs. The first proposed changes for regional/local staffing met some resistance overall, but the most vocal protests about lack of county-based staff was with the 4-H area. As this pushback was tracked, something had to be done to compromise for the good of the whole plan. An acceptable alternative was devised and that compromise perhaps saved the entire change effort from derailment.

A second example was the response to a system wide survey of staff implemented in August and September 2004, nine months after the implementation of the regional centers. The survey was sponsored by the Minnesota Association of Extension Educators and reflected considerable pockets of discontent with Extension administration. In response, Extension administration created the Vitality Task Force with the aim of developing recommendations for "making Extension a more vital and impactful organization" (Martenson 2005). The task force included 17 representatives from Minnesota Association of Extension Educators (MAEE), Extension Faculty Consultative Committee (EFCC), Extension Staff Consultative Committee (ESCC), The Circle (an association of professionals of color), and administration. The group made a series of recommendations related to improving communication flow and dialogue, recognizing impacts, growing into new roles, honoring diversity, working toward unity, and measuring how well we are meeting promises made to our stakeholders. This process helped administration identify a number of issues that still needed attention. As these were addressed, morale rebounded.

Identifying gatekeepers. Mapping the various external audiences in categories of "positive/ neutral / negative" was helpful on questions such as: locations for listening sessions around the state, where to target media releases and editorials, or which specific stakeholders needed more one on one attention from the Dean/Director.

Building coalitions. The implementation team helped track the individual parts of the change efforts but also kept an eye on the big picture: wins, gains, meeting deadlines, etc. Particularly challenging were the months the legislature was in session. Several highly charged legislative hearings could have been the demise of the entire effort. Through the patience and wisdom of Dean/Director Charles Casey who took the brunt of the often contentious questioning, and through the methodical efforts of the tracking/adjusting process, appropriate modifications were made and the plan for regional/county Extension stayed on course.

Summary and Future Research
Summary

For readers who anticipate or are in the midst of organizational change efforts of their own, here is a quick summary of the things that worked well for Minnesota. Recognizing that Extension operations vary across the country and every state has a unique external constituency; the following list would tend to have universal applicability:

- Define and support external relations roles inside the system and tapping outside expertise as needed;

- Have a firm date for implementation and letting that target drive the tempo;
- Recognize that staff morale issues can make or break external relations efforts;
- Keep everything focused on the goal of keeping the plan alive;
- Don't underestimate the power of the media to influence public opinion;
- Identify and stick to a few clear and concise key messages;
- Stay on the offense as much as possible; don't let others frame the debate;
- Use multiple communication tools to answer FAQs and debunk myths and rumors;
- Put the top leader out front and provide him/her with good back-up support;
- Train, coach, practice being effective communicators throughout the system;
- Balance information gathering with making decisions in a timely way;
- Use both data and stories to support key messages and respond to critics;
- Communicate well with central administration and with staff inside the system as well as externally; and
- Learn from mistakes and celebrate victories as you move toward the end goal.

Future Research

Two major questions that need further research in making large organizational changes in Extension are:

1. Can CSREES provide external relations resources or support multi-state teams to help states facing the need for major restructuring?

2. Can CSREES or other groups support research on the effectiveness of different external relations efforts for major organizational changes?

Chapter 5

Specialized Extension Educators

George Morse and Adeel Ahmed

Specialization is what makes us productive.

Charles Wheelan, 2002

Nearly every Cooperative Extension Service talks about their educators being much more "specialized" than in earlier years. However, the terms "Regional Extension Educator" and "Extension Field Specialist" have no common meaning across states. Minnesota's history of using the term "specialized Extension educators" demonstrates how loosely the terms "specialized" and "specialist" have been used with Extension field staff.

Starting with the county cluster model in 1987 (Chapter 2), the Minnesota county Extension Educators each self-selected a specialization to cover in their cluster of counties. However, the "specialized" Extension Educators in the county cluster model were very different from the specialized educators in Minnesota's new regional/county model. Until 2009, the Iowan Extension Educators were called 'Extension Field Specialists'; yet, their structure did not allow as much specialization as in the new Minnesota model where the educators are simply called 'Extension Educators in (name of their specialty)'. Now the Iowa field educators are called 'program specialists' and have roles similar to the Minnesota REEs. "District/ Area Specialists" are defined by USDA only as "those persons who are responsible for a highly specialized segment matter for a district of the state" (USDA 2008). Further, the USDA definition assumes these positions report through a District Program Leader or a District Director. Yet, the Minnesota Regional Extension Educators often cover the entire state and appear to be more specialized than the USDA definition for "District/Area Specialists." To date, there is no literature that defines the features of a "Specialized Extension Educator" or empirically measures the impacts of specialization.

In this chapter, initial steps are taken to fill this gap. An explicit conceptual definition is given of a "specialized Extension Educator." The characteristics of the Regional Extension Educators in Minnesota before and after the 2004 restructuring are defined and empirically measured.

Definition of Specialization

In order to define "specialized Extension Educators" it is necessary to clarify some key concepts, including: (1) area of expertise, (2) statewide program team, (3) program leadership, (4) scholarship, (5) outreach education, and (6) community of interest.

Key Concepts

Area of expertise (AOE). An area of expertise is analogous to an academic discipline, but typically is broader than most disciplines. The Crops AOE in Minnesota includes people from five academic departments and one center (Agronomy and Plant Genetics; Applied Economics; Bioproducts and Biosystems Engineering; Entomology; Soils, Water and Climate; and the Water Resources Center). The Community Economics AOE in Minnesota includes people from two academic departments and one center (Applied Economics; Design, Housing and Apparel; and the Tourism Center).

Statewide program team. This is a team designing and implementing a statewide program. Most teams consider the delivery of programs a responsibility of the team and not just the individual. If an individual agrees to deliver a program on a specific date and becomes ill, someone else from the team covers the commitment to deliver the program. In a few cases, the person covering has to travel from a considerable distance to handle this obligation. The concept is that the public expects the program to go on and prefers a substitute to a cancelation.

The team, generally, includes campus faculty from several different academic disciplines and REEs from around the state. Some teams include REEs from several areas of expertise. The statewide delivery of a program might be done by one field specialist, by a team of field specialists, or a combination of field specialists and campus faculty. However, the key is that the program is available throughout the state.

Program leadership. Leadership for a statewide program provides the initial needs assessment and market research, arranges the funding for the program, develops the curriculum, markets the program, teaches, and evaluates. As a program leader, an individual would do one or more of these tasks for a statewide program. Once a workable system is established on each of these, other team members follow the new approaches. This process of implementing established programs is called program management.

Scholarship. Four types of scholarship are relevant for Extension programs: (1) the scholarship of application, (2) the scholarship of integration, (3) the scholarship of discovery, and (4) the scholarship of teaching (Boyer 1990). More details are provided on scholarship in Chapters 9 and 11.

Outreach education. Outreach education has many definitions and formats. In this book, it refers to educational programs provided to individuals not enrolled in for-credit programs at the University. Most of these programs are delivered in communities around the state rather than at the University.

Community of interest. The term 'communities of interest' refers to groups with common interests around the state, e.g. pork producers, economic development professionals, low-income nutrition advocates, environmentalists, etc. Working with communities of interest shifts the programming focus from the traditional focus on a geographic community, such as a county or several counties, to specific audiences at a statewide level. In some programs, the community of interest and the geographic community overlap to a considerable degree. In Community Vitality, there is considerable overlap since many programs require participation from a wide cross section of local leaders. In many agricultural programs, individuals in a community of interest are the target audience rather than groups in a community. In the agricultural programs, there is less overlap between the communities of interest and the geographic communities than in most Community Vitality programs.

Definition of Specialized Extension Educator

Given the above definitions, it is now possible to define a specialized Extension Educator. The definition used in this book is as follows:

> *A specialized Extension Educator concentrates on an area of expertise, provides leadership on a statewide program team that develops and delivers outreach educational programs for a community of interest, and contributes to the scholarship related to outreach education.*

Not all specialized Extension Educators deliver programs throughout the state. They are part of a statewide program where the core deliverables are the same statewide and that delivery is a team responsibility and not just an individual one. There are some adjustments to the core deliverables to fit local situations, with as much as 50 percent of a local program being unique to the local area. In some cases, local expertise is used.

While a conceptual definition of specialized field staff is necessary, it is not sufficient. To understand the differences in specialization between educators, empirical data are needed on the differences in specific features that define specialization.

Survey of Regional Extension Educators

A number of defining features can be used to measure the level of specialization of Regional Extension Educators, reflecting the policies adopted in the regional/county model. These features could be used to describe the level of specialization in any Extension Service. To collect data on these characteristics, the authors implemented a survey of Minnesota educators.

To determine the differences between specialization in the county cluster delivery system and the regional/county delivery system, all Minnesota Extension Regional Extension Educators (REEs) were surveyed in January 2007. REEs were asked to respond to questions about their work in 2001 under the Minnesota county cluster model. Then, they were asked identical questions about their work in 2006 under the new regional/county system.

The Minnesota REEs perceptions of the county cluster and regional/county models provide direct comparisons between the two systems. This approach avoided the difficulties of comparisons between states, which have different terminology, initial structures, different audiences, and needs. Focusing on Minnesota, before and after the 2004 change, also avoided the problems of securing approval for human subject review in multiple states.

In July 2002, Minnesota Extension had to reduce the number of staff. While Extension reorganized the number of specializations in 2002, it maintained the basic county cluster model. After only 18 months, Extension implemented the new regional/county model. The authors asked Regional Educators to describe their work before the changes started (in 2001) and two years after the implementation of the regional/county model (in 2006). These dates were chosen to avoid the transition period.

Since the focus of this book is specialization and regionalization, only the Regional Extension Educators were surveyed. The roles and responsibility of the county positions did not change and they were not surveyed, even though they are very important to the regional/county model.

All 129 REEs were surveyed with a response rate of 79 percent. The 102 regional educators that responded were representative of all five of the Capacity Areas in Minnesota Extension as shown in Table 5.1.

Table 5.1:

REE Response Rate by Capacity Area, 2007

Capacity Areas	Percent of Total Regional Educators (N = 129)	Percent of Respondents in Survey	Response Rate by Capacity Area
Agriculture, Food and Environment	30	29	79
Community Vitality	15	14	74
Family Development	20	22	85
Natural Resources and Environment	13	12	71
Youth Development	22	23	83
Total	100	100	79

Note: Data in column 1 are from the University of Minnesota Extension Human Resources Directory (May 2007).

To determine face validity, the draft survey was circulated among several experienced Extension members. To ensure reliability, three steps were taken. First, the survey was pre-tested with eight persons, using a face-to-face approach suggested by Dillman (1978). Second, to allow anonymity, a question on the area of expertise was omitted since it would have allowed identification of individuals when combined with time on the job. Third, the survey was administered by the University's Office of Management Services (OMS). OMS removed all individual identifiers before sending results to the authors. This anonymity also allowed respondents to be more candid in their responses, increasing the reliability of the results.

To increase participation, the authors provided advance notice to both supervisors and REEs on the survey and its purpose. Two follow-up reminders were sent by the OMS to those who had not completed the survey.

Defining Features of Minnesota Regional Educators

Specialized Regional Extension Educators in Minnesota have the following defining features:
1. are located in regional centers rather than county offices;
2. cover larger geographic areas than non-specialized educators;
3. are not funded by counties but rather by state funds, federal funds, or by other organizations;
4. focus on a specific area of expertise;
5. have high scholarship and promotion expectations; and
6. are supervised by state specialists in their area of expertise.

Regional Centers for Specialized Educators

The Regional Extension Educators (REEs) are located in one of 18 regional centers located around the state. For the location of these offices, see Minnesota's website (www.Extension.umn.edu). These locations were selected to create the greatest access to programming around the state. Unlike Alabama, where the regional educators are located in county offices, none of the Minnesota REEs are in county offices. Iowa had a system much like Alabama until April 2009, when it shifted to one like Minnesota. However, the Iowa educators, called "program specialists," will have virtual offices (University Extension 2009).

Specialized Educators Cover Larger Areas

Another hallmark of specialization is the size of the geographic area covered by an Extension educator. The larger the geographic area a field staff Extension educator covers, the more specialized the educator can be. Specialization within a single county would often result in more capacity on the area of expertise than there is local demand.

In 2006, nearly half of REEs worked statewide depending on the type of program (Table 5.2). In both the Agricultural and Natural Resources programs, over 90 percent of REEs worked statewide, which reflects the nature of their programs that are largely aimed at individual decision-makers. Counties purchased a number of local agricultural educators to work only in their county or in two neighboring counties (Chapter 6).

In contrast, the Community Vitality REEs covered an average of nine counties each, reflecting the participation of a cross-section of community leaders. In Family Development, the eleven Health and Nutrition REEs supervise about 100 nutrition education assistants. The family development REEs serve an average of seven counties, each providing educational leadership, and supervision.

The 4-H program has 11,000 adult volunteers who contribute greatly to the success of the program but require coordination from the local 4-H coordinators. The 30 4-H REEs supervise the local program coordinators and provide educational leadership to the 4-H program in an average of three counties. Sixty-three percent of the REEs, not counting the 4-H REEs, worked statewide. From this perspective, two thirds of the Regional Extension Educators in Minnesota really are state specialists.

Table 5.2:
Counties Covered by Minnesota REEs, 2006

Counties Covered	AFE (%)	NRE (%)	CV (%)	FD (%)	YD (%)	Total (%)
1 to 2	3	0	0	0	17	5
3 to 4	7	0	0	9	54	15
5 to 6	0	0	0	9	4	3
7 or more	0	8	86	54	17	30
State wide	90	92	14	27	8	47
Total Percent	100	100	100	100	100	100
N	30	12	14	22	24	102

Source: Survey of REEs in March 2007 (Morse and Ahmed 2007).

AFE = Agriculture; NRE = Natural Resources; CV = Community Vitality; FD = Family Development; YD = Youth Development

Table 5.2 includes the results for all REEs working in Extension in 2006 and not just the REEs who worked for Extension prior to the restructuring. In 2006, the pattern for the number of counties covered by the established REEs, those who were working for Extension in 1999, followed almost exactly the same one as for all REEs in 2006, with a difference of only 1 to 3 percent in each category of counties.

There were major changes in the number of counties covered between 2001 and 2006, as shown in Table 5.3. In 2001, 58 percent worked in four counties or less. Only the respondents (74) who worked in Extension in 1999 or before are included because it gives a more accurate picture of the geographic distribution in 2001.

Table 5.3:
Counties Covered by Minnesota REEs, 2001

Counties Covered	AFE (%)	NRE (%)	CV (%)	FD (%)	YD (%)	Total (%)
1 to 2	13	33	30	27	88	36
3 to 4	26	11	30	27	6	22
5 to 6	30	11	0	14	6	15
7 or more	17	12	20	32	0	18
Statewide	13	33	10	0	0	9
Total	100	100	100	100	100	100
N	22	7	9	20	16	74

Source: Survey of Minnesota REEs in March 2007 (Morse and Ahmed 2007). AFE = Agriculture, NRE = Natural Resources, CV = Community Vitality, FD = Family Development, and YD = Youth Development. The 74 educators in this table are ones who worked for Minnesota Extension in 1999 and continued to work for it in 2007.

The shift in numbers shown between Tables 5.2 and 5.3 reflects the change from geographic communities to communities of interest. In Community Vitality, the two types of audiences overlap much more than in Agriculture and Natural Resources.

The new Minnesota REEs are filling the gap spanning role, connecting the research oriented state specialists and local generalists. This gap spanner role had been played earlier by the M.S. level state specialists who had been located on campus in academic departments, as described in Chapter 2.

Table 5.4 summarizes the changes in geographic coverage from 2001 to 2006. In 2001, only 27 percent of the educators covered seven counties or more compared to 80 percent in 2006. In contrast, in 2001, 36 percent of the educators covered only one or two counties compared to only 5 percent of the REEs covering 1 to 2 counties in 2006. Furthermore, if all regional educators had been shown in

Table 5.4, rather than just those who had worked for Extension in or before 1999, the distribution for 2006 is very similar and not statistically different at the 10 percent level.

Table 5.4:
Percent Counties Covered by REEs, 2001 and 2006

Counties Covered by Educators working in both 2001 and 2006	Before Restructuring in 2001 (%)	After Restructuring in 2006 (%)
1 to 2 counties	36	5
3 to 4 counties	22	12
5 to 6 counties	15	3
7 or more counties	18	30
Entire State (87 counties)	9	50
Respondents (N)	74	74

Source: Morse and Ahmed 2008. The 74 educators in this table are ones who worked for Minnesota Extension in 1999 and continued to work for it in 2007.

Specialized Educators Not Funded by Counties

The source of funding for educators is another important characteristic of specialization. When a portion of the funding for county-based educators comes from counties, specialization is not as likely. There are pressures for the educators housed in counties to answer questions outside their area of expertise. In 2006, Minnesota REE funding came primarily from state and federal sources and not from counties, making it much easier for the educators to specialize. A few REE positions were funded by communities of interest, with the funding encouraging rather than discouraging focus.

Focus on Area of Expertise

The opportunity for REEs to focus on a specific area of expertise is a basic principle of the division of labor, which is a fundamental characteristic of specialization (Chapter 2). Table 5.5 shows the 16 Areas of Expertise to which the 129 REEs were assigned as of 2007.

Table 5.5:
REEs by Area of Expertise, Minnesota, 2007

Capacity Area/ Area of Expertise	Regional Educators
Agriculture, Food and Environment	
Crops	10
Livestock	9
Ag Business Management	7
Food Safety	7
Horticulture	5
Natural Resources and Environment	
Water Resources	8
Natural Resources	6
Environmental Sciences	4
Housing Technology	1
Family Development	
Health and Nutrition	11
Family Resource Management	8
Family Relations	6
Youth Development	
4-H	24
Community Youth Development	5
Community Vitality	
Leadership & Civic Engage.	10
Community Economics	9
Totals	129

Source: University of Minnesota Extension Staff Directory, 2007

There are four components of Extension field staff specialization related to focus:

1. organization by area of expertise;
2. statewide program teams;
3. planned number of programs; and
4. academic training of Regional Educators.

Organization by area of expertise. The focus for REEs became much tighter after the 2004 reorganization. Almost three quarters of the REEs reported the opportunity to "focus on my area of expertise" was either more (31%) or much more (43%) because of the specialization. In contrast, in 2001, many REEs worked in several different areas of expertise (Table 5.6).

Table 5.6:
REE "Specialists" Working in Other Capacity Areas, 2001.

Capacity Area of "Specialization"	Time Spent in Other Capacity Areas (%)	REEs Working in Other Capacity Areas (%)	Primary Other Capacity Area Areas
Community Vitality (CV)	53	64	AFE & YD
Natural Resources & Environment (NRE)	48	66	AFE & YD
Agriculture, Food & Environment (AFE)	24	53	YD & CV
Youth Development (YD)	20	41	FD & CV
Family Development (FD)	18	16	YD

Source: Survey of Minnesota REEs by Morse and Ahmed, 2008

While Extension Educators in every capacity area spent some time working in areas of expertise outside their "specialization," this was more common in some capacity areas. Nearly two-thirds of the Community Vitality REEs worked outside of their "specialization" and spent over half time (53%) working in another Capacity Area (Table 5.6). Two-thirds of the natural resources REEs worked in other capacity areas about 48 percent of the time. This data suggests that these two capacity areas were the least specialized of the five prior to the new regional/county system. The primary reason for this in the Community Vitality Capacity Area is that most of the Extension Educators who self-selected to "specialize" in Community Vitality had been hired originally as either agricultural or 4-H educators and expected by their county stakeholders to give this work priority. Given this lack of focus, it is not surprising that many state specialists in Community Vitality and Natural Resources did not view the Extension Educators as likely partners for statewide programming.

Statewide program teams. The development of statewide program teams helped focus the work of Regional Extension Educators. To encourage this shift in focus, Capacity Areas were asked to develop statewide program teams on their major programs and then to write program business plans. The statewide programs done before 2004 were done primarily by state specialists. At the county or county cluster level, the history was one of local programs being done by individual Extension Educators or small teams. The first step in the planning process was to form statewide program teams. It is not surprising that the identification of individuals willing to participate on the program teams was perceived as the most important benefit of the program business planning by both the REEs (73%) and the state specialists (71%).

Two related questions confirm the enhanced opportunities to work in teams and to provide statewide leadership. Sixty-three percent of the REEs who were with Minnesota Extension before 1999 responded they had more opportunities to work on a team in the new system compared to the old one. In addition, 64 percent perceived greater opportunities to provide leadership to statewide programs in the new system.

Planned number of programs. Focus on a manageable set of programs is essential for specialization. Few educators can become experts in every issue and every program within their area of expertise. The development of effective Extension programs requires background research on the audience's needs, development of curriculum, pilot efforts, evaluations, and continuous improvement. Without program focus, Extension educators have neither the time nor resources for investing in program quality.

An Extension program is defined as all the educational activities aimed at the same educational objectives and the same target audience. A program is likely to consist of a number of different educational events and activities, such as workshops, popular press releases, applied demonstrations, websites, webinars, and field days (Seevers, Graham, Gamon, and Conklin 1997).

In 2002, Minnesota Extension had over 208 "programs." Many did not fit the above definition and were individual events within a program. By 2005, Minnesota Extension, through the program business planning process, reduced the number of programs to 59. In part, the number of programs fell because many individual events that were really a part of a program had been labeled as programs. In addition, the number of programs fell as those programs that had been done only in one or two counties were not included. In a few cases (vital aging, sheep production, and diversity training), programs were discontinued as areas of expertise realized they simply did not have the resources to do a program statewide.

Areas of expertise could submit as many programs as they wished, provided they assembled a program team and wrote a program business plan. These two requirements encouraged teams to think carefully about both the needs of their audiences and their capacity to deliver.

Academic training of regional educators. A further feature important to greater focus and specialization is that the requirement that the

REE's advanced degree must now be related to his or her area of expertise. This ensures that field staff has the basic knowledge in a specific academic discipline necessary to interact well with the campus faculty. This is also important to enhancing scholarship and program quality.

In 2006, ninety percent of REE respondents had either a master's (79%) or Ph.D. (11%) degree related to their area of expertise. In 2001, Minnesota Extension required a master's degree for an REE position but often the degree was in adult education or other topics unrelated to the area of expertise. Now there is high alignment between the degree and area of expertise.

Promotion and Scholarship Requirements for REE

If program leadership and scholarship are important elements of the REEs' promotion criteria, the REEs must specialize in order to be successful. In 2006, Minnesota Extension adopted a new promotion policy of requiring a promotion within six years for regional educators. The primary criteria for promotion were program leadership, outreach teaching, and scholarship. The details of the new promotion system are presented in Chapter 9. To meet these criteria within six years, the REEs need to specialize much more than in the county cluster system in order to move an idea from a concept to accomplishments in program leadership and scholarship.

Supervision by State Specialists

This might be the most important change in the Minnesota regional/model. Specialized Regional Extension Educators now are supervised by experts in the REE's area of expertise rather than by District Directors. Each of the new supervisors, called Area Program Leaders, supervise all REEs across the state in a given Area of Expertise. In the old system, District Directors supervised everyone within a given geographic area, regardless of their Area of Expertise.

Reasons for change. The major reasons for the change were as follows:

1. It was impossible for District Directors to provide relevant coaching on subject matter or target audiences to REEs in 16 different Areas of Expertise;

2. The transactions costs for creating a statewide program team was very high since every Area of Expertise team(usually eight people) had nine supervisors (eight District Directors and one Capacity Area Leader); and

3. The policy and procedural differences between Capacity Areas made it very difficult for District Directors to coach and enforce these policies and procedures.

Supervisor shares expertise. Since one of the key functions of a supervisor is to coach extension educators, the greater specialization expected from REEs required supervisors with expertise in the same field as the educators.

Table 5.7 shows the background of the Area Program Leaders who supervise the REEs. The agribusiness management (ABM) area of expertise will be used as an explanation of this table. The first column shows both the number of REEs supervised by the Area Program Leader and the number of State Specialists in the Area of Expertise. The ABM Area Program Leader supervised six regional educators in 2007 and another 13 faculty worked in ABM (column 1, Table 5.7). In two of the Areas of Expertise, 4-H and Health/ Nutrition, the majority of the other persons are program coordinators and program assistants.

The second column in Table 5.7 shows the department or the capacity area in which the Area Program Leader worked and whether or not the individual was a tenured faculty member. The Area Program Leader for agribusiness management was a tenured faculty member in the Department of Applied Economics. In 2007, all of the Areas Program Leaders in agriculture were tenured faculty members while none were in the other capacity areas.

Column 3 shows the office location for the Area Program Leaders. For the Agribusiness Management Area Program Leader, the office was in the Department of Applied Economics on the St. Paul campus of the University of Minnesota.

Area program leader differences. The Area Program Leader's time allocated to this job varied by area of expertise. In the Agriculture, Food, and Environment Capacity Area (AFE), the five area program leaders are tenured faculty and have 25 percent appointments, as well as having responsibilities as state Extension specialists, campus teaching, and research. The AFE Capacity Area had three additional area program leaders, located in regional centers to supervise the 40 county-based agricultural educators and Master Gardener program coordinators. Several of the other areas of expertise had full-time area program leader positions.

The reason for the differences in the roles of the area program leaders between Agriculture and the other Capacity Areas are that there is a higher ratio of state specialists to REEs in agriculture. To have the full respect of the state specialists, it was important to have tenured faculty as the area program leaders in agriculture. This required part time area program leaders in agriculture since it was not possible to find existing tenured faculty who wished to devote full time to this and Extension could not afford to establish new full-time positions.

The agricultural area program leaders coached the Extension educators, reviewed their annual plans of work, organized training sessions, helped them prepare for promotion, and recommending salary increases (common with all Capacity Areas). In contrast, the area program leaders in other areas had more direct involvement in program development.

Table 5.7:

Area Program Leaders by Area of Expertise, MN, 2007

Area of Expertise	REEs/ Total # Others in AOE [a]	APL's Home Unit/Tenure [b]	Office Location
Agriculture, Food and Environment (AFE) Capacity Area			
Agribusiness Management	6/13	Applied Econ. / Tenured.	St. Paul Campus
Crops	9/33	Agronomy/ Tenured	St. Paul Campus
Food Safety	8/3	Food Sci. & Nutrition / Tenured	St. Paul Campus
Horticulture	6/30	Horticulture/ Tenured	St. Paul Campus
Livestock	8/24	Animal Sci./ Tenured	St. Paul Campus
County Educators (2 APL)	33/ na	AFE	Albert Lee & Crookston
Master Gardener	7/29	AFE	Andover
Youth Development (YD) Capacity Area			
4-H Club Program (3 APLs)	31/113	YD	Farmington, Marshall, and Moorhead
Community Youth Development	5/26	YD	St. Paul Campus

Source: Table derived from Morse and O'Brien, 2006. a/ Others are primarily state specialists except for 4-H; b/ Academic departments or capacity areas.

Table 5.7 (continued):

Area Program Leaders by Area of Expertise, MN, 2007

Area of Expertise	REEs/ Total # Others in AOE [a]	APL's Home Unit [b]	Office Location
Family Development (FD) Capacity Area			
Health and Nutrition	11/108	FD	Campus
Family Relations	5/1	FD	Andover
Family Resource Management	9/9	FD	Campus
Community Vitality (CV) Capacity Area			
Community Economics	9/9	CV	Campus
Leadership & Civic Engagement	10/4	CV	Campus
Natural Resources and Environment (NRE) Capacity Area			
NR Management	6/13	NRE	Campus
Housing Technology	1/4	NRE	Campus
Water Resources	5/10	NRE	Campus
Environ. Science Ed.	3/3	NRE	Campus
Total Area Program Leaders = 19	167/474	5 in Academic Dept.	12 on Campus

Source: Table derived from Morse and O'Brien 2006

a/ Others are primarily state specialists except Health and Nutrition;

b/ The Area Program Leaders in these three capacity areas reported directly to the Capacity Area Leaders rather than academic departments.

These differences in the roles of area program leaders demonstrate Minnesota Extension central administration's commitment to decentralized decisions on the details of the structures, reflecting the decentralized nature of academic departments.

Hiring process controlled by capacity area leaders. Decisions about the qualification and the selection of individual REEs are now made by area program leaders and ultimately by the Associate Deans for the five Capacity Areas. In all cases, they utilize search committees that include citizen stakeholders as well as other REEs and state specialists. However, unlike the traditional model and the county cluster model, the final decisions are no longer made by counties. Having the final decision, counties often controlled the area of expertise determination, making it difficult to offer a balanced portfolio statewide. The portfolio was particularly challenging to balance when counties needed to cut funding.

The original selection of educators to be REEs in the new system was from the pool of existing educators. Extension administration reassigned 130 REEs to the new regional positions, the maximum number that could be funded with state and federal funds. Those not reassigned were given layoff notices.

The process of doing the assignments had a series of steps. First, Extension determined the number of REEs in each Capacity Area, based on the current percentage allocations. No attempt was made to redistribute the number of REEs by Capacity Area, even though some argued for this. With all of the other changes, Extension administration felt it was politically unwise to change these allocations. Youth (i.e. 4-H) was given a large number of REEs, reflecting both the current situation and the political reality that 4-H is one of Extension's most public programs. Once the total number of FTEs per Capacity Area was determined, all educators were given an opportunity to indicate their preferences for Capacity Areas, Areas of Expertise and for Regional Centers. Then the Associate Deans for the Capacity Areas were also given a chance to indicate their preferences for the field staff they wanted in each of the Areas of Expertise. Once the Dean/Director had approved the final selections, each of the selected Educators was asked if they would accept these reassignments.

This process sounds a lot easier than it was. Remember that the total number of field Extension personnel were cut by 13 percent, from 597 to 518 field employees of all types (Morse and O'Brien 2006). For more discussion of these changes, see Chapter 6.

Conclusions and Future Research

Conclusions

In this book, a specialized Extension Educator is defined as an educator concentrating on an area of expertise, providing leadership on a statewide program team that develops and delivers outreach educational programs for a community of interest, and contributing to the scholarship related to outreach education.

To measure the defining features of specialized Extension Educators, a survey of the Minnesota Regional Extension Educators was implemented three years after the initiation of the new regional/county model. These data, together with personnel data, show the Minnesota regional educators in the model are much more specialized than in the county cluster model. A few pieces of data are highlighted to summarize the findings.

1. Seventy-nine percent of the M.S. level educators are located in regional centers in Minnesota's new regional/county model compared to none in the county cluster model;

2. Forty-seven percent of the M.S. level educators cover the entire state in the new model compared to 10 percent under the county cluster model;

3. All of the M.S. level educators with regional or statewide responsibilities in the new model are funded by state and federal funds compared to none under the county cluster model;

4. All of the regional educators in the model are more focused than were in the county cluster model; and

5. All of the regional educators in the model are supervised by area program leaders who are state specialists compared to none in the county cluster model.

Future Research

Extension administrators often claim that their Extension Educators are much more specialized then they were earlier. However, when details are compared, the nature and level of specialization is often very different. If the Cooperative Extension System wants to sort out the benefits and costs of regionalization and specialization of its field staff, it will need to first develop common conceptual and empirical measures of specialization and then apply these to different regional systems.

The exploratory research in this book starts that effort by comparing specialization under Minnesota's county cluster regional model with specialization under its new regional/county model. Cross-sectional analysis between states would improve our knowledge of the impacts of specialization.

Chapter 6

Benefits and Costs for Counties

George Morse

It ain't so much what you don't know that gets
you in trouble.
It is what you know that just ain't so.

Josh Billings
1818-1885

Some readers might think there are no longer county offices in Minnesota. However, as Josh Billings would say, it "just ain't so." Sixty-two percent of all field positions, and 59 percent of all full time equivalents (FTEs), are located in the county offices. Two of the largest programs, 4-H and nutrition education, have many staff who work in county offices. Counties pay the costs of all the staff located in the county offices except for the nutrition education assistants. This means the counties are paying for all the costs of 267 county based staff, including support staff, program coordinators, and educational assistants as well as educators. Obviously, county support remains a critical part of Extension's success in Minnesota.

This chapter explains the benefits and costs for counties for the Minnesota model. It compares the number and type of local positions before and after the restructuring and then estimates the positions likely without the restructuring. Next, the most common types of county-based positions in the Minnesota model are described. The role of the Regional Directors and Area Program Leaders in working with the counties is examined. After the discussion of implementation difficulties, conclusions and future research are discussed.

Benefits for County Governments

The change in the relationships between Extension and the counties started with a state budget crisis and its impact on county governments. In 2004, counties cut their budgets for Extension by 28.5% or a statewide total of $4.6 million dollars (Morse and O'Brien 2006). To serve people in all counties, Extension adopted the Minnesota regional/county model as described in Chapter 3. One of the major features of this Minnesota regional/county model was the establishment of regional educators to work in all parts of the state, using state and federal funds. Counties could buy additional local educators if they were willing and able to do so.

For counties, the primary advantages of the new model are:

1. greater choice in the selection of local positions;
2. greater clarity on the roles of local staff;
3. continuing programming support from regional educators in all parts of the state; and
4. greater flexibility in funding for the counties.

Greater Choice in Local Positions

Under the county cluster model (before 2004), counties and Extension jointly decided on the types of positions to locate in a county. While counties had considerable voice on the priorities, Extension needed to balance the types of positions across several counties. With the new Minnesota model, each county could purchase exactly the type of position or positions it was willing and able to purchase. Since the counties no longer had to support the regional educators, they could use their funds on those local positions that were of their highest choice. This resulted in many 4-H youth development and agricultural positions being purchased. Many states consider this move to be a risk to the overall support for land grant outreach through Extension, fearing it will result in less local support for some programs. Minnesota's decision was based on a belief that our county "customers" know best what services they need from us, and that they will be more satisfied customers when they get what they pay for.

Greater Clarity in Roles of Local Positions

Counties also had greater clarity under the new model on what "their" local educators or program coordinators would be doing. In the past, the educators were expected to work in county clusters about 25% of their time. While many county stakeholders liked the availability of educators from outside their county, some worried that the exchange system might not be fair. In other words, was the exchange equal? The Minnesota regional/county model leaves the decisions on working with neighboring counties entirely to the counties. Some counties elected to share one agricultural educator with another county.

Continuing Programming Support

Programs available from the regional educators were not contingent upon having local educators. For example, even if a county did not have a local 4-H program coordinator, the youth in the county could be members of a 4-H club. As described in Chapter 12, the access to specialized educators and programming increased.

George Morse

Greater Flexibility in Funding For the Counties

Counties reduced their funding for Minnesota Extension by $4.6 million in 2004; this was a direct result of the large cuts in state funding. While the funding has increased every year from 2004 to 2008, the Minnesota model system gives counties more flexibility in their funding than the previous county cluster system. Changes in funding in one county are less likely to have impacts on neighboring counties, as was the case in the county cluster model.

Costs to Counties

The costs to counties fall into three categories: (1) fees paid for University of Minnesota Extension employees working in county offices, (2) salaries of clerical support staff in county offices, and (3) office space and operation expenditures.

The fees for the local positions do not vary by the location in the state or the salary of the individual employee. The fees for 2008 full time positions, as set by Extension administration, were: $80,600 for County Extension Educators and County 4-H Directors and $62,700 for County 4-H Program Coordinators and Master Gardener Coordinators.

These fees covered the salary and fringes, program supervision, travel (mileage, meals, and lodging), in-service training within program area, payroll, and accounting services. The county provides support staff, office space, telephone, computer, network connections, software, and general office supplies.

Fees for part-time positions are directly proportional to the amount of time. Some positions, including 4-H program coordinators, restrict these positions to a minimum of half time.

All of these positions are University of Minnesota employees and supervised by either program leaders or Regional Extension Educators.

Nearly all of the 4-H positions are program coordinators rather than Directors. The Director positions are held by senior 4-H educators who preferred to stay in the county. In a few cases, counties were willing to pay higher fees to ensure these individuals stayed in their counties. Their roles cover the work of 4-H program coordinators but also have some additional system responsibilities.

Some rural counties complained about the fees, which were high enough to cover travel, training, and other support needed as well as salaries and fringes. Extension insisted on paying people in all parts of the state the same so that rural areas would not be disadvantaged in the quality of the applicants for these positions.

In the first few years, a number of the local positions were filled by individuals with a great deal of seniority and higher salaries. Because the fees were lower than some salaries, Extension lost money on some positions while making money on others. Naturally, the counties with lower paid staff wanted to reduce their fees. This was not feasible and Extension successfully resisted this.

The fees have increased about 11 percent from 2004 to 2008, or an average of 2.7 percent per year. In addition, the number of positions has increased slightly, from 114.1 FTEs in 2004 to 122.8 FTEs in 2008, not including the nutrient education assistants and the clerical staff (Werner 2009).

As this book goes to press, there is another major state shortfall in Minnesota, as in many states. The Minnesota Extension contracts with counties on a calendar year for these positions. For FY2009, six counties had increases in their contracts with Minnesota Extension and five had slight decreases. One county eliminated the 4-H program coordinators (Thorstensen 2009).

Changes in Extension Positions

Some stakeholders think the Minnesota regional/county model resulted in deep cuts in field jobs. This conclusion is erroneous for two reasons. First, some stakeholders only considered the reductions in county offices and not the increases in regional offices. Second, many stakeholders compared the number of positions before and after the restructuring, forgetting that the $7 million budget reduction would have lead to major cuts even without any restructuring.

Next, a discussion of these changes in employment is presented. The bottom line is that the field staff in the Minnesota regional/ county model was over 30 percent higher than it would have been under the county cluster model (Morse and O'Brien 2006).

Before and After Comparisons

Table 6.1 shows the changes in county and regional positions before and after the 2004 restructuring. Nearly half of the Extension field staff moved out of county offices while the regional centers gained 203 positions. The net change was 79 positions (13%) in the field.

While Table 6.1 shows what happened before and after the restructuring, it misses the point. What would have happened if no change in structure had been made? It is clear that a $7 million cut (13%) of the total Minnesota Extension budget would result in deep cuts in employment.

Table 6.1:

County and Regional Employment Changes, 2003 to 2005

Type Position	Total Positions (FTEs)		Change	
	Before (2003)	After (2005)	FTEs	Percent
Local positions	589	307	-282	-48
Regional Positions	8	211	203	+2538
Total	597	518	-79	-13

University of Minnesota Extension local and regional positions
Source: Morse and O'Brien 2006

With and Without Comparisons

To examine the employment impact of the restructuring, it is necessary to compare the employment "with" the new policy and "without" it. These comparisons are called "with and without comparisons" because they compare the results without the policy versus with the policy.

Table 6.2 shows this comparison for both the counties and the regional positions. Column 2 in Table 6.2, labeled "With Change in 2005 (FTEs)", reflects the same changes shown in column 2 in Table 6.1. However, Column 1 in Table 6.2 shows estimates of what was likely to have happened without the change in structure. The assumptions for estimating Column 1 in Table 6.2, the "Without" case, were:

1. Counties may be reluctant to lay off the clerical support staffs, who unlike the other individuals in the county were county employees rather than university employees. Thus, it was assumed the 175 county staff members that were in place in 2003 would remain in their positions in 2005 if there had been no restructuring.

2. Extension administration would fund as many local positions as it could afford after the cuts from the state and counties, even funding some positions in counties that cut all funds to cover local educators. This assumption had two parts:

   a. Extension would fund 4-H positions in most counties due to popular demand and pressure; and

   b. program coordinators for 4-H would be hired rather than Extension educators because the coordinator salaries were lower. Eighty full-time equivalent program coordinators were assumed for 2005 without the restructuring.

3. Since nutrition education assistants were funded largely from federal funds, it was assumed that the restructuring would not change the number of these positions.

4. With no change in the structure of Extension, it was assumed all field administrators would remain in place. Hence, the 53 field administrative positions that existed in 2003 were assumed to continue in 2005.

5. Once Extension administration started to fund positions in counties providing no funding, there would be a bandwagon effect, with all counties refusing to fund any positions and accepting as many as Extension would fully fund. Based

on this assumption, there would have been 85 Extension
Educators without a change in structure.

Table 6.2:

Staff With and Without Shift to Regional/County Model

	Without Change in 2005 (FTEs)	With Change in 2005 (FTEs)	Change (FTEs)	Change (%)
County-based Educators	85	34	-51	-60
4-H program coordinators	80	80	0	0
Nutrition education assistants	89	89	0	0
Specialized Regional Educators	0	130	130	NA
Total Program Staff	254	333	+79	+31
County support staff	175	104	-71	-41
Regional support staff	0	49	49	NA
Field administrators	53	32	-21	-40
Total Field Administration	228	185	-43	-19
Total Field Staff	482	518	36	+7

Source: Morse and O'Brien 2006 (Univ. of MN Extension)

This would have reduced the total number of educators and program coordinators that could be funded. If 4-H had been fully staffed, there would have been little else that Minnesota Extension could have done. On the other hand, if some counties did fund local positions, it was assumed they would not want to share their educators with other counties that did not fund any local positions. In effect, the system would lose its initial steps toward regionalization and specialization.

In total, it is estimated Extension would have lost 107 positions in 2005 under the old system compared to 79 that were lost under the new system. Naturally, it is difficult to know if the estimates of what would have happened without the change are accurate. The above assumptions are more reasonable than assuming that there would have been no job cuts under the old system. The only way Extension could have tested the validity of these assumptions was to make no changes in structure and see what happened. While this approach would certainly have been easier on the Extension administrative team, it could have lead to more serious cuts.

Based on this analysis, the three most plausible employment consequences of adopting the Minnesota regional/county model as compared to simply staying with the county cluster model are as follows:

1. Minnesota Extension field employment is 7 percent higher;
2. the number of educational positions, including both educators and program assistants, is 31 percent higher; and
3. the number of Extension educator positions is nearly double.

Number and Variety of Local Positions

The number and type of positions varies considerably by county. These differences are now examined.

Total Number of Positions per County

In 2008, every county has a local office with the number of staff varying from one in Cook County to 20 in Hennepin County. As shown in Table 6.3 only seven percent of the counties had two or fewer people in the county office. Nearly two-thirds of the counties had either three or four people. Twenty-one percent of the counties funded five to seven individuals and seven percent of the counties had from eight to twenty employees.

Table 6.3:
Minnesota Extension Positions in County Offices, 2008

Number of Positions Per County	Number of Counties	Percent of Counties
One	2	2
Two	4	5
Three	35	40
Four	22	25
Five	9	10
Six	4	5
Seven	5	6
Eight to Twenty	6	7
Total	87	100

Source: University Minnesota Extension Staff Directory 2008

Number by Type of Local Positions

Table 6.4 shows the distribution of these University of Minnesota employees by the type of positions. The Nutrition Education Assistants are funded by the federal government. All of the other positions are funded by the county, without any state or federal funds. Support staff and 4-H program coordinators are the most common positions, both being in 94 percent of the counties. Forty percent of the counties paid for agricultural educators and/or master gardener coordinators. For the 46 counties with four or more employees, only three lack this basic staffing. One of those, Ramsey County, is the location of St. Paul that has an urban 4-H office that handles 4-H programs.

Table 6.4:
Type of Minnesota Extension Employees per County, 2008

Positions per County	NEA[a] (%)	Support Staff[b] (%)	4-H PC[c] (%)	Agr and Master Gardener (%)	Other areas (%)
Zero	7	6	6	59	95
Shared	0	0	0	5	0
One	75	72	76	30	5
Two	13	16	13	5	0
Three or more	6	6	6	1	0
Total Jobs	123	113	101	31.5	13.5

Source: University of Minnesota Extension Employee Directory 2008. a/ NEA = Nutrition Education Assistants; b/ Support staff are the only ones hired directly by the county government. All others are University of Minnesota Employees; c/ 4-H PC = 4-H Program Coordinators.

Only five percent of the counties have paid for positions outside 4-H and agriculture. Some readers, working in community development, family development, or natural resources, might see the low percentage in the final column as a negative thing. However, the number of educators working full time in each of these areas must be compared to the county cluster system. In Minnesota's Community Vitality Capacity Area, there are now 19 full time Extension Educators compared to four full-time people before the new system. Before the new system, there were no full-time Extension Educators in community economics. Now there are nine, all with academic training in economics, business administration, or public policy.

All of the Extension staff members in counties are University of Minnesota employees except the clerical staff. Ultimately, counties decided to lay off over 40 percent of their clerical staff since there were fewer educators to support. Reducing clerical staff allowed counties to fund more educators and program coordinators.

Nutrition Education Assistants

The Minnesota Nutrition Education Program (NEP) is a $12.6 million program funded by the federal government with matching funds from state and local entities. In 2006, the NEP helped over 57,000 Minnesotans complete a six-hour course on nutrition and food resource management. Evaluations of changes in behavior by participants in 2006 found that 75% of the youth, 78% of the adults, and 77% of the seniors improved their diet quality (NEP 2007).

The Nutrition Education Program was taught by 123 Nutrition Education Assistants (NEAs). The NEAs are paraprofessionals who were originally part of the target audience. The Regional Extension Educators in Health and Nutrition teach the NEAs both the nutrition content and active teaching methods.

While the nutrition program had the largest number of people in county offices (about a third), it differed in one fundamental aspect from the rest. The counties only paid for this program with in-kind contribution, about 20 percent of the cost. However, in 2008, counties contributed $2.8 million to in-kind match (Ha 2008).

County Employed Support Staff

The second largest group of employees in county Extension offices is the support staff, with 113 in 2008. These individuals are the only ones in the county Extension office employed directly by the county. Extension provides training and support for these individuals because they are important to the productivity of the local educators and program coordinators. This group is also the first contact for many new Extension participants who call or stop by the Extension office. To assist them in this role, the Regional Directors have organized training on answering questions, on coaching people to call the Farm Information Line or the Answer Line, described in Chapter 8, and on making referrals to either county educators or regional ones.

4-H Program Coordinators

The 4-H program coordinators are the third largest group of Minnesota county Extension workers, with 101 coordinators in 2008. The county pays the full costs for these positions.

About 26,000 Minnesota children participate in 4-H clubs and nearly 260,000 Minnesotan children participate in other 4-H events. While the original programs focused on agriculture and home economics, current 4-H programs emphasize citizenship, science, technology, and healthy living. About 11,000 adult volunteers provide leadership to these programs with the help of University of Minnesota Extension's 100 4-H program coordinators and its 26 4-H Regional Extension Educators.

The 4-H program coordinators work on 4-H club program management, coaching the 11,000 4-H volunteers, and working directly with the 26,000 youth in 4-H clubs and the 260,000 youth in other 4-H events. Every 4-H REE supervises and coaches about four 4-H program coordinators. In addition, the 4-H REEs provide leadership in new program development, testing new outreach teaching methods, and scholarship to improve the programs. In 2008, only five counties lacked 4-H program coordinators. The children from those counties can participate in 4-H programs. The local clubs in these five counties do not have nearly as much direct assistance since there is no program coordinator. Many of the program coordinator positions are part-time, ranging from 50 to 80 percent.

Local Educator Positions

Over 70 percent of the county-based Extension Educators and program coordinators are in agriculture or the Master Gardener program. Thirty-one counties (36% of all counties) paid for agricultural production or horticultural educator positions in 2008. Eight of these counties also paid for Master Gardener positions, described below. Another five counties relied on the regional educators for production agriculture but had local Master Gardener Coordinators. In the other Capacity Areas, there were 8 county-based positions in Family Development, three in Natural Resources, and 2.5 in Community Development. These counties ranged from four employees to 22 with six as the median number of employees, compared to a median of four employees in all counties. Five of the thirteen counties had one of these positions without an agricultural position. These results demonstrate the ability of counties to make choices that fit their local needs.

The role of the Local Extension Educator (LEE) and program coordinator (PC) positions are very different from those of the Regional Extension Educators (REE). Table 6.5 outlines the overall expectations for these positions and the general practice.

Local programs are major responsibilities **(M)** of the county-based educators, program coordinators, and nutrition education assistants. State specialists and REEs sometimes assist with these programs but have only small responsibilities **(S)** for local programming. Technical assistance is done largely (M) by the local educators. They sometimes rely on the state specialists and REEs as sources of information but the local positions do most of the direct work with farmers and other participants.

Volunteer coordination is one of the major responsibilities (M) of both the 4-H program coordinators and the Master Gardener coordinators and is not a responsibility (N) of the state specialists and the REEs. Both the local educators and the Nutrition Education Assistants have some responsibilities (I) for volunteer coordination in local programs. The Local Extension Educators have no research or scholarship expectations. Campus state specialists have major responsibilities for doing research while Regional Extension

Educators have only intermediate levels of responsibility for research.

Table 6.5:
Responsibilities of Positions, MN Regional/County Model

Role	LEE [a/]	PC [b/].	NEA [c/].	REE [d/]	SS [e/]
Local Programs	M (Major)	M	M	S	S
Technical Assistance	M	N	N	S	S
Volunteer Coordination	I (Intermediate)	M	I	N	N
Research	N (None)	N	N	I	M
Statewide Program Develop,	S (Small)	N	N	M	M
Statewide Program Delivery	S	N	N	M	I to M

Code: a/ Local Extension Educators, b/ Program Coordinators in 4-H or Master Gardener Program, c/ Nutrition Education Assistants, d/ Regional Extension Educators, e/ State Specialists

Local Extension Educators help on program development in some cases, but it is small (S) part of their responsibilities. Both the campus state specialists and the Regional Extension Educators have major responsibilities for statewide program development.

Master Gardener Positions

The Master Gardener Program trains people to educate others in the community about gardening. Thirteen counties hired Master Gardener Coordinators to organize the volunteer efforts of these

Master Gardeners. Each person in the Master Gardener program must complete 45 hours of training in a series of 12 meetings over a nearly a month's time. The Master Gardeners must agree to volunteer 50 hours during the first year, helping others with gardening questions. After the first year, they are expected to volunteer 25 hours per year. During 2007, over 1,800 Master Gardeners donated an average of 58 hours each to their communities, totaling over 106,000 hours (University of Minnesota Extension 2007b).

Before the move to the regional system, the County Extension Directors (CED) coordinated the work of the Master Gardener volunteers in several counties. Since the CED positions were eliminated in the 2004 reorganization, the Master Gardeners found themselves without any organizational assistance from Extension. As counties hired local coordinators, Extension hired a statewide Master Gardener Program Manager to provide training, coordination, and supervision to this group.

Promoting Local Positions

Counties are the major customers for local positions. In addition, other groups sometimes sponsor local positions. The task of promoting and arranging the local positions differs between these two types of positions.

Promoting County Position

Shortly after the Minnesota model started in 2004, there was no policy about who should be the primary contact with counties to discuss new positions. Should it be the Area Program Leaders because they could best describe the types of work that a position could handle? Alternatively, would this create competition between the 16 different areas of expertise? Should it be Local Extension Educators already in the county because they knew the county commissioners? On the other hand, would this generate a conflict of interest for the LEEs when the counties wished to shift the types of local positions they funded? Should it be the Regional Directors because they could be a single contact for the commissioners and who would not have any conflicts of interest?

Since counties prefer dealing with one person whom they know and trust, the primary contacts are now the Regional Directors. The regional directors often work jointly with one or more program leaders when necessary. However, the Regional Directors are the primary contact with counties.

Promoting Other Local Positions

Other local positions are funded by foundations, state agencies, commodity groups, or others interested in sponsoring a major educational effort. Typically, the area program leaders (APLs) are the primary contact for these types of positions since the APLs generally have worked closely with these sponsors in the past. Further, there is not as much overlap in these sponsorship relationships as with the positions funded by counties.

One example of these other positions is in the Community Vitality Program Area, where six local individuals (5 FTEs) were hired through a grant from the Northwest Area Foundation to work on poverty issues (Senese 2008). Another example is in Natural Resources, where one of the local positions on forestry is jointly funded by Blandin Foundation. Another natural resources program on storm water was funded jointly by the Minnesota Pollution Control Agency, the Metro Council, and Watershed Districts (Pardello 2008). In the agricultural area, the Corn Growers Association and Soybean Growers Association have funded a full-time regional educator (Cuomo 2008).

Since the statewide program teams can more easily support these local positions, Extension has become a more attractive partner with foundations and state agencies. The Minnesota regional/county model allows quicker administrative decisions because all the members of a program team report to one supervisor rather than to several. This facilitates negotiations with these new sponsors. The number of local positions funded by other groups will probably increase because of these advantages. .

Speed Bumps with Local Positions

Any large change like the shift from a county cluster model to the Minnesota regional/county model is apt to have a few speed bumps. From the very start, the local agricultural educators felt second-class relative to regional educators. There are five possible reasons for this:

1. The REEs were selected first because of differences between the counties and the University fiscal years;
2. The counties were encouraged to fill the local positions from the educators not selected as REEs, to minimized non-renewals;
3. The REE positions are more similar to those of state specialists than to the traditional LEE, suggesting these were promotions;
4. Extension administration spent more time in defining the roles and solving problems with the new REE roles than on the local educators' roles; and
5. The local positions did not have a promotion system that allowed advances in rank while REEs did.

Local educator satisfaction. Schmitt and Bartholomay (2009) explored the agricultural Local Extension Educators (LEEs) and the Regional Extension Educators (REEs) perceptions of Minnesota's new regional/county system. Using a retrospective pretest approach, they surveyed the 16 LEEs and 16 REEs. They examined 16 measures related to job satisfaction and job performance. The performance measures explored how the old versus the new systems influenced the educators' ability to use their skills, the opportunities for collaboration, views on supervision and autonomy, and opportunities for teaching and research.

The REEs perceived the new system as advantageous in 13 of 16 of the variables while the LEEs perceived only five of the variables as advantageous. One of the statements in the survey was, "I am satisfied with my position as an REE or LEE." Ninety-four percent of the REEs agreed (50%) or strongly agreed (44%). In contrast, only sixty-four percent of the LEEs agreed (43%) or strongly agreed (21%).

The overall picture from the Schmitt and Bartholomay (2009) study confirms the finding from Morse and Ahmed (2007 and 2008) that the REEs are very satisfied with the new regional/county system. For LEEs, it appears that they are lukewarm to the changes. Schmitt and Bartholomay suggest this is because the LEEs "viewed this change as more of a reassignment than a promotion" while the REEs saw their new positions as a form of promotion.

Although this was the picture in 2007, the LEEs might be more satisfied with their positions now, as they have adjusted to the changes and as there is turnover in these positions.

Conclusions and Future Research

Conclusions

Counties are an essential part of the Minnesota model. About 62 percent of all the Extension personnel in the field are in county offices where they are fully funded by counties, except for the nutrition education assistants. All of the positions are University employees with the exception of the county support staff, who are county employees.

Since the state funds and manages the portfolio of regional educators and allows counties to select any mix of local positions, counties now have greater clarity and choice in the types of positions they fund. Most of the local educators work in 4-H, nutrition education, and agriculture.

Future Research

Many questions need additional research. Some of these are outlined below.

1. What factors influence the county demand for local 4-H coordinators, master gardener coordinators, agricultural educators, and other types of educators?

2. What factors influence the demand by foundations, state agencies, commodity groups, and other groups to support either local or regional educator positions?

3. Are local positions also more specialized? If so, how do the characteristics of this specialization differ from the characteristics of specialized regional educators?

4. Do counties with local positions see more programming from the statewide program teams?

5. What is the public value of the local educators and how is it measured?

6. How does the county portion of the Minnesota regional/county influence the public value and support for the state funding of regional positions?

7. How do the number of local positions in Minnesota compare with the number in other states, holding constant population, income, and other demand variables?

Chapter 7

Extension Program Business Plans

Thomas K. Klein and George Morse

*A culture of discipline is not a principle of business;
it is a principle of greatness.*

Jim Collins 2005

Program business plans were an essential part of moving from the county cluster delivery model to the regional/county model. Fifty-four of fifty-six program teams successfully developed program business plans during the first six months of the new system. Now the program business planning process is well accepted and respected by Regional Extension Educators (REEs) and by campus state specialists.

This chapter describes what Minnesota Extension required for program business plans and the response of the teams. The reasons Minnesota Extension mandated that all programs have written program business plans are explained. The support and technical assistance provided to the program teams is outlined. The acceptance by REEs and state specialists of the program business-planning concept is reported. Finally, conclusions and future research are discussed.

Program Business Plans: What Happened?

There were three phases to the program business planning during the first three years of the reorganization. In the first phase, program teams were required to develop their initial written program business plans immediately after the start of the new system. About a year later, the teams were expected to select two aspects of their original plan that needed further implementation, one related to their educational mission, and one related to financial sustainability. This second phase was called "Mission and Money." In late 2006, during the third phase, program teams were encouraged to develop standard one page executive summaries of their program business plans that included a public value statement.

Initial Program Business Plans

In December 2003, a month before the new regional/county model started, all program teams were asked by the Associate Dean/ Director of Programs to develop a written program business plan. These plans were to contain the elements in traditional Extension program planning (Seevers, Graham, Gamon, Conklin 1997) with a few important exceptions and changes in emphasis.

Elements in Extension's Program Business Plans. While the plans varied widely, all had these common features:

1. The plans were statewide, but the programs were delivered locally and regionally;
2. Each plan was developed by a team of regional educators and state specialists;

3. The final approval for the program business plans was with the Associate Dean of the Capacity Area in which the program resided; and

4. The emphasis was on identifying the statewide team, defining the target audience, and stating the educational goals and approaches rather than the financial aspects.

Since organizing program information in a business plan was new for most program teams, a template was provided. Appendix D shows the initial outline suggested to program teams. However, the individual Capacity Areas were given considerable flexibility to vary this outline. Appendix E provides an example of the program business plan for the Retail Analysis and Development Program. Over time, the best program business plans added information on most of the plan elements shown in Table 7.1.

Differences from traditional plans. One of the most important changes from the traditional program development model is that program teams, not individual extension educators, were required to develop the programs and to document the programs in written program business plans. The teams were expected to include REEs from around the state, campus-based state specialists, and non-tenured faculty. The programs were expected to draw on the University's research base and consider the statewide needs rather than focus on the needs of an individual county or a set of a few counties. Agricultural and natural resource programs focused on the counties where a specific crop or species was grown.

Table 7.1:
Elements of an Extension Program Business Plan

Primary Element	Description
Executive Summary	Educational Objectives & audience Public and Private Value Delivery methods, locations and price, Why Extension? Key Contact and website
Program Team Members	Identification of regional educators and campus-based state specialists on team
Educational Goals	Description of the changes in outputs, outcomes, and impacts expected from the program.
Target Audience	Clear identification of the program's target audience, including estimates of size.
Market Research on Target Audience Needs	Identification of audience needs, availability of non-Extension programs to address these needs, feasibility of developing and delivering a program, and Extension's comparative advantage in doing a program
Promotional Plans	What tools will be used to encourage high participation?
Logic model and Research-base	What is the educational theory that links inputs to outputs, outcomes, and impacts? What is the research-base for the materials being taught?
Public and Private Value	Private value, the value to the participants, is essential for ongoing participation. Public value, the value to non-participants, is essential for taxpayer support.
Implementation Plan	Who plays which roles, when and where? Types of events and delivery methods?
Evaluation Plans	Types of output, outcome and impact evaluations completed and planned
Financial Plan	Goal of these plans was to maximize participation in the short-run and to ensure high quality programs with long-term financial viability.

Identification of the target audience was done early in the planning process – before the needs assessment and priority setting. This is the reverse of the traditional recommendation for county-based educators (Seevers, Graham, Gamon, Conklin 1997; Martenson 2002; Caravella 2006). This change in order was necessary because of the focus of programs on communities of interest rather than on geographic communities. By identifying the target audience first, it is possible to involve them more deeply in the needs assessment and the priority setting work (Savanick and Blair 2005; Martinson, Hathaway, Wilson, Gilkerson, Peterson, Del Vecchio 2006).

The program business plans also were asked to examine the competitive position of the program. Historically, many Extension staff felt no other agency could substitute for their programs, and that Extension's programs were much better; therefore, comparisons with other programs are invalid. However, the public is the judge of this, not the providers. The relevant question is, "What does the target audience see as a potential substitute for the Extension program?" Minnesota Extension administration asked program teams to identify their program's comparative advantage as a way to foster a better understanding of the competing offerings.

Every program team had to address the double-bottom line of mission and money. While most of the plan was about the educational mission, there was a financial plan component to enhance the sustainability of the program. The traditional Extension program development model does not name this as a component (Seevers, Graham, Gamon, Conklin 1997). In the past, many Extension field staff and specialists felt the financial component was not a part of their responsibility, but one that Extension administration should handle. Yet, the program teams know what external revenue sources (user fees, sponsorships, grants, etc.) are most appropriate for their target audience. Hence, each program team was asked to include a financial plan as part of their overall program business plan. When the program teams generated more revenue than their non-salary expenses, the team could retain the funds and use them to invest in future programs.

Some REEs and state specialists saw the financial element as *the major component* of the program business plans, but Minnesota

Extension administration did not. Rather, Extension administration constantly stressed that if there were trade-offs between mission and money, the educational mission should come first. At the same time the line: "No money, no mission" was used to stress that long-term viability had a financial component. The initial confusion probably stemmed from the novelty of being asked to consider the financial aspects at all.

Mission and Money Updates

A year after the initial plans, each program team was asked to review their plan and to develop more detail on two aspects of their plan. One aspect had to relate to the educational mission and one had to relate to the money (or financial plan). The other requirement was that they write a description of their work, which would be posted online and shared within Extension.

This "Mission and Money" approach was used for three reasons. First, it helped the program teams think about their programs as more than individual events but as multi-year efforts. Enhancing an existing plan demonstrated that outstanding programs are built over a number of years. Second, the Minnesota program teams had just come through three years of major organizational and professional changes and needed some continuity and stability. Third, this repetition provided stronger links to the implementation efforts.

Public Value Statements

The public value statements summarize a program's logic model and its impacts on society, as shown in the two examples in Chapter 10. In 2006, program teams were asked to develop or update their public value statements and prepare an executive summary of their program business plans. The statements were developed based on training provided by Dr. Laura Kalambokidis (2004), Extension Economist in the Department of Applied Economics.

There were two reasons for including these public value statements. First, Extension administrators needed a brief summary of each program to communicate the value of the programs. Second, this process provided another look at the original business plans, encouraging tune-ups but not requiring them. As Collins (2005) explains, changes in any culture require building momentum by repeated efforts.

Why Program "Business" Plans?

Several years prior to the restructuring, a county extension educator from Soybean County (not the real name) moved to a new regional position at one of the Agricultural Research and Outreach Centers. When asked how he felt about the position, he lamented the lack of contact with farmers on a day-to-day basis. He said, "When I was in the county office, six to eight farmers a day dropped in to visit me. That really helped keep me in touch with local needs and people. Now, almost no one drops in. That makes it hard to know exactly what programs to develop." Essentially this educator found himself in the same situation as most state specialists. He needed to find ways to proactively reach out to audiences rather than conduct programs in a reactive mode. The program business plan was the vehicle for REEs and state specialists to grapple with the changes in programming required by the new financial, political, and demographic conditions. Extension was being pushed to function within new constraints and expectations and needed new ways to understand and reach their audiences.

For four years prior to the restructuring in 2004, Minnesota Extension Dean/Director Charles Casey had emphasized the importance of high quality Extension programs and the need to generate additional revenue. The program business plans provided a means to address both the program quality and revenue concerns. Specifically, the program business plans helped each area of expertise do the following:

1. identify the primary communities of interest and target audiences on a statewide basis;

2. develop statewide programs in collaboration with specific communities of interest;

3. evaluate how many programs it could handle and focus on those where it had a comparative advantage;

4. improve collaboration between regional extension educators and state specialists from relevant disciplines;

5. explore ways to ensure the financial sustainability of programs; and

6. program business plans addressed a broad organizational need for accurate program information.

Communities of Interest and Target Audiences

In a 1995 strategic planning workshop for Extension's community development programs, the first question posed by the session leader was, "Who is the primary audience for your programs?" The immediate answer was, "Everyone!" Not all programs had this much difficulty in targeting their audiences, but many wanted to serve more groups and cover broader topics than they could realistically handle. This resulted from the attitude that it was not politically prudent to tell local constituents Extension could not tackle everything.

In-depth needs analysis or market research with specific audiences was not feasible for educators working in the county cluster model. The process of preparing a program business plan was the first step for program teams to reach a consensus on the primary audiences and to define what work could realistically be accomplished. As reported later, this was one of the most successful aspects of the planning efforts.

Under the new regional/county model, the Community Vitality Capacity Area has done an excellent job in identifying their audiences, even setting an example for other areas.

Statewide Programs and Program Teams

Prior to 2004, educators located in county offices had to give primary attention to the needs of their home county. It was very difficult for them to participate on a sustained basis in statewide programs that focused on an issue of statewide importance. While there were occasional examples of statewide program teams, most of the collaboration came after the program was delivered and individual efforts were aggregated into a "team" report. This individualistic approach was understandable given the funding, county offices, and county-centric culture in Extension. Program business plans became a bottom up way for field staff to agree on statewide team goals, approaches, and their individual roles.

Comparative Advantage and Focus

Extension's primary source of comparative advantage is the close link between REEs and researchers on campus. Without these close ties, between Extension and research, the community colleges or the state's Department of Agriculture would be logical parent organizations. Before the program business plans, Minnesota Extension had a very large set of county-based programs, many of which were not tied closely to a research base.

As program teams explored the source of their comparative advantages and their ability to sustain high quality programs, the teams made decisions on which programs would yield the greatest public benefits and should be continued. The key point is that the decisions flowed from the bottom up and not the top down. Teams decided on the programs to put forward and the manner in which to write up the plans.

Collaboration between Campus and Field Staff

Prior to 2004, there had been a growing gap between campus-based state specialists and field based educators. The tendency was for each to "do their own thing." This gap challenged a fundamental claim of Extension work: that Extension's localized educational programming is directly based on university research. The broad responsibilities of field staff (anything and everything the county expected the local educators to do) clashed with the focus required of campus faculty. A state specialist, who developed a program in response to a county educator's request and then saw only a few educators use the program, often was unwilling to make similar investments later.

This gap made it difficult to explain Extension programs to legislators, interested customers, and potential partners new to Extension. Some Extension programs were guided and delivered almost exclusively from campus, making it difficult for field personnel to explain the program to county funders and local customers. Other programs varied extensively from county to county or from educator to educator raising questions about accessibility, quality, cost, and consistency.

Essentially, there were two Extension Services in Minnesota, one from campus and another in the field. Questions challenging the role of Extension were surfacing more frequently in Minnesota and other states (Johnsrud and Rauschkolb 1989; Harriman and Daugherty 1992; King, D. and Boehlje 2000). Program business plans were one way to have a bottom-up definition of the collaboration between campus and field staff. It was intended to force the development of a consensus on the priorities and roles of each of the parties.

Financial Sustainability

Traditionally, financial sustainability was viewed as an administrative responsibility that did not involve educators. The "double-bottom line" term was used to provide a framework to address the dual responsibilities for educational outcomes and financial sustainability (Morse and Smith 1999; National Center for Social Entrepreneurs 2006). The program business plans provided a means for program teams to evaluate options for generating additional revenue while still seeking to build program quality and maximize the number of people served.

Organizational Needs

When the regional/county model started in January 2004, Extension administration did not have a complete menu of programs provided or who worked on each program. The newly appointed regional directors wanted consistent program information they could present to county commissioners, County Extension Committees, interested citizens, and potential funders. Campus faculty wanted a reliable description of their work that did not over-promise their time or the potential benefits of their research. Field educators wanted to be able to tell interested audiences what programs were available.

Extension's External Relations unit and the Dean/Director wanted a concise comprehensive summary of program information that could be used to respond quickly to requests from legislators, university officials, news media, and potential partner organizations. Extension Accounting wanted a complete list of programs that would be used for setting up the chart of accounts and reporting financial results. These demands for information traditionally resulted in reactive efforts to pull together a list of programs or write up stories about select programs. Campus based faculty and field educators were particularly vulnerable to repeated requests for the same information from different units. This repeated individual requests approach was understandably irritating and often resulted in inaccurate information. The program business plans offered a shared solution to each of these needs.

Implementation Challenges

As readers working in Extension will recognize, it was a major culture shift for Extension staff to develop program business plans that: (1) were statewide, (2) identified communities of interest as the target audience, (3) did market research that considered capacity, comparative advantages and needs rather than simply needs, and (4) were written documents available to the entire team and their supervisors. Even though this was a major cultural shift, 54 of 56 programs successfully did the work in the six months. The following elements helped Extension achieve this success:

1. A clear mandate from Extension Administration that every program team develop a written program business plan within six months;

2. Incentive funding tied to the completion of the plans;

3. Formation of a team of Business Advisors in the Resource Development Unit to support program teams as they worked on the plans;

4. Support from the Extension Dean/Director and Dean of the College of Agriculture, Food and Environmental Sciences; and

5. Support from the Capacity Area Leaders.

Mandate to Develop Program Business Plans within Six Months

Extension Dean Casey agreed that the program teams needed to do this for the reasons outlined earlier. Other Extension leaders saw the looming financial pressures and went along with the plan. It was important that the plans were developed within the first six months to guide the shift from a county-based or county cluster delivery system to a regional system. Otherwise, REEs might try to work at the regional level in the same way they had at the county level, a formula for confusion and failure.

Funding Incentive

Linking a portion of the funding for the Capacity Areas to the completion of the program business plans was one of the more effective (and least popular) implementation tactics. These funds went to the Capacity Area Leader, who could use them for investments in any programs. Completing the program business plans was an expectation for the program teams and they did not directly receive any of these funds. This provided a major incentive for the Capacity Areas Leaders to push their teams to complete the plans, to provide training, and to furnish technical assistance as needed. A plan was considered complete when the Capacity Area Leaders felt it was ready to turn in to Extension's Associate Dean for Programs.

Potentially this approach could have created a conflict of interest for the Capacity Area Leaders by providing incentives for them to approve inadequate plans so they could secure the funding. This was not a concern to the authors because of two factors. First, the Capacity Area Leaders wanted their teams to develop strong programs and recognized the value of this tool. Second, the Capacity Area Leaders were told that their plans would be shared with their peers. This provided peer pressure to have strong plans.

Resource Development Unit Business Advisors

The Resource Development Unit focused on three adaptations of the standard business planning process that were important for an organization in its first efforts at formal program business planning. The Resource Development Unit:

1. customized the business planning process to Extension's educational needs;
2. supported program teams' work on their plans rather than teaching planning to the teams; and
3. set priorities within the planning tool (Klein and Morse 2007).

Customized process. To customize the planning process, the Resource Development Unit contracted with the Center for Farm Financial Management to develop an online template to guide teams on key questions and items to cover in outreach education business plans. The template built on the Center's existing farm business planning expertise and software. The Center's credibility with Extension educators was a plus in getting people to look at the template.

The program business plans were developed in a decentralized way. Extension administration left the evaluation of the plans to the five Capacity Areas Leaders. This approach was used to avoid a time consuming debate over the standards and to allow the different Capacity Areas to modify the template to meet the needs of their team and program. Just as states are sometimes seen as the laboratory for democracy, the Capacity Areas were seen as a laboratory for improving Extension program business planning.

Support the teams not the process. To support the teams, Extension offered them free assistance from external consultants and four internal Resource Development Unit business advisors. Only one of the four Resource Development Unit business advisors had business training and experience, the others were provided with crash courses on business planning. Initially, the Resource Development Unit advisors were nervous about their lack of experience. However, this was turned into an asset, as the advisors became credible examples that educators without business training could handle the basics of program business plans (Klein and Morse 2006).

A series of orientation meetings were held with the Capacity Area Leaders and the Area Program Leaders, the direct supervisors of the REEs, about the nature and the philosophy of the program business plans. This group was essential in encouraging their REEs and campus faculty to take this effort seriously. Frequent communications from both Extension administration and the deans of the colleges emphasized the importance of this planning.

For most of the areas of expertise, the area program leaders played a key role in helping program teams develop their plans while the Capacity Area Leader did not get directly involved. However, in the Agricultural Capacity Area, the Associate Dean, Michael Schmitt, was heavily involved because the state specialists often saw the programs as "theirs" not Extension's. Since the state specialists out-numbered REEs by over two to one in Agriculture and they reported to academic department heads rather than to area program leaders, some faculty members were unwilling to contribute to the planning. The Agricultural Capacity Area Leader provided direct leadership to the development of these programs business plans and assigned a staff person in his office to work directly with him and the teams.

This was a major step in encouraging skeptical state specialists to participate.

Prioritize the elements. Some elements of the program business plan were prioritized over others. For instance, an accurate description of the people the program intends to serve (the target market) and identification of the partner organizations were viewed as more important than financial projections in the initial planning. It was accepted that the plans would not be perfect in this first effort. As expected, there was great variation in the initial plans. Extension administration hoped that teams would learn from each other as they noted these differences.

All this sounds easy. It was not. First, only two of the Resource Development Unit staff had any business experience. A third person with business experience was hired part-time. The other three advisors had extensive Extension experience and backgrounds in communications, video production, and web publishing. Second, some outspoken REEs and state specialists aimed their dissatisfaction with the policy toward the business advisors. Patience, respectful persistence, and support from Extension leadership overcame the resistance.

Support from the Deans

Dr. Charles Casey, Dean/Director of Extension, played four very important roles in the program business development. First, he approved Associate Dean/Director George Morse's plan to mandate that teams develop plans, a bold move given the culture of Extension. Second, he allowed the Associate Dean to tie completion of the plans to the allocation of $750,000 in program funding. Third, after the first eight plans were drafted, Dean Casey read them, sent personal notes to the teams commenting on the plans, and wrote in his weekly newsletter column about how impressed he was with the plans. Fourth, Dean Casey also shared the information with other collegiate deans that lead to broader support and their encouragement of department heads and campus based faculty to support the writing of the plans. The visible attention of senior leadership in the form of the newsletter and notes was a turning point in getting the next group of reluctant teams on board. Requests for assistance to the Resource Development Unit increased markedly in the following several weeks.

There was one block of reluctant campus and field educators. In the Agricultural Capacity Area, it appeared that about half of the programs might not submit business plans. Unlike the other Capacity Areas, there were more tenured campus faculty members on the program teams. Initially, many of the tenured faculty rebelled at the idea of the written plans. The faculty worried about the time required and increased accountability to Extension. Many of these faculty members already had well developed programs, although not written program plans. Hence, they saw little benefit from the program business planning exercise. In addition, some saw a potential risk of additional programmatic and financial accountability.

When the Dean of the College of Agricultural, Food and Environmental Sciences, Charles Muscoplat, heard about the resistance and that it would cost the Agriculture Capacity Area as much as $100,000 in incentive program funds, he met with the Extension faculty and department heads in each department. He expressed the expectation that the teams would complete the plans on time, asking if they would ever let anyone on a research appointment operate without a research proposal, or teach a class if they had no course syllabus. Then he questioned how they could let faculty do Extension work without a written plan. After that, plan writing accelerated in Agriculture and all but two of the 26 Agricultural teams met the deadline. The last two teams completed their plans six weeks later, without receiving the incentive funding. A deadline is a deadline.

Capacity Area Leader Support

Capacity Area Leaders serve in a role analogous to academic department heads in the new system. In this role, they held a great deal of power and were in a position either to block the implementation of the program business planning initiative or to see it successfully implemented. Early on, they did have some reservations about the feasibility of requiring all teams to do these within the first six months. However, they became enthusiastic supporters.

Case Studies on Program Business Plans

The authors spent much of their time working with groups on this issue for six months. Thomas Klein, Director of the Resource Development Unit, was in charge of the team providing technical assistance to the program teams. George Morse, Associate Dean for Programs, had proposed the plan and was the chief administrative advocate for it at the Dean's level. On the program teams, individuals spent varying but significant time organizing their ideas and information into a written plan. What were the outcomes? Moreover, was this investment worth it?

The outcomes of the program business plans were evaluated in two ways. First, six teams (of the 56) were interviewed for their reactions and recommendations. Second, all REEs and state specialists were surveyed for their feedback.

Members of the six program teams were interviewed by Thomas Klein. The principle findings from these interviews were:

1. initially, most disliked writing program business plans for various reasons;
2. the planning process was the platform for teams to reach agreement on essential issues; and
3. the planning process and the plans produced benefits for the program team.

Initial Dislike of Program Business Plans

Initially, there was significant skepticism about the business planning effort. All the people interviewed mentioned the initial dislike for the planning. For some, it was as basic as their objection to the word "business." They did not like using business terms to describe Extension work and did not believe in using business tools in Extension. The "business" term was used for two reasons. First, it implied discipline that often was missing in many Extension planning efforts. Second, it implied the need to consider the financial aspects of the program in the plan. If Jim Collins' monograph *Good to Great and the Social Sectors* (2005) had been available when we did the initial business plans, we probably would have used this as a key resource. Further, we might not have called them business plans. But a rose by any other name...

Some faculty and REEs noted that the plans shifted power away from individuals and to the program teams. Some liked this team approach to program management, the specialization of roles it allowed, and the back-up coverage it provided. Others disliked the loss of individual independence and the responsibility of meeting team commitments and expectations. In five of the six teams, the initial dislikes gave way to appreciation of the benefits of the plan for the team members.

Essential Discussions

A major benefit of the plans was the improved understanding among campus and field personnel. The key to this was having discussions on priorities, values, opportunities, and concerns. Writing the program business plan focused the discussions and established urgency for reaching a broader team understanding. One educator describes the plans as "The conversation we should have had a long time ago." They also saw the practical benefits of having more program information written down and of having consistent and accurate program information widely available. The program business plans made cooperation easier, resulted in fewer misunderstandings, and avoided redundant efforts.

Benefits of Program Business Plans

The following benefits were stated in the interviews.

1. Integration of individual efforts of team members and alignment of the components of the program improved through the discussions and the writing of the plans.

2. The program business planning methodology brought financial issues into view. These issues previously were often not considered part of the program teams' responsibility and were difficult to discuss. The plan provides a framework for discussing financial and other operational issues.

3. An Extension wide list of programs became available, with information on who works on which programs and a summary of each program, improving communication with stakeholders.

4. Program teams that actively engaged in the program business planning effort are pleased with the results and use the plan. Five of the six would recommend the writing of program business plans to colleagues. One of the five would recommend program business planning only if certain preconditions existed, namely that the team was already working together somewhat effectively. If the program team is dysfunctional, the planning effort produces limited results.

Teams that disdained the planning usually delegated the work to a few individuals and saw few benefits. Teams that have widely disparate elements among their personnel and in their programs saw some benefits but were not satisfied with the results.

The five who recommend program business plans see the plan as a useful tool. For example, some cut and paste sections of the plan for grant proposals. Some have established operating rules that resolve marketing issues and are using the plans to improve implementation.

Survey Results on Business Plans

While the above case studies suggested positive results, are these attitudes toward program business plans widespread? To examine the use of the plans and the attitudes of the program team members, twelve questions were included in the 2007 survey of all REEs described in Chapter 5. Seventy-nine percent of the 129 REEs responded to the survey with the respondents being very representative of the full population.

State Specialist Survey

In January through mid-March 2009, George Morse conducted a separate survey of 116 state specialists, asking questions about the program business planning process and other aspects of the new regional/county model. This survey went to all state specialists, both tenure-track and non-tenure track, located on campus or at the Research and Outreach Centers. After the survey received University of Minnesota Institutional Review Board's approval on the human subjects review, a web-based survey, using SurveyMonkey, was sent to the 116 state specialists, with one follow-up for non-respondents. Fifty-five individuals responded for a response rate of 47.4 percent. Of these, 42 provided data on their tenure-track status and were useable, for a response rate of 36.2 percent. About three-fourths (73.8%) of the respondents were tenured or tenure-track faculty. Not all of the questions asked of REEs were asked of state specialists.

Business Plans Availability

While all of the programs had written business plans, how many programs were sharing them widely? Had some plans been developed and then put on the shelf? Were there some REEs who did not know how to get a copy of the plan? To check availability the following question was asked: *Are copies of your program teams' business plan(s) available to all team members (either online or in print)?* Over 90 percent of the regional educators said their team's plan was available. While only 2 percent said "no", an "uncertain" response is essentially the same thing as a "no" since it indicates the educators were not using the plan enough to even know where to find a copy. This was surprising, since some Extension administrators have been reluctant to share the plans widely. In most cases, the plans were not shared beyond the program team.

Frequency of Using Business Plans

Skeptics of the program business planning felt that the teams probably completed the plans to earn the incentive funding and then put them on the shelf. To check usage, the following question was asked: *How often does your program team discuss or use one or more components of the business plan and either formally or informally revise it to meet new circumstances?* Forty-five percent of the REEs used the plan every six months or more often. Sixty-eight percent used them at least once a year (Table 7.2).

Table 7.2:
Frequency of Using the Business Plans, REEs, 2007

How often does your program team discuss or use one or more components of the business plan and either formally or informally revise it to meet new circumstances?	Percent of REEs
3 or 4 times per year	28
About every six months	17
Once a year	23
Once every two years	14
Never	6
I don't know	13

Source: Survey of Minnesota Regional Extension Educators, March 2007 (Morse and Ahmed 2007).

The responses of "never," "once every two years," and "I don't know" indicate very low levels of use. A third of the REEs were not really using the program business plans. Although this non-use is high, having two-thirds use the plans is a major cultural shift from 2001.

State specialists were not asked this question but were asked how frequently they would recommend updating the plans. Since the REE results for these two questions were closely correlated, it seemed reasonable to focus on the later one. Furthermore, individuals are not going to recommend frequent updating if they do not use the plans.

Recommendations on Frequency of Updating Plans

A complimentary question was asked: *"How frequently would you recommend that your program team formally review and update its program business plan?"* This was probably the most surprising result in the survey, with only seven percent saying "never" or practically the same thing of "every five years." Equally surprising was that 60% felt it should be formally updated every year or more often (Table 7.3).

State specialists were not as enthusiastic about program business plans, with about one-third of the tenure-track faculty saying never (16%) or every five years (16%). Interestingly, of the non-tenure track state specialists responding, only had 9 percent indicated "never." However, this means that nearly two-thirds of the tenure track specialists and 90 percent of the non-tenure track specialists would update their plans every three years or more often.

Why would state specialists be less enthusiastic than the REEs or non-tenured faculty? If Extension's success relies on the close linkage between state specialist research and field staff application of the research, this difference in opinions is worth examining in the future. There are at least three hypotheses that merit future discussion or research. The first hypothesis is that tenured faculty have never been accountable to Extension and objected to program business plans or other requirements that open the door to greater accountability in the future. The second hypothesis is that some state specialists were skeptical about the abilities of the REEs to deliver programs as well as a specialist and did not want to engage fully with REEs in shaping the REEs' specialists role in Extension programming. A third hypothesis is that state specialists were worried that the REEs new specialized roles would diminish their own roles as the team experts and the individuals who brought back new ideas from national meetings.

Table 7.3:
Recommended Frequency of Updating Business Plans

"How frequently would you recommend that your program team formally review and update its program business plan?"	REEs (%)	State Specialists	
		Tenure-track (%)	Others (%)
Never	4	16	9
Every five years	3	16	0
Every three years	31	45	55
Every year	51	19	36
Every six months	9	0	0
Uncertain	2	3	0
Respondents (N)	102	31	11

Source: Survey of Minnesota Regional Extension Educators, March 2007 (Morse and Ahmed 2007) and survey of Minnesota Extension state specialists in January to March 2009 by George Morse

Benefits of Program Business Plans

To learn how the plans benefited the teams, REEs were asked to agree or disagree with a series of nine statements. The specific question was, ***How has the process of developing and updating*** *the program business plan impacted you and/or your program team?"* The responses are shown in Table 7.4.

Table 7.4:

Impacts of Using Program Business Plans, 2007 and 2009

"How has the process of developing and updating the program business plan impacted you and/ or your program team?"	REEs (% agree or strongly agree)	State Specialists	
		Tenure-track (percent agree or strongly agree)	Others (percent agree or strongly agree)
Clarified our target audience	76	47	73
Helped identify who was on program team	73	70	100
Helped in preparing my individual plan of work	71	NA [a/]	NA
Helped our program team work more closely as a team	63	50	73
Helped us identify our comparative advantages	63	NA	NA
Helped us learn more about our costs	62	53	64
Helped us clarify our public value	59	NA	NA
Helped team evaluate alternative delivery methods	48	47	45
Gave us text to use in grant applications	42	NA	NA
Helped REEs focus	NA	43	73
Respondents (N)	102	31	11
Year Surveyed	2007	2009	2009

Source: Survey of Minnesota Regional Extension Educators, March 2007 (Morse and Ahmed 2007) and survey of Minnesota Extension state specialists in March 2009 by George Morse. a/ NA = not asked.

Clarified the target audience. For REEs, the process of clarifying the target audience was the most beneficial aspect of the program business planning, with 76% agreeing or strongly agreeing the process helped them. Almost as many (73%) non-tenure track state specialists agreed. Nearly half of the tenure-track state specialists also saw the business planning process as beneficial in clarifying the audience. However, it is not a surprise that the tenure track specialists were lower since they already had very specialized target audiences while the field staff did not.

Identify program team. Moving from individualist efforts to statewide programs required knowing who was on the team. As shown in Table 7.4, over 70% of all three groups found this helpful. While this may seem a simple benefit, the fact that the team membership was not clear before this testifies to the gap that had developed between state specialists and field educators. In the course of writing the plan, individuals decided in which team(s) to participate. There were no mandates from Extension administration on what program teams should be formed, or how many people should be selected for each team. Hence, individuals self-selected to work on teams of their choice.

Preparing annual plan of work. The regional educators found this the third most helpful aspect of the program planning process, with over 71 percent agreeing or strongly agreeing with the statement (Table 7.4). This is not surprising since REEs had some apprehension about their new roles as specialists. The program plans helped provide a framework for their work.

Helped teams work together. More than half of all groups named this as a benefit of the planning process, reinforcing the comments about essential discussions from the case studies (Table 7.4).

Comparative advantages. Nearly two-thirds of the regional educators felt the process helped them better understand their comparative advantages relative to other educational programs.

Learn about costs. Over sixty percent of the REEs and non-tenure track specialists and over half of the tenure track specialists found the business planning process helped them better understand their costs. One team was shocked when they estimated the cost per participant to be over $1,000 and went back to the drawing board to redesign the program and bring costs down using an alternative delivery method and working to increase participation.

Clarify public value. Almost sixty percent of the regional educators agreed the process helped them better understand the public value of their programs.

Evaluate alternative delivery methods. Slightly less than half reported the planning process helped them evaluate alternative delivery methods.

Text for grants. Over 40 percent of the regional educators found the planning process useful in providing text for grants. Probably this low percentage reflects the history of limited involvement by REEs in grant writing.

Focus for regional educators. This question was asked of state specialists, because prior to 2004, they often expressed concern about the lack of focus by Extension educators. The survey of state specialists was done in the spring of 2009, five years after the initial program business plans were developed. Seventy-three percent of the non-tenured specialists and 43% of the tenure-track specialists felt the planning process had helped the REEs focus.

The REEs also reported that the new regional/county system gave them more opportunity to focus. Seventy-four percent of the REEs responded that they had more (31%) or much more (43%) focus on their area of expertise (Morse and Ahmed 2008).

Conclusions and Future Research

Conclusions

While program business plans were met with initial resistance and skepticism, they are now viewed as valuable tools by most regional educators and state specialists. The early survey results indicate that program business plans can be a good mechanism to help align divergent perspectives and interests among campus and field personnel. The planning process creates an opportunity to identify and resolve key issues. In particular, it helped teams agree on the target audiences and team membership.

The planning process fosters sharing of information, clarification of roles and responsibilities, identification of financial issues, and is a good vehicle for communicating program information to team members, administrators, and stakeholders. A key benefit to regional educators was that it helped them prepare their individual plans of work.

Program business plans are an alternative to starting over from scratch as suggested by some. It is practical and effective to use this business-planning tool to improve Extension management and programming. Business planning skills in other settings are transferable into the Extension world.

It appears that the process of writing program business plans is much more feasible with a regional/county delivery model than with a county cluster model. Statewide collaboration is essential to the process and feasible for regional educators located in regional centers. A longer-range view, which is required to justify the establishment of good program business plans, is feasible since the regional educators are funded by state and federal funds rather than county funds. A scholarly approach is possible since the regional educators are supervised by specialists in their area of expertise.

There is one problem with which the program business planning process in Minnesota is still grappling -- transparency. While the program business plans are posted on the web in some capacity areas, some program teams are unwilling to share their plans with regional directors, department heads, and service units (HR, Finance, Resource Development Unit, External Relations, and Diversity). Some teams will not share their plans with regional educators and faculty in other capacity areas or other program teams; at best, this is a peculiar attitude for people in an educational institution.

If transparency and access improved, the quality of the plans would gradually improve, simply through learning from peers and peer pressure. Stakeholders would be more likely to understand Extension's work and its value. Easy access to the plans of other teams would result in the more frequent discovery of potential partnerships across Areas of Expertise and among programs. The availability of the business plans to department heads and faculty would help them better understand the needs of Extension and allow them to be supportive of outreach programming.

Future Research

A number of questions about the program business plans can only be answered over time. Some of these are:

1. How many programs have updated their program business plans since the last mandated update in 2006?

2. What incentives or leadership is needed to encourage program teams to update their plans?

3. Do program teams continue to believe the program business planning process provide benefits to them in future years?

4. Are there alternative formats for doing the planning that are more consistent with the educational mission of Extension? For example, is the Collins (2005) approach for social sector planning an option?

Chapter 8

Regional Support Systems

George Morse and Larry Coyle

Nobody need learn. Survival is not compulsory.

~W. Edwards Deming, 1992

The support systems required for the Minnesota regional/county model are different from a traditional county or county cluster delivery system. New systems are needed for: (1) distributed education or distance education programs, (2) telephone answering systems, (3) online program registration, (4) sales of publications and products, (5) needs assessment and market research, (6) tracking participation, (7) grants for new program initiatives, (8) training educators, (9) program planning, and (10) promotion systems for Regional Extension Educators. The first eight systems are covered in this chapter, while program planning was covered in the previous chapter and the promotion system is covered in the next chapter.

Distance Education Systems

With the University of Minnesota Extension's move to a regional/county model, the role of distance education and distance delivery assumed much greater importance for reaching both internal and external audiences. The new regional/county model means that Extension Educators had more responsibility for program development and delivery, necessitating technology enhanced staff development opportunities and team meetings. Simultaneously, the shifting of Educators from county to regional offices increased the importance of distance education in providing access to programs for geographically dispersed external audiences.

The term distance education dates back to when the primary method available for distance program delivery was via the US mail. However, technology-based terminology, such as e-learning or learning technology, is problematic as well. Technology may be the enabler, but as Collins points out in *Good to Great* (2001), technology by itself is not "the answer." Nevertheless, it can be a powerful tool to advance organizational objectives. In addition, just as the mail carrier did not define the early distance education systems, neither does the Internet define distance education today. Perhaps *distributed education* is more descriptive, but whatever it is called, this section will describe the critical role that educational and communications technology plays in Minnesota's regional/county education system.

A Hybrid Approach to Distributed Education

An underlying assumption for Minnesota's distributed education system is that Extension will provide improved access to citizens, specialists, programs, and information with a blend of face-to-face and distance education and/or communication. For needs assessment, online surveys supplement face-to-face contact with citizens. Research updates are delivered via webinars to provide improved access to campus-based researchers. Both instructor-led and on-demand online classes provide increased access to programs. Minnesota uses these and other new access methods to compliment and supplement, not replace, traditional Extension methods. However, in order for this approach to work, the technical and human infrastructure needed to be put in place.

Infrastructure for Distance Education

Minnesota Extension decided success in distance education depended upon a technology infrastructure that would work for a mobile workforce, strong human capacities in technology, and quality assurance.

Technology infrastructure for a mobile workforce. When the regional/county model was introduced, there was understandable concern that most programming would be concentrated in the new eighteen regional centers. To allay that fear, the plan called for a mobile workforce that would take programming out into the region and across regions. At the time of the regional transition, the University of Minnesota Extension's existing technology infrastructure was largely place-based. Landline telephones, office computer networks, and even the distance education facilities in use at the time (satellite downlinks, ITV sites) did not support mobility.

Fortunately, Minnesota's regional restructuring came during a time of rapid increases in broadband Internet adoption across the state (Center for Rural Policy and Development 2008). The Internet evolved from primarily a one-way information medium to two-way communication directly reaching into many homes and businesses. To take advantage of these trends, Minnesota significantly restructured its technical infrastructure. The regional office technology plan included:

1. Laptop computers with wireless capability and cell phones for all educators, campus based specialists, and administrators phased in over three years;

2. Broadband Internet connectivity in all regional offices with standard authentication across the system so that educators and state staff can sign on in any region;

3. Standardized local computer networks in all regional offices for interoperability and ease of maintenance; and

4. A conference room in each regional center equipped for web conferencing (used primarily for internal communications and staff training).

Extension in Minnesota, as in most states, is heavily dependent on the technology infrastructure of the University at large, the state of Minnesota, and on tools provided through consortia, such as American Distance Education Consortium (ADEC) and eXtension. A major part of Minnesota's strategy, therefore, is to work closely with these partners to insure that Extension's needs are 'at the table' when major infrastructure decisions are made at the University and with consortium partners.

Human capacity. Like most states, Minnesota faculty, staff, and administrators have a wide range of experience, interest, and skills in the use of educational technology. Minnesota Extension takes advantage of widely available technology skills training from the University and elsewhere. Minnesota Extension is also using a learning community approach to professional development in distance education methodology and pedagogy. This approach takes advantage of peer-to-peer learning across the organization as well as expert resources from across the University and beyond. The community is supported by an online collaboration site and webinars to share best practices, lessons learned, and showcase examples.

Quality assurance. For anyone involved in distance education, some of the most frequently asked questions are about the quality of distance or hybrid programs. The issue of comparative learning outcomes (distance education vs. face-to-face teaching) has been largely laid to rest (Russell 2001). Russell found that when course materials and teaching methods are held constant, there were no significant differences between student outcomes in distance education courses and traditional face-to-face courses. This became known as the "No Significant Difference Phenomenon." Moreover, comparative studies with new technologies continue to add to the evidence (Russell 2008). However, the more interesting questions in distance education revolve around *quality* of the learning design. Minnesota is piloting a set of research-based design standards and a peer review process for distance education and hybrid programs.

More work to be done. In order for Cooperative Extension to best leverage the potential of technology, states must develop a comprehensive and integrated strategy for the applications of information technology. Twigg (1995) has long warned of "bolt-on" technology where distance education is isolated as a separate effort from our existing processes. She advises that "superficial thinking" will lead to increased costs with little gain in productivity or learner access. As Twigg advises, Minnesota Extension is hard at work "rethink(ing) all the old trade- offs and invent(ing) new designs for our working lives." In many respects, the widespread adoption and integration of new educational technology delivery methods throughout the organization remains the biggest challenge.

Programs Available Online

Webinar series. A webinar, or web seminar, is a single event or series and includes synchronous interaction among learners and educators—that is, communication in real time such as in an online "chat." Examples of this are: (1) the PORKcast Online Seminars, held on a quarterly basis for pork production managers and owners; (2) the seminars on "Building Extension's Public Value," held for Extension professionals; and (3) the seminars on "New Directions for Youth Development" for youth work professionals.

Online courses. Online courses can be either: (1) "on-demand" (allowing learning any time and at your own pace) or (2) offered over a specified period, using a course management system (e.g. Moodle, WebCT, Vista), and including asynchronous communication (communication at any time online or via email) among learners and educators. Examples of on-demand courses are: (1) Introduction to

Animal Agriculture, for new agribusiness management staff and 4-H youth; (2) FINPACK Online Training for producers and agricultural professionals; (3) Healthy Bees for bee keepers; (4) Natural Resource Learning Modules for landowners; (5) Alcohol Use on Campus for the parents of college students; (6) Parents Forever Online Train the Trainer Course for professionals who want to teach the "Parents Forever" course; (7) Serve it Up Safely Online for certified food managers; and (8) Youth Work Matters for youth work professionals or volunteers. The Master Gardener Core Course is offered online (as well as face to face) from mid-January to early May.

Online communities. Online communities offer a form of virtual networking where individuals with similar interests (learning, professional networking, etc.) can 'meet' and exchange ideas. Currently this is largely an internal learning tool.

Internet. As Extension shifted to more statewide programs in 2004, the philosophy used to manage Extension's website shifted. Previously, Minnesota Extension had used the state's website to cover topics not covered by programs. This philosophy changed to one of focusing on information related to the programs being offered. This was done for several reasons. First, covering topics on the web suggested that Minnesota Extension had the expertise to deliver information and programs on this topic in local face-to-face meetings or via consultations. In many cases, this was not true. Second, when Minnesota Extension linked to attractive sites provided by others it implied the quality of the information had been reviewed and was endorsed by Minnesota Extension. In some areas, Minnesota Extension did not have the expertise or time to do this review. Third, the 2005 initiation of eXtension provided individuals with an option for additional information, which had not been available earlier. Thirty-two Minnesota state specialists and REEs are members in sixteen eXtension working groups, called communities of practice.

Each program has a webpage, which gives a brief description of the program, lists upcoming workshops, and team member's contact information. Each site also lists a series of items related to the program, such as related programs, related websites, related materials, news items, newsletters, and research summaries prepared in academic departments. For an example of this, see the beef production program website (http://www.extension.umn.edu/BeefProduction/).

The website is not only essential for a regional model; it is easier to keep up-to-date because there are clear lines of responsibility on who should provide information to up-date each page.

Telephone Answering Lines

During Dean Casey's summer 2003 State Advisory Committee meeting, the fourteen members from across the state endorsed the overall concept of the regional/county model. However, they kept coming back to one set of questions Extension administration could not answer, "What happens if a county cannot hire a local agricultural educator and a farmer has a question? Whom does he call? Does he call a regional educator or a state specialist or is he just out of luck?"

These questions were not about programs but the provision of information for answering specific questions. Because of this discussion with the state advisory committee, two support systems were developed:

1. Farm Information Line, a free 800 number for agricultural questions; and
2. Answer Line, a free 800 number for household questions.

Farm Information Line

This 800 number takes calls from farmers in any part of the state and provides answers to their questions (See www.extension.umn.edu). The line is open from 8:30 am to 1:30 pm Monday-Friday. At other times, questions can be left on an answering machine. Answers are returned within one business day. While many questions can be answered on the spot, others require some research by the educators and a call back. To achieve some economies of scale, once a team member has answered a question on a new issue, they post the answer on the Extension website to facilitate the process for other team members. This also allows some farmers to check the website directly.

Examples of the questions answered by the Farm Information Line are:

1. What should I pay for land rent in my area?
2. How much fertilizer should I put on my horse pasture?
3. The leaf tips on my oats are turning white. What is causing this?
4. With all the recent rain, will extra nitrogen benefit corn?
5. What kind of farm record keeping and accounting software is available?

The Farm Information Line is staffed by a team of county-based agricultural educators on a rotating basis. The time of the local educators working on the Farm Information Line is paid by the state Extension office. A side benefit of using the part-time local educators is that increases their time.

Initially, there was some concern among some county educators that counties would see the Farm Information Line as a substitute for a local position. Instead, the Farm Information Line has helped to promote the value of the county positions. If a call comes from a county that has a local educator, the Farm Information Line Extension educator answers the question, refers the caller to the local educator, and notifies the local educator for potential follow-up.

Answer Line for Household Questions

The Answer Line is an 800 number phone system to address individual questions related to home and family issues such as safely cooking, canning, and freezing foods, cleaning stains and mildew from homes and clothes, and other issues (www.extension. umn.edu). While nearly every county has Nutrition Education Assistants, the focus of their work is on low-income families. Since few counties purchased local Family Development positions, there was a gap in the availability of someone to answer questions on family development issues. The Answer Line addresses this gap. In addition, educational programs, provided by the regional educators, were still available to residences in every county.

A slightly different approach for staffing this 800 number was taken than with the Farm Information Line. In this case, the University of Minnesota Extension contracted with Iowa State University Extension to handle these free 800 number phone calls. After all, the information on these topics is nearly identical in Iowa and Minnesota and there are major economies from this collaboration. However, the Answer Line team does answer the phone with "University of Minnesota Extension" and does steer people to the Minnesota website and to available Minnesota resources. During 2007, the Answer Line responded to 5,533 phone inquiries from Minnesota.

The volume of phone calls has been declining in Iowa for several years as more people shift to the internet so, it is unclear how long these answer lines are necessary. However, they helped tremendously with the transition from a county delivery model to a mixed county-regional model.

In summary, these answer lines have increased access to direct assistance for those which lack access to the internet. Getting an individual answer via these answer lines might even be more effortless than contacting a local educator.

Online Program Registration

Three factors make online registration necessary in a regional/county system: 1) program teams had members located around the state; 2) sharply lower numbers of field support staff; and 3) high levels of public access to the internet. The advantages to the program teams of online registration are as follows:

1. reduces the amount of support staff and cost required to handle registration while improving communications with customers;

2. allows the program team to customize the questions asked of potential participants so they can better plan specific parts of the program;

3. provides program teams from across the state access to data on the levels of enrollment and the names of participants on a real-time basis;

4. provides University of Minnesota financial and security protection ;

5. posts the registration option directly on the workshop website or is easily embedded into email marketing campaigns; and

6. supplies options of group discounts, wait listings, and emailing participants.

Possibly the major benefit of online registration is that ensures that program teams will not be in violation of financial or security regulations, which are very expensive for each violation.

The participants benefit from this system in the following ways:

1. The transactions have credit card security;

2. enrollment can happen at any time of day from home;

3. there are multiple payment options;

4. participants receive auto-confirmation of their enrollment; and

5. maps and directions are provided online.

The cost of using the online registration system varies with the fee charged in the program. Free Extension programs are not charged anything at all. In 2008, all other programs are charged a fee that ranges from $4.30 for a program fee of $20 to $7.88 for a fee of $200. However, compared to other available systems on campus of $10 to $15 per person, these are small fees. The amount per participant has three components: (1) $3.50 base fee, (2) 40 cents fee for using a credit card, and (3) 2 cents per dollar (actually 1.99 cents) for using a credit card. The balance of the funds is deposited automatically into the program accounts designated by the program team.

Participants are not limited to registering or paying online. If individuals mail in their registration, Extension staff members enter them in the system.

Since this option was adopted in 2006, over 50 program teams have used the system, with all being repeat customers. The majority of the programs using the online registration system have been from the agricultural capacity area (Anderson 2009).

Selling Publications and Products

Program teams sell a large number of publications, DVDs, and other educational materials to compliment their programs. In the past, many of these sales were handled at the county level. This required large inventories to be stockpiled in each county and often the estimates of needs were either too high or too low. It also required keeping change on hand in each county and careful accounting for sales. Today, much of these sales are done through the Minnesota Extension Store.

The Extension Store handles twenty-nine different functions for each product or publication, including warehousing (3 functions), inventory management (6), order fulfillment (10), and financial services (10). For example, under financial services the Extension Store makes sure the sales comply with both the latest university rules and the latest tax requirements. Furthermore, it ensures the credit card transactions comply with security requirements, avoiding the risks of fines.

Minnesota's Extension Store charges a shipping/handling fee for all orders unless the program team is covering all the costs and providing the item free. For all other items, the 2009 fee is 15 percent of the selling price. This fee covers the costs of warehouse space, order fulfillment fees, extra shipping fees, insurance, credit card fees, phone, and computer system charges. Order fulfillment fees include the cost of the warehouse (non-extension) staff picking the item out of storage, packing it, applying postage, and updating Extension's order fulfillment software with information that the order has been filled and has been given to the appropriate delivery service (USPS, UPS, or FedEx). Hence, an order of $10 would cost a total of $11.50. This is the price of the item delivered to the door of the person ordering it so it is probably less expensive than driving to the county Extension office to pick it up. Most orders reach customers in Minnesota within two days. Customers can pay extra for overnight delivery if they wish.

Customers can order online at any time (24/7), by mail, fax, and email, or by phone during business hours. There is an 800 number for contacting the Extension Store.

Minnesota Extension administration does not charge any fees for the labor in the Resource Development Unit that runs the Extension Store. Extension staff labor includes entering items into the Store, running the online catalog and shopping cart software, managing sales tax collection and remittance, managing purchasing card industry data security standards (PCIDSS) compliance, processing payments, complying with University external sales policies and procedures, inventory management, customer service, credit card reconciliation, and distribution of income back to the owners of the publications.

While this service is essential in the traditional model, it became more important in the new regional model for the following six reasons:

1. counties no longer had to carry an inventory of materials;

2. county staff no longer had to worry about financial reporting to the University, charging sales tax or keeping adequate change available;

3. the workload for county support staff was reduced, an essential step considering the heavy cuts in their ranks due to the budget crisis;

4. users can receive their publications within two working days without the costs and time for traveling to a county office;

5. customers can order materials anytime (24/7) from their homes; and

6. program team members can check sales rates and inventory levels easily online.

During 2007, the Extension Store handled 12,000 publications, videos and other educational materials and fulfilled over 5,000 orders. Over $450,000 dollars were returned to over 30 program teams.

As Minnesota moved to a regional/county model, there was concern that the level of publications sold would fall due to fewer county-based educators and fewer support staff. In addition, many expected the greater emphasis on the internet to cut into demand for printed publications. However, the volume of publications has actually increased from 2003 to 2007 (Anderson 2009)

Needs Assessment and Market Research

In order to secure program participation, the program has to be relevant to the needs of the audience, be offered at a teachable moment, and be perceived as effective. To achieve this relevance, timeliness, and effectiveness requires two major components: (1) understanding the needs of the public in sufficient depth and in a timely matter, and (2) the staff capacity to respond to the needs identified. Without the former, Extension staff will spend their time and resources on irrelevant issues. By focusing attention on areas of expertise with capacity to respond, more programming is likely to happen.

A typology of Extension program needs assessment is shown in Table 8.1.

Table 8.1:
Types of Extension Program Needs Assessment

Source of Citizen Input / Capacity of Extension Staff	Capacity Not Considered	Capacity Is Considered
Geographic Communities (i.e. counties or districts)	Traditional County or county cluster Needs Assessment	Matching Needs Assessment
Communities of Interest	Long-Run Market Research	Short-run Market Research

County Cluster Needs Assessment

In the county cluster or county needs assessment, representatives from a geographic community (such as a county or a group of counties) provide feedback on program priorities for their area. The focus is on the needs expressed by this group and not on the capacity of the team.

Generally, local Extension staff attempt to recruit a broad cross section of individuals to participate. In some cases, the results are aggregated to clusters of counties or multi-county districts (Martenson 2002) since the purpose were to identify statewide priority areas rather than specific programs. In Minnesota, leadership for this effort came from county extension directors prior to July 2002.

Matching Needs Assessment

This approach gets its name from matching local needs with existing Extension programs. The purpose of this form of needs assessment is to indicate which of many potential existing programs might best fit the needs of the county or district in the next year or two, rather than to identify any new areas of work. This approach recruits a broad cross section of individuals from geographic communities in a fashion similar to the county cluster model just described.

In the first year of Minnesota's new regional/county model, a number of key Extension leaders were very insistent on a needs assessment that was geographically based. Because of the problems outlined above, the senior author, in his role as Associate Dean/Director, together with the Associate Deans for Capacity Areas, adopted this "matching needs assessment." The matching needs assessment had the following steps:

1. each program team developed a list of programs which would be available in areas with sufficient demand;
2. the Regional Directors shared these lists of programs, together with some program explanation, with the citizens participating in the needs assessment process;
3. the citizens were asked to rank the top ten programs they would like to see offered in their county, but were told that the process was indicating a preference and not buying or "ordering" a program; and
4. once the data was returned to the program teams, they were asked to develop a short written plan that outlined how they would respond to the indications of interest.

Program teams that had geographically based audiences used the matching data to direct the location of their programs. For example, several of the community vitality programs needed a cross section of community leaders from a given geographic area for the program to be effective. The matching needs assessment provided an excellent starting point for these community vitality programs to explore potential communities.

Program teams that had audiences of individual farmers or other types of individuals did not find the data from this exercise as useful. These teams tended to rely more on the feedback from industry groups than a broad cross-section of local leaders since the industry leaders typically could give them feedback that is more accurate on their needs.

This matching needs assessment approach was adopted because it would allow a much more timely response than the other approaches would allow. It was quicker because it used existing programs and resources. Since Extension had just completed two years of restructuring, Extension administration felt it was important to deliver on whatever was promised and to do it quickly. Further, since the program teams were new ones and had not worked together on program delivery, it seemed more practical to practice the statewide delivery on known programs. However, the matching approach did not open the door for new issues and audiences as with the traditional approach and the long-run market research. Essentially, the "matching needs assessment" is a form of merchandising, i.e. selling what you already have on hand.

The matching needs assessment approach had mixed results because many of the program teams had shifted their focus to communities of interest. The senior author's conclusion is this approach works better with programs where the community of interest and the geographic community overlap, such as in Community Vitality. The data from this needs assessment approach was least useful to programs in Agriculture, which usually has audiences of individual decision-makers rather than working with community groups. Hence, the use of this type of needs assessment should be optional by program team in order not to build expectations among the traditional stakeholders, which are unlikely to be met. However, the groups electing not to use this system should provide a executive summary of the market research or needs assessment results to Extension Administrators, mid-level administrators such as Regional Directors and Area Program Leaders and eventually to all program team leaders. Further, they should provide information on the web, or by other means, of the upcoming meetings and events they have over the next three to six months.

Long-Run Market Research

Long-run market research considers the following questions when setting program priorities:

1. What are the social problems and trends that suggest the need for outreach education programs?
2. Based on these problems and trends, and the available research, what types of Extension programs would campus faculty recommend over the next five to ten years?
3. In light of these problems, trends, and local concerns, what types of Extension programs would citizens in a community of interest recommend?
4. What non-Extension education programs are available now to address these issues?
5. What is Extension's comparative advantage relative to other non-Extension outreach programs for developing a new outreach program?
6. What additional faculty and/or field staff resources would need to be added to implement this new program?
7. How would additional staff be funded (new public appropriations, private sponsorships, participant fees, or reallocations)?

The long-run market research version of needs assessment allows the development of new programs and issues, but focuses on a specific community of interest rather than on everyone in a geographic community. The community of interest includes people throughout the state with similar interests. For example, the dairy industry, including farmers, input suppliers, farm service professionals, and processors could be a community of interest. Alternatively, the community of interest could be defined more narrowly, such as organic dairy farmers, or small organic dairy farmers. While each of these is a theoretical possibility, it is not practical to sub-divide the groups too finely.

Focusing on a community of interest allows greater depth of exploration of issues. While the traditional county cluster or county needs assessment can indicate that community economics is a topic of interest, both the long run and short-run market research can indicate what particular aspect of community economics is of interest (i.e. economic development, public finance, costs of community services, regional economic impacts, and land use issues). In addition, market research can help the area of expertise team identify which specific aspect of a topic needs attention. For example, in economic development, is the primary concern related to business retention and expansion, to evaluation of tax incentives for business attraction, to industrial clustering, to entrepreneurship, or to other topics?

Since Extension promises to provide unbiased research-based outreach education, each program needs some campus faculty input to ensure the curriculum has a solid research base. Newly hired tenure-track faculty members are usually offered an appointment with some research time. Faculty members on these types of appointments focus their research on one or two areas for long periods of time (5 to 15 years) simply because good research requires time. With this type of focus, it is difficult to shift to completely new areas of work quickly. For example, a faculty member working within the community economics area of expertise, might shift from doing business retention and expansion to working on regional economic impacts, but he is unlikely to shift to taxation issues in public finance and very unlikely to shift to agri-business management issues. Taxpayers benefit from faculty members becoming highly specialized experts and striving to be the best in their fields. Yet this specialization by faculty means that changes in focus are slower than often is pictured in the traditional county or county cluster needs assessment.

The long-run market research often takes several years to complete as contrasted with the much quicker traditional and matching needs assessments, which often involves only a few meetings.

Short-run Market Research

The short-run market research type of needs assessment is limited to questions one through five listed earlier under for long-run market research. The only difference from the long-run market research is that the short-run market research assumes a fixed supply of campus faculty and the field staff resources for the program. In this approach, as with the long-run market research, the feedback occurs almost continuously rather than happening annually or at one or two meetings. The approaches used vary widely, depending on the history of the program, the relationship of the Extension staff to the leadership in the community of interest, and the manner in which programs are delivered. Programs delivered through face-to-face workshops often use post meeting evaluation forms to both evaluate the current workshop and to seek ideas for future programs and workshops. Programs with close connections to the leadership of the target audience often use needs assessments conducted by these groups. Often, Extension will help to draft the needs assessment instruments administered by organizations serving the target audiences. Both the research and the popular literature provide input to this market research.

Tracking Program Participation

Just as one-third of all Minnesotan workers are driving across county lines to jobs (Center for Rural Policy and Development 2009), many Extension participants have been crossing county lines for years to participate in specialized educational programs. By tracking the zip code of the participants, it would be possible to estimate the number of participants in each event and in each program area served by county. Knowledge of the number and type of participants served has the following benefits:

1. Minnesota Extension could demonstrate that it was serving people from all parts of the state, even if some had to travel to a neighboring county;

2. regional directors would have data on the program services provided to the people in the counties they covered without needing to ask for reports from individual program teams; and

3. program leaders could monitor whether counties were served adequately and take corrective action if necessary.

MyPrograms Reporting System

The MyPrograms reporting system was developed by Minnesota Extension to address the needs of both the communities of interest and the county stakeholders for data on participation. The goals of the MyProgram reporting system were to:

1. provide an on-line catalog of programs for Extension's public website;

2. ensure constancy in the branding of programs throughout the state;

3. provide current information on participation in recent programs for Extension administration;

4. provide data on the number of participants in a given program by the county of residence of the participants; and

5. improve the accuracy of the data.

The adoption of MyPrograms has been uneven. Due to complexity of the Extension system and the programming needed, there were some early technical problems. This resulted in some Extension leaders discouraging their program teams from using the system initially and these areas have never fully adopted the system. The system, however, offers great promise in providing the type of data called for the Extension Excellence program (Archer, Warner, Miller, Clark, James, Cummings, and Adamu 2007).

Grants for New Program Initiatives

In late 2003, Extension administration decided to set some broad criteria for program investments and then leave all decisions on specific program investments with the five Associate Deans for Capacity Areas. This approach was used because the administration felt decisions within Capacity Areas would result in better choices than decisions made by a centrally named committee.

To allocate the funds between the Capacity Areas, each area was given funds for program investment, contingent upon the completion of the program business plans. Once the program business plans were submitted and the funds were allocated, the Associate Deans had complete discretion in how they used the funds to enhance programs.

In 2006, Minnesota Extension shifted to a compact system. The Associate Deans submitted proposals to the Dean/Director Beverly Durgan for initiatives to make program improvements. The University of Minnesota also had a compact with each college, including Minnesota Extension. In this process, the Associate Deans competed for the opportunity to submit proposals in Minnesota Extension's overall proposal. One example of a successful compact request was the award of $500,000 in recurring funds for Community Vitality to expand the number of REEs in community economic development area of expertise from four to nine and to add a ninth REE position in the leadership and civic engagement area of expertise. These two teams then developed regions of about nine counties, each that had one REE in community economics, and one in leadership. In most cases, these REEs also provided statewide leadership for one particular program in addition to working on all programs in their assigned counties.

Training for Specialized Regional Educators

The nature of the training shifted as Minnesota Extension started hiring regional educators with degrees related to their area of expertise. Recall from Chapter 5 that the hiring process for Regional

Extension Educators shifted to the Capacity Area Leaders and Area Program Leaders rather than final decisions made by counties. Rather than Master's degrees in adult education being common, most REEs now have training in their assigned area of expertise. This changes the types of training needed.

Professional training increased considerably in 2006 compared to 2001. Most of the training in 2006 was organized or encouraged by the Area Program Leaders and program teams at Minnesota. This included training by Minnesota Extension (89% of the REEs responding), short duration workshops (84%), and training by other University of Minnesota units (44%). However, the greatest increase came in training at national association meetings, nearly doubling from 2001 to 2006. Thirty-six percent of the REEs attended training at national meetings in 2001 compared to 64 percent in 2006. While over one-quarter took online courses or training in other states, this declined slightly. For-credit courses declined even more, probably reflecting the fact that most regional educators had completed their Master's degrees. The data in this paragraph are from the 2007 REE survey (Morse and Ahmed 2008).

By wide margins, the REEs felt the training they received in 2006 was more helpful to their programming than what they received in 2001. Forty-four percent felt it was more helpful in 2006 compared to 12 percent who felt it less helpful (Morse and Ahmed 2008).

Training on teaching methodology paints a different picture however. Eighty-six percent of the established REEs, those hired before 1999, had either a degree in teaching or related subject (47%) or some formal training (39%). The REEs hired after the start of the new regional/county system (2004), had much less formal training on teaching methods. Only 58% had some formal training on teaching methodology (Table 8.2)

Table 8.2:

Training in Teaching Methodology, Minnesota REEs, 2007

Level of Training	Established Educators (hired before 1999) (%)	New Educators (hired in 2004 or after) (%)
I have a degree in teaching or related subject	47	26
Some formal training received as part of professional development or in a credit class	39	32
No formal training but prior experience in teaching	9	32
No formal training nor prior experience	5	10
Respondents (N)	74	19

Source: Morse and Ahmed 2008.

Half or more of the REEs are interested in additional training on distance education, scholarship, program marketing, and program evaluation (Table 8.3). The high ratings for distance education reflects the greater distances covered by REEs and the history of Minnesota Extension leadership on educational efforts by Larry Coyle, distance education specialist.

Training on scholarship was ranked second in importance. Given the new promotion requirements, this is expected. The third and fourth training concerns were related to program marketing and program evaluation.

It is not a surprise that there was little interest in additional training on program business plans, given the emphasis on these from 2004 to 2006. Most teams feel comfortable in updating these plans as needed. The results in Chapter 7 indicate that program business planning is understood and accepted as part of the culture now. Likewise, many REEs feel comfortable with their skills in engagement, program management, and service. These three items are part of the promotion criteria but are in the second priority category. This might also explain their lower ranking.

Table 8.3:
Professional Development Needs, Minnesota REEs, 2007

Please select which of the following items you would like more professional development or staff training on.	Percent of REEs
Distance education methods	63
Scholarship	57
Program Marketing	54
Program evaluation	50
Program leadership	46
Use of software applications (e.g. Excel, Powerpoint, MyPrograms)	40
Extension teaching methodology	38
Engagement	31
Program Management	23
Program Business Plan Development	10
Service	8
Respondents (N)	98

Source: Morse and Ahmed 2008.

Conclusions and Future Research

Conclusions

A regional delivery system requires modifications in support systems such as distance education, telephone answering systems, online program registration, product distribution, needs assessment and market research, tracking participation, grants for new initiatives, field staff training, program planning, and promotion in rank systems. While each of these support systems might be useful for traditional county or county cluster delivery systems, they are essential for a regional/county model.

Future Research

Some of the unanswered questions are:

1. How does the type of regional/county models influence the ability to develop and implement distributed education programs?

2. Which market research approaches are most valuable in different types of regional delivery systems?

3. How do the features of regional/county models influence the ability to do in-depth market research?

4. How do diverse regional/county models and different degrees of specialization influence the nature of training needed by regional educators?

5. How do these support systems affect program quality, scholarship by regional educators, access to Extension programs, and public support?

6. What are the most feasible types of program participation tracking systems that yield high quality data?

Chapter 9

Scholarship and Promotion Policies

George Morse

Clearly, the time has come not only to reconsider the meaning of scholarship but also to take the next step and consider ways by which the faculty reward system can be improved.

Ernest L. Boyer, 1990

New promotion policies, which were adopted for Regional Extension Educators in 2006, are a key feature of the Minnesota regional/ county delivery model. Scholarship will be given special attention in this chapter because it became one of three primary criteria in the new system and because it is the greatest change in expectations from earlier promotion criteria.

The chapter starts with a discussion of Minnesota Extension's core values since they are the basis for the revised promotion system. Ernest Boyer's definitions of scholarship are discussed, followed by the history of earlier attempts by Extension in Oregon and Wisconsin to incorporate Boyer's perspectives on scholarship into promotion standards. The process Minnesota Extension used to change its promotion system is reviewed, followed by the promotion policy adopted.

Core Values and Promotion

Importance of Core Values

An institution's core values define its enduring values that do not vary with changes in the times. Collins and Porras (2002) define core values as "the organization's essential and enduring tenets, not to be compromised." Together with the organization's fundamental mission, the core values provide direction to employees when there is uncertainty on specific issues.

At universities, the two primary ways for helping new employees understand the core values of an institution are the annual reviews and the promotion process (Weiser 1996). Both offer opportunities to discuss successful work outcomes and preferred methods of work. Not only do these processes provide opportunities for transmitting the core values from supervisors and experienced educators to inexperience ones, they provide an opportunity for discussion between peers about the standards and expectations at all ranks.

In Minnesota, as with many Extension Services, the educators hold academic rank at three levels (assistant, associate, and full professor). In Minnesota, these ranks are prefixed by the term Extension to differentiate them from tenure-track professors.

Minnesota Extension's Core Values

Below is a list of the core values used to develop the promotion criteria for the University of Minnesota Extension (Casey, Morse, and Markell 2004)

1. Extension's highest value is to serve Minnesotans by helping them learn to address critical issues to improve their lives.

2. Scholarship and research guide Extension educational programs.

3. Extension upholds the land-grant mission of the University of Minnesota, providing people throughout the state access to University research and scholarship, and brings their wisdom and insights to the University.

4. Extension values personnel development of our staff and organizational learning.

5. Extension honors the strength that comes from diversity of staff and audiences.

6. Extension works in teams, with each participant contributing unique and specialized skills to achieve common ends.

7. Extension holds itself accountable for making a difference in the lives of Minnesotans.

These core values reflect a long-standing aspect of Minnesota Extension and are similar to the core values in most other states. Two of these core values are spelled out in more depth in this book. Core value 6 (above) is the central feature of the new system as reflected in Chapters 3 to 9. Additional attention will be paid to scholarship (core value 2) because it reflects the greatest departure from Minnesota's earlier promotion system.

Scholarship in Extension

Types of Scholarship

Ernest L. Boyer, in *Scholarship Reconsidered: Priorities of the Professoriate* (1990), challenged the traditional view that scholarship is identical to research and measured by publications. After an analysis of trends in higher education, Boyer writes, "We conclude that for America's colleges and universities to remain vital a new vision of scholarship is required" (Boyer 1990). Boyer proposes four types of scholarship.

Scholarship of discovery. The scholarship of discovery is the most traditional view of scholarship, defined as research to generate new knowledge. As the name implies, the scholarship of discovery requires being the first one to develop a new theory of about the way things work and then to empirically test the validity of this theory or parts of it. Most of the research published by faculty fits within the scholarship of discovery.

Scholarship of integration. Boyer defines the scholarship of integration as giving,

> meaning to isolated facts, putting them in perspective. By integration, we mean making connections across the disciplines, placing the specialties in larger context, illuminating data in a revealing way, often educating nonspecialists too (Boyer 1990).

Integration generates new knowledge by combining the knowledge from several different lines of research into something new. Boyer argues that it is "serious, disciplined work that seeks to interpret, draw together, and bring new insight to bear on original research." Unlike the scholarship of discovery, which is searching for new knowledge, the scholarship of integration is asking what the existing knowledge means, especially when considered from a multi-disciplinary perspective.

Scholarship of application. The scholarship of application uses the knowledge generated in either the scholarship of discovery or the scholarship of integration to solve a problem. Boyer (1990) suggests the primary question in scholarship of application is, "How can knowledge be responsibly applied to consequential problems?" The scholarship of application usually starts with a practical problem rather than with a theoretical one.

Scholarship of teaching. Teaching is the processes of helping students learn new knowledge, skills, attitudes, and aspirations. Often, the public value of teaching depends on the degree to which students not only learn new knowledge but also adopt new behaviors. The scholarship of teaching is implemented by using one or more of the other forms of scholarships on the process of teaching.

Importance of Scholarship to Extension

Each of the forms of scholarship is important to Extension and demonstrates the importance of Extension being located within a University.

Comparative advantage. The close ties that Extension has with academic departments are seen as its primary comparative advantage over other outreach organizations. Extension originally evolved from the needs of the Agricultural Experiment Stations to communicate better their research findings to farmers (Rasmussen 1989). Hoag (2005) suggests Extension's competitive advantage has shifted from its ability to deliver information to individuals who lacked access to information to that of "delivering high-quality, research-based, unbiased information, and education."

Since Extension is part of a research university, this facilitates the connections to all forms of scholarship. Most state Extension specialists also have research appointments that give them opportunities to do all four types of scholarship (discovery, application, integration, and teaching). Few other outreach institutions have as close ties to these four forms of scholarship.

Collaboration with campus faculty. When campus faculty and Extension educators work closely together, the problems identified by the educators often lead to scholarship of application. However, when the existing knowledge base is inadequate to solve the problems, this scholarship of application can lead to new efforts in the scholarship of discovery.

Continuous improvement. The scholarship of teaching is essential for continuous improvement in the effectiveness of Extension pedagogy. Likewise, the scholarships of discovery, integration, and application provide the new content necessary for developing programs that draw repeat participants and build public value.

Credibility within the university. Some faculty members are skeptical about the intrinsic worth of the academic titles for Extension Educators. Clear and rigorous promotion criteria also increase the credibility of the titles among both faculty and Extension educators. In Minnesota's prior system, few Extension Educators knew the rank of their peers. The titles were not a status symbol in the same way that academic titles are for faculty.

Participant value and public value. Better Extension program quality leads to better impacts for participants and greater public support from taxpayers. Each type of scholarship leads to stronger program quality. The scholarship of application helps program teams bring the best of current scientific knowledge to the outreach program. The scholarship of teaching ensures the program is delivered in the most effective manner, given the audience and the context. When Extension educators find there is no research available on a problem, they can encourage more scholarship of discovery. The public value to federal taxpayers of a Minnesota Extension program depends on scholarship about that program. Evaluation articles about a Minnesota program can assist Extension Educators in other states assess the appropriateness of a program or a new educational methodology. This allows the educators in other states to upgrade their programming efforts without all the original investments in time and resources.

Scholarship Disincentives

If a symbiotic relationship between scholarship and extension programming were the norm in most states and most programs, the world would be a remarkable place. Unfortunately, these close connections are rare and growing rarer over time. The M.S. level state specialists who served as spanners between field educators and campus researchers (Rogers 1995) have largely disappeared from campuses. With their loss, the scholarship connections have been severely weakened. Even before their disappearance, there were disincentives for state specialists to do scholarship. George McDowell (2001) suggests many extension specialists fail to do scholarship for the following reasons:

- Time saving – if you can get away with winging it, why not?

- Self-preservation- when information is particularized to a user via a personal consultative type of relationship, the first and primary source to which the information is attributed by the user is the person of the extension specialist, not the institution he represents. Extension specialists use that proclivity by clients associated with personalized distribution of extension information to build direct personal political support.

- Avoidance of scrutiny-if you don't write it done, it is a lot easier to get away with fuzzy economics, biology, or engineering, actual misinformation, and /or undefended opinion.

- Frustration-if you can't get scholarly credit for it anyway, why bother (McDowell 2001).

McDowell further emphasizes, "If the slogan for the researcher is 'publish or perish' then for the extension scholar it is, "publish or you have no program" (2001). He points out that written material, while not sufficient for a program, are necessary not only for doing the educational work but also for capturing political support and for the evaluation. Finally, he concludes: "It is hard to know who is worse for the land-grant system, the researcher who does irrelevant research or the extension specialist who has no program" (McDowell 2001). While George McDowell was writing about campus based state specialists, the same concerns could be expressed about field-based specialists.

Scholarship in Other States

This review will focus on Oregon State University Extension and the University of Wisconsin Extension since the Minnesota Extension task force on promotion adapted aspects from these two states.

Oregon Extension: In the late 1990s, Oregon State University adopted Boyer's view (1990) of scholarship. The definition of scholarship used in Oregon is, "creative intellectual works that is validated by peers and communicated" (Weiser and Houglum 1998).

All field educators were assigned to an academic department for promotion evaluation. However, Oregon has had some difficulties with the implementation. McGrath, who is an advocate for scholarship, writes:

> After 10 years, the integration of Extension agents into academic units remains the number one concern of OSU field faculty (personal communication). Extension agents are frustrated by the apparently conflicting demands of academia for durable scholarly products and the expectations of their clientele for action and impact. They are frustrated by the lack of alignment between a performance appraisal process, which focuses primarily on excellence in the performance of assigned duties, and a promotion and tenure process, which focuses heavily on scholarly accomplishments (McGrath 2006).

Two major institutional features of the Oregon experiment seem to hamper the acceptance of the scholarship requirements for field educators. First, the field educators are all located in a county office, which makes it difficult for them to specialize. In county offices, it is more difficult for them to devote time to scholarship. Second, their annual plans and their promotions are evaluated by different groups of people. Their annual plans of work are evaluated by county office "staff chair" with input from the program leaders and department heads. Their promotion documents are evaluated by the department heads with inputs from the program leaders and county chairs. Even though the formal criteria are similar, the cultures of these two groups are very different. This means that the field educators face two sets of signals on success criteria rather than the promotion process being a comprehensive multi-year review on the same criteria as the annual review. As a result, McGrath suggests that the resistance of field educators to a more scholarly approach to outreach is expected for the following reasons:

- Extension educators tend to be relational and have a strong bias for active rather than reflective learning. They may not have the training or the inclination to engage with highly analytical approaches to learning. Scholarly activities may not be the best use of their skills.

- Extension educators are committed to inquiry-based, collaborative learning. They argue that if we become too focused on hypothesis testing in the community, we may lose sight of the importance of listening and participating as learners. Extension educators question the value of scholarship to their clientele.

- Community-based educators live and work in a very distracting learning environment. Regardless of how we define scholarship, it is difficult for county Extension agents to find a quiet place and the quality time needed for reflection, analysis, and writing. They are busy "doing their job."

- Extension educators are overwhelmed by the urgent demands of their clientele and community stakeholders (McGrath 2006).

Wisconsin Extension. The University of Wisconsin-Extension started exploring ways to incorporate the Boyer concepts on scholarship in the early 1990s. The Wisconsin Extension definition of scholarship is, "creative intellectual work; reviewed by the scholar's peers who affirm its value; added to our intellectual history through its communication; and valued by those for whom it was intended"

(Wise, Retzleff, and Reilly 2002). Upon promotion, Wisconsin Extension Educators also receive tenure.

Educators views of scholarship. Vlosky and Dunn (2009) report on a survey of a national sample of Extension educators. Slightly more than three-quarters of the respondents indicated they are expected to do scholarship as part of the Extension job. However, less than half felt their institution had clearly defined scholarship expectations. The educators felt service was more important than scholarship but perceived their institutions as rewarding scholarship more than service.

Revising Minnesota's Promotion System

Previous Minnesota System

Minnesota Extension has a long tradition of providing academic rank, but not tenure, to Extension educators. The ranks ranged from instructor to professor. One of Minnesota Extension's Dean/ Director Charles Casey's first assignments to the author was to work with a committee of educators to revise the promotion process. At the first meeting of the committee, the author asked why there was promotion in rank for educators. After a long pause, with more than a few raised eyebrows, an educator replied, "For the money." Many heads nodded in agreement. Educators received a permanent increase in their base pay each time they were promoted. When the author asked about the primary criteria for promotion, someone responded, "About three years in rank."

After working with this system for two years, the author believes the motivations for rank were more admirable and the criteria more meaningful than the above discussion implied. Yet, the criteria and process had a number of problems. First, the performance expectations for each of the criteria were vague, only specifying that the "quality in depth and experience should increase with each succeeding level of academic rank (University of Minnesota Extension Service 2001). Second, the criteria on extension research are limited to the scholarship of application, rather than the full set of scholarship concepts. Third, there was no promotion clock and no negative consequence if an educator never applied for promotion. Consequently, some never did apply. Fourth, the review process did not include any tenured state specialists, contributing to the gap between these groups. Fifth, the review committees were composed of educators in an Extension district from all areas of expertise, making it more difficult for them to evaluate the relevance and quality of specialized programming. Sixth, letters included in the portfolio of materials generally were viewed as letters of support from colleagues and program participants rather than evaluation letters. Seventh, the annual plan of work requirements were not tightly integrated with the promotion requirements.

The old system remained in place during the first year of the Minnesota new regional/county system simply because it was impossible to design and implement a new promotion system in the middle of the shift to a new system.

Charge to Task Force

In June 2005, a fourteen-person task force was named and charged with revising the promotion guidelines to be certain they were consistent with Extension's core values and principles. The charge included the following:

1. Developing standards related to each level of promotion in rank for University of Minnesota Extension Service staff and the concomitant means of measuring and documenting an individual's contributions. These standards and measurement approaches must be consistent with our core values.

2. Developing a shared understanding of a conceptual model of engaged scholarship—from discovery to teaching to integration to application—and their relationship to the standards of promotion and means of assessing contributions.

3. Recommending a process for requesting, reviewing, and determining promotion in rank for the University of Minnesota Extension Service (Morse 2005).

Task Force Membership

Jim Collins (2001 and 2005) suggests the most important step in any major project is "getting the right people on the bus." To achieve this, the author spent many hours identifying the group below and recruiting them individually. The fourteen-member task force had at least two representatives from each capacity area as well as regional educators, program leaders, and administration. Two of the state specialists were tenured faculty. The composition of the group was important to its credibility as well as to its deliberations. The membership was:

Dale Blyth, Associate Dean for Youth Development, chair

Timothy Arlt, Area Program Leader, county agricultural positions

Charles Blinn, Forest Resources Extension specialist

Phillip Glogoza, Regional Extension Educator, Crops

Diana Martenson, Organization and Program Development Specialist

Leslee Mason, Director, Minnesota Extension Human Resources

Kent Olson, Applied Economics state specialist and Program Leader

Patricia Olson, Associate Director, Family Development

Ryan Pesch, Regional Extension Educator, Community Economics

Cindy Petersen, REE, Family Resource Management

Michael Reichenbach, REE, Natural Resource Management

Barbara Roberts, Exec. Administrative Assistant in Human Resources

Donna Rae Scheffert, Leadership Development Specialist

Jennifer Skuza, Director of Urban 4-H Programs

Suspension of Promotions

Extension administration announced a one-year suspension of the promotion process in 2005 to allow the task force time to complete their work, seek feedback from REEs, and allow time for REEs to prepare their documentation for the new criteria. To facilitate the process of sharing information, the task force was responsible for the first afternoon of the 2005 October annual conference. The final report was due to the Associate Dean/Director on March 30, 2006.

Task Force Deliberations and Initiatives

For ten months, the Task Force met at least monthly and often twice per month. The members reviewed the existing literature on scholarship and promotion in preparation for these meetings. Subcommittees were developed to explore specific issues. Input was sought from different groups within Extension. An email survey of educators was done to learn current perceptions about scholarship and promotion (Olson, Skuza, and Blinn 2007). The task force invited Dr. Lorilee Sandman, University of Georgia and a national expert on the scholarship of engagement, to speak at the 2005 annual conference. This was followed by a panel from the Task Force. To reinforce these presentations, the task force prepared a fact sheet on scholarship for the conference attendees.

To build their understanding of scholarship issues and promotion, members of the task force attended a national meeting on outreach scholarship as part of their deliberations. They also surveyed all the REEs to ascertain their understanding of scholarship. To provide explicit proposals for Extension staff and administration, the task force developed a detailed set of written recommendations. The sixty-page report provided rich detail for reactions.

Survey of Educators

A sub-group of the promotion task force did a survey of extension educators (Olson, Skuza, and Blinn 2007). The survey had a 75 percent response rate from regional educators, with 91 useable surveys. Furthermore, the response was representative of the five capacity areas. Early in the survey, the authors asked the regional educators an open-ended question on the definition of scholarship to learn their views, before it was "officially" defined. Further, they tried to determine what criteria regional educators felt was important for defining a piece of work as scholarship. Only 50 percent felt that scholarship had to be "reviewed by peers" while 89 percent felt it must be "valued by intended audience." The authors provided eight statements that were consistent with Boyer's four definitions of scholarship and asked the regional educators if they agreed with these. The regional educators did overwhelmingly, showing they understood the basic types of scholarship.

The most surprising finding from their study is that regional educators reported "that 29 percent of their time was currently dedicated to scholarship; the median was 20%" (Olson, Skuza, and Blinn 2007). This is nearly double the level of applied research (12.9%) which regional educators reported in 2007 (Morse and Ahmed 2008). Several have suggested that the difference is in the definition of scholarship and applied research. Olson, Skuza, and Blinn found that 75 percent of the educators used scholarship of application while only 12 percent contributed to the scholarship of discovery, almost identical to the level found by Morse and Ahmed (2008). While 81 percent of the regional educators felt scholarship should be a promotion expectation for them, only 47 percent felt that scholarship should be a promotion expectation for county educators.

When asked about the extent various factors should influence performance evaluations or promotion in Extension, the regional educators rated scholarship fourth in importance, preceded by program management and delivery, program development, and program evaluation (Olson, Skuza, and Blinn 2007). This attitude toward the importance of scholarship reflects the attitude found nationally by Vlosky and Dunn (2009).

Minnesota's Promotion Policy

Promotion Criteria

Scholarship, while a very important criteria and the one with the greatest change, was not the only criteria in the new Minnesota Extension promotion policy for REEs. The new policy had the following six criteria:

Primary Criteria:
- Program Leadership
- Extension Teaching
- Scholarship

Secondary Criteria:
- Engagement
- Program Management
- Service

Minnesota Extension's promotion policy provides an explicit definition on each criteria plus a discussion of each one's key elements and sample indicators. The definitions are presented below:

Program leadership. "Program leadership is the intentional creation and continuous improvement of high-quality, financially viable educational programs that have impacts on knowledge, skills, attitudes, and behavior. It involves the full cycle of deliberate processes, from defining need to evaluating impacts and making adjustments" (University of Minnesota Extension Service 2006).

Extension teaching. "Extension teaching is a complex function that occurs in many ways. In all cases, it creates conditions for learning to take place so the learner can change knowledge, attitudes, and/ or skills and behaviors. It involves interactions between the teacher and learner" (University of Minnesota Extension Service 2006).

Scholarship. Scholarship is defined in a fashion similar to Ernest Boyer (1990) rather than simply as research or publishing. The Minnesota definition is as follows:

> Scholarship is creative intellectual work that contributes significantly to knowledge in the discipline and has impact, is communicated and valued, and is reviewed by peers (University of Minnesota Extension Service 2006).

Engagement. "Engagement is integral to Extension. It is the process of connecting with communities and stakeholders to understand better their needs, use their resources, and build their capacity. Engagement can be demonstrated through the program leadership, extension teaching, and scholarship as well as program management. Engagement is viewed as a distinct criterion for promotion to highlight its value and contribution to our work" (University of Minnesota Extension Service 2006).

Program management. "Program management is how Extension delivers programs. Once programs and their curriculums are developed, they need to be managed and delivered in an effective and efficient manner. There is some overlap between program leadership and program management. Leadership focuses on doing the right programs at the right time, while program management focuses on doing the program right" (University of Minnesota Extension Service 2006).

Service. "Service is professional assistance provided outside the regular realm of the position description but that relates to the individual's professional training and experience" (University of Minnesota Extension Service 2006).

Performance Expectations by Rank

Criteria alone are not sufficient to evaluate promotion candidates. In addition, performance expectations are needed. These are inherently quantitative in nature but almost never explicit. For example, in academic departments, a favorite question of new faculty is, "How many journal articles do I need to get tenure?" Likewise, when faculty members are reviewed, it is common to hear senior faculty member say, "He has published a large number of articles in highly rated journal and merits a promotion." Both of these involve quantitative judgments. While very few departments, if any, have written expectations on the quantity of peer-reviewed articles, there typically is a consensus on the range. It is not written down for a very good reason. The value of articles ranges widely depending on the journal in which it is published, the quality of the article, the timeliness, and the reaction of readers. Hence, it would be impossible to develop a fair formula that explicitly defines the number. The same problem exists on all the other criteria for academic faculty. Yet, there are standards. Here is what Minnesota Extension did for the regional educators.

Significant and distinguished contributions. For promotion to Extension Professor, the candidate has to demonstrate a *significant* contribution in one of the three primary criteria (program leadership, Extension teaching, or scholarship). Likewise, promotion to Extension Professor requires a *distinguished* contribution in one of the primary three criteria. Evidence of contributions must be provided on all six criteria mentioned above.

Consistency across capacity areas. A major concern was the definitions of *significant versus distinguished* contributions. In academic departments, the consistency in the interpretation of promotion standards needs to hold across individuals within the department and not between departments. The measures of performance in the Department of Applied Economics are so different from those in the Department of Theatre, Arts and Dance that faculty in these two departments are not going to compare notes to determine if they were treated fairly in promotions. This is more or less true for any two disciplines, even within the same college. However, the regional educators from different areas of expertise share office space together. In the past, they have been in the same promotion system with the same review committees in a district. If the "significant" standard in one capacity area became higher than the "distinguished" standard in another capacity area, the regional educators would find the system unfair. This would make it hard to maintain the system.

Unlike academic departments that have had a long history of implicitly defining performance standards, Minnesota Extension's new promotion system had no such history. Consequently, there was great potential for the uneven use of the "significant and distinguished contributions" standards.

The author, who was the senior administrator in charge of the promotion process during its first year, was very concerned that unevenness in its application between capacity areas would destroy the credibility of the new system. As a proactive step, the author established the following process to ensure consistency between capacity areas.

1. Three individuals outside the promotion process were recruited to review one of the three primary criteria for all candidates;

2. They were asked to develop tables which displayed the accomplishments of each candidate on a row with specific output measures in the columns;

3. All names were to be removed from the above table so that the results were anonymous beyond these reviewers;

4. The rows were to be organized in a random fashion rather than by capacity area or even by whether the candidates were applying for Associate Extension Professor or Extension Professor;

5. The reviewers were not to indicate whether they felt the individual had a significant contribution or a distinguished contribution.

Completing these tables was easiest for the scholarship criteria and most difficult for the leadership criteria. However, the process pointed out the inadequacy of the documentation in many applications. Once these tables were complete, the author convened a meeting with two individuals from each capacity area: (1) the Associate Dean for the capacity area who submitted the final letter of transmittal and (2) the capacity area's promotion committee chairperson. These individuals were given the table on scholarship. Then they were asked which individuals should be promoted to Associate Extension Professor and which ones should be promoted to Extension Professor. Remember, there were no names, no capacity area, nor area of expertise data on the tables. No data were provided on the length of time in service or any other identifiers, which would have made it possible for the group to identify individuals. After they completed their individual work, they were asked to indicate publicly their decisions and why. A discussion followed on the differences and the reasons for them. This process was repeated with the teaching and leadership criteria.

While the group initially had reservations about the above process, they were assured that the Extension Human Resource Director had reviewed the planned exercise and approved it. As expected, the process sparked considerable discussion. Judging from the results from the first year of promotions, it also avoided the potential problem of differing expectations by capacity area.

Post decision review. After the completion of the 2007 promotions, the above team was reassembled by the author to do a review and explore changes for the next round. Overall, the group found the system worked very well. However, there were some minor changes on the process for handling letters. The majority of the discussion focused on training to help regional educators be successful in the promotion process.

Promotion Evaluation Process

The evaluation process differed from the early system in six important aspects: the nature of the review committee, the voting by educators, the type of promotion letters, the letters of transmittal, promotion clock and the timeline expectations, and an academic rank review for senior REEs.

Review committee. In the old system, the review committees were composed entirely of educators from the district in which the educator worked and were appointed by the District Director. In the new system, there was one statewide review committee for each capacity area, which was appointed by the capacity area's Associate Dean. The new committees had three regional educators with rank senior to the person seeking promotion and one tenured or tenure-track faculty member. The recommendations of this committee were advisory to the capacity area's Associate Dean. However, their letter of recommendation was part of the full promotion file.

Voting by educators. In the old system, all educators in a district with rank senior to the candidate voted on whether the person should be promoted. In the new system, only the review committee votes. This approach was taken to encourage more informed voting.

Promotion letters. In the old system, colleagues and program participants wrote letters of support for candidates. In the new system, the capacity area Associate Deans solicits letters from peers both within Minnesota and nationally. These individuals are asked to evaluate thoroughly the candidates against the criteria.

Letters of transmittal. The capacity area Associate Deans write the letter of transmittal to the Associate Dean/Director rather than these letters being written by District Directors. The Associate Deans can either confirm the conclusions of their review committees or offer their own independent conclusions.

Promotion clock and timeline expectations. All Extension Assistant Professors are given six years to be promoted to Extension Associate Professor. Educators who are not promoted within this timeline are considered to be performing unsatisfactorily and are not renewed. Tenure is not granted to regional educators since the University of Minnesota does not allow tenure for Professional and Administrative employees. Once REEs achieve the Extension Associate Professor rank they are encouraged to work towards the Extension Professor rank but this is not required.

Annual Performance and Promotion

The annual performance review criteria are identical to those for the promotion process and the final decision-makers in both cases were the same. The direct supervisors, who reported to the Capacity Area Leaders, do the annual reviews and help coach the REEs as they prepared for their promotion. The Capacity Area Leaders make final decisions on annual salary increases and on recommendations for promotion. This approach is used to avoid the problems experienced in Oregon with two sets of criteria and two sets of decision-makers.

Coaching

Philosophy. The philosophy of the promotion and annual reviews can be summed up as a long distance run with a goal of all members of the team reaching the end rather than as a competition to sort out the strong from the weak. The goal of the promotion system is to help all regional educators develop their abilities to contribute to higher quality programs. It is not simply to select high performers. This philosophy requires active training and coaching.

Training and mentors. Two types of training are needed for success in the promotion system: 1) training on the process of developing documentation, and 2) training on skills related to the six criteria. Educational materials were developed by the program leaders on ways to break down scholarship into manageable steps. For example, one unit on scholarship illustrates how regional educators can start doing scholarship by doing presentations within their team on their work and getting it peer reviewed. Then the REEs can revise the presentation or develop a paper and share it with their larger group of peers in the capacity area, again getting a peer review. Future steps would be developing papers or presentations for regional professional meetings, national meetings, and journal articles. While this progression is very standard for most academic faculty, it has not been a tradition for most Extension Educators.

Conclusions and Future Research

Conclusions

Minnesota Extension's new promotion system for regional educators has much more explicit criteria than the old system. The primary criteria are program leadership, extension teaching, and scholarship. The secondary criteria are engagement, program management, and service. Scholarship received the greatest attention in the process of making the changes, and in this chapter, because it was a new criterion.

The new promotion process is done within capacity areas rather than geographic districts, involves representatives of both REEs and state specialists within the capacity area, and includes a promotion time clock.

The new promotion system is not used for county positions because it would be impossible for county educators to focus sufficiently to be successful under this system. Further, if the county educator failed to achieve the Associate Extension Educator status in six years, the rules would require they receive a non-renewal, even if they were considered very successful by local leaders. Clearly, this is not desirable.

Future Research

A number of interesting research questions remain related to promotion, regionalization, and specialization. A few of these are:

1. How do variations in promotion systems for Extension educators impact differences in program quality, scholarship, public value, and public support?

2. How is the feasibility of different promotion systems for REEs influenced by the type of regional system?

3. Which types of scholarship contributes the most to the outreach-teaching mission of Extension?

4. How does additional scholarship by Extension field educators impact Extension's standing within academic units at the University?

5. What types of training do extension educators need to enhance their scholarship?

PART III

PRELIMINARY RESULTS

Chapter 10

Program Quality Results

George Morse

How can a new administrator...have any idea of what vision they should have for excellence in the state Extension program if there are no established metrics?

Chester P. Fehlis, 2005

Has Minnesota's regional/county model and increased specialization by Regional Extension Educators led to improved program quality? While the literature on specialization (Chapter 2) suggests that it should, what has been the experience in Minnesota several years after it shifted from a county cluster delivery model to a regional/county model?

In this chapter, rudimentary results on the hypothesis that specialization leads to enhanced program quality are explored using the Minnesota experience with its county cluster educators (before 2004) to its experience with the specialized regional educators (after 2004). After alternative definitions and measures of Extension program quality are reviewed, this framework is used to examine the changes in Minnesota. Data for examining this question come from surveys with Minnesota's regional educators and state specialists.

Definitions of Quality

National Definitions

Striving to deliver effective outreach educational programs has been a hallmark of the Cooperative Extension System since its beginning. This section reviews the major efforts to define program quality and excellence in Extension. From the very beginning of Extension, there are examples of this search for excellence, including the early agricultural institutes, movable schools, farm trains, and short courses done by professors from the early agricultural schools (Rasmussen 1989).

More recently, the national Extension leadership has conducted intensive reviews of Extension's effectiveness. Major reviews of Extension by national leaders were conducted in 1948, 1958, 1968, 1983, and 1991 (Ratchford 1984; Seevers, Graham, Gamon, and Conklin 1997). These reviews focused on the relationships with farm organizations, the broadening the scope of programming, the partnerships with USDA and the colleges, and the issue-based programs. Research on public perceptions and participation were conducted in 1982 and 1995 on national samples (Warner and Christenson 1984; Warner, Christenson, Dillman, and Salant 1996). These two studies measured rates of participation in programs, user satisfaction and public support, but not program impacts. While each of these reviews had implications for excellence and quality in programming, none defined it explicitly.

However, the search for excellence has not been easy. M. F. Smith of Maryland (1991) suggested three reasons why it is difficult for Extension to reach agreement on outcome and impact measures: (1) time lags from programming to impact; (2) multiple factors influencing outcomes and impacts; and (3) inadequate social science methodology. Smith suggests a set of 25 indicators to measure the relevance, process quality, and utility of Extension programs.

Likewise, some discussions of excellence have not provided clear definitions. In 1999, the Kellogg Commission on the Future of State and Land-Grant Universities issued a report that suggested ways universities could become more engaged with the public. Yet, the Kellogg report did not define program excellence per se.

Recently, Chester P. Fehlis, Director Emeritus, Texas Cooperative Extension Service, pointed out that, "Extension is one of the few nationwide organizations or businesses that does not have defined metrics for success" (Fehlis 2005). In response to his challenge that the Extension system define and measure excellence in Extension programs, the Extension Committee on Organization and Policy (ECOP) appointed a task force (Archer, Warner, Miller, Clark, James, Cummings, and Adamu 2007). The task force developed a matrix of 61 criteria based on two different conceptual frameworks. The first framework uses language and concepts most common in academic departments at universities and the second framework uses language and concepts most common in outreach education in Extension.

ECOP's Measuring Excellence in Cooperative Extension Task Force identified the first seven criteria in the following list as the most important measures of excellence and the next thirteen as the next most important. The most important criteria were:

1. changes in knowledge, attitudes, skills, aspirations, and behavior;
2. scholarship on best practices/exemplary programs;
3. use of diverse stakeholder input to shape programs;
4. economic impact of programs;
5. recognition by the University of Extension as the major component of outreach/engagement;
6. client satisfaction; and
7. funding for Extension.

The next most important criteria were:

8. meeting client needs/access;

9. proactive/responsive programming;

10. systematic program development and evaluation process;

11. university students recruited/enrolled;

12. Extension scholarship recognized by the University;

13. applied research to solve problems;

14. documenting programs through peer review;

15. grants and contracts for applied research, Extension, and strengthened research/Extension efforts;

16. enhanced public good (environmental and social impacts);

17. financial support of Extension in relation to university support;

18. return on investment;

19. leveraging resources; and

20. external funds generated.

The other 41 criteria are available at the Extension Excellence website (http://www.ca.uky.edu/ECOP/index.htm). Next, the efforts at defining quality in Minnesota are considered.

Minnesota's Quality Efforts

Minnesota Extension also has a long history of concern with program quality and effectiveness. Early attempts to define and implement quality in programs are described by Abraham (1986)and Patton (1985).

In the early 1990s, Minnesota had a major project to define quality. Mueller (1991) describes a set of 28 criteria developed to measure four different phases of an extension program: problem selection (10 criteria), commitment (8 criteria), strategy implementation (4 criteria), and review/sunset (6 criteria). In 1990, Dean Borich announced a major restructuring to enhance excellence by increasing specialization of field staff.

From 1996 to 1999, Extension Dean/Director Katherine Fennelly used a competitive grants process to promote program evaluation. From 1999 to 2005, Extension Dean Charles Casey made program quality a central feature of his administration, speaking about it frequently. In 2004, Dean Casey invested $750,000 in program improvements for capacity areas that had developed program plans showing how they would operate in the new regional system.

In 2006, the author lead an effort to explore whether the "best in the business concept" (Collins 2005) applied to Extension and its implications for evaluation (Morse and Martenson 2005). It became clear that Minnesota Extension was involved in four types of businesses: 1) educational programs, 2) answering questions, 3) providing technical assistance, and 4) connecting groups.

In 2006, Extension Dean Beverly Durgan approved the hiring of two new professional evaluators, resulting in four full-time professionals. In 2008, Dean Durgan used her State of Extension speech at the October annual conference to urge all program teams to increase their evaluation efforts.

Next, a series of quality indicators, which are consistent with the regional/county model, are described.

Regional Program Quality Indicators

Program quality indicators must be consistent with the overall goals and approach of the delivery system. Thus, this section presents a modified version of the framework described by Mueller (1991). As with the earlier Minnesota framework, this one focuses on the central questions and key indicators at each phase of program development and delivery. Next, the questions and indicators are presented for each program phase.

Phase I: Needs Assessment and Market Research

Key question. What societal problems exist for our target audiences that could benefit from outreach educational programs?

Quality indicators. (1) Important statewide issue not already covered by other educational groups; (2) Program focuses on specific problems; and (3) Problem is at a teachable moment.

Phase II: Planning - Capacity to Deliver

Key questions. (1) What needs to be done to make a visible change in the problem? (2) Does Extension have the capacity to make a difference in the problem in the time necessary?

Quality indicators. (1) Program has a team with sufficient expertise and time to develop and deliver it; (2) Clearly defined logic model explains the program's educational theory; (3) Research base exists and can be incorporated; (4) Extension has the credibility with the target audience to be effective; (5) Target audience and key stakeholders are involved; and (6) Implementation of program (content, frequency of exposure, delivery effectiveness, team capacity) is sufficient to make a difference in the problem.

Phase III: Program Delivery

Key question. How well is the program being delivered?

Quality indicators. (1) Program management facilitates adaptations in implementation when necessary; (2) Program teams use peer reviews and stakeholder data to review ways to improve the quality of teaching, enhance customer satisfaction, and increase measures of KASA outcomes; (3) Program teams use peer review to evaluate ways of reducing costs, such as the appropriate use of technology and distance education; and (4) Programs evaluate means of increasing external revenues, consistent with the program mission and effective demand.

Phase IV: Output Evaluations

While the evaluation questions should be asked before starting the program, they are typically addressed during and after events.

Key questions. (1) What is the demand for the program? (2) How many people will participate?

Quality indicators. (1) Number of educational events held; (2) Number of participants; (3) Participants per event; (4) Participants per hour of educator time; and (5) Cost per participant.

Phase V: Outcome Evaluations

Key question. Did the program improve participants' knowledge, skills, attitudes, or behavior?

Quality indicators. Teams use pre- and post-surveys, observational surveys, peer review, etc. to document outcomes.

Phase VI: Impact Evaluation

Key questions. (1) Did the program contribute to improvements for participants, i.e. private value? (2) Did the program contribute to improvements for non-participants, i.e. public value?

Quality indicators. Teams use prior studies on similar programs, case studies, quasi-experimental studies, and benefit-cost analysis to document public value impacts.

Summary on Regional Quality Indicators

The regional program quality indicators, just defined above, differ from Minnesota's 1991 approach in two major ways. In Minnesota's regional/county model, program teams consider both needs assessment and capacity to deliver programs rather than just the needs of their audiences as was common in the county cluster model. In addition, the new indicators consider the public value to non-participants in addition to private value to participants.

The three major efforts at defining quality (the ECOP Extension Excellence, the 1991 Minnesota quality indicators, and this book's regional program quality indicators) all examine large numbers of factors. In addition, they all focus much of their attention on internal processes to improve quality. In contrast, the next definition of program quality focuses on Extension's customers and funders.

The "Best Program" Quality Definition

Extension program participants and taxpayers are the ultimate jury on a program's quality. If participants judge the quality to be high, especially relative to the time and financial costs, then their levels of involvement will be greater. Taxpayers will support public funding when they believe the programs are effective in creating economic, social, and environmental changes that benefit them as well as the participants.

The regional program quality indicators focus on the steps that Extension educators must consider to have a high quality program. While these indicators can be helpful to Extension staff trying to improve program quality, they are too complex for participants, government officials, or taxpayers. Moreover, high success on the first three phases of the regional quality indicators could be inconsistent with the benefits perceived by participants and by taxpayers.

Benefits to participants alone are not sufficient because of the way Extension is funded. If Extension were funded only by user fees, then knowing the private value, or the benefits to participants, would be sufficient. However, between 80 and 90 percent of Extension funding comes from the public sector, making it important to consider public value (Kalambokidis 2004). The public value is defined as the benefits to non-participants that benefit indirectly from the impacts of the program.

The total benefits of an Extension program are the sum of these two factors: (1) the total private benefits from a program; and (2) the total public value from a program. The total private benefits are simply the sum of the average benefits per person times the number of participants. The total public value could be estimated as the average public benefit per program participant times the number of people in the public who benefit indirectly. While public value is probably not a consistently increasing function of per capita private value, it is likely to increase as the number of program participants increases.

Given these definitions of private and public value, the "best program" quality definition is:

> *The best program on a given issue (a common audience and the same educational objectives) is the one that delivers the greatest total benefits (with benefits not necessarily measured in dollar terms) per dollar of investment in Extension.*

The phrase, "with benefits not necessarily measured in dollar terms," is included because some non-economists jump to the conclusion that this definition calls for measuring all benefits in dollar terms. While there are advantages to measuring the benefits in dollar terms, resulting in a benefit/cost analysis, this is not essential. Benefit/cost analyses can be done on educational programs (Shonkoff and Meisels 2000; Brent 2006; Reynolds and Fletcher-Janzen 2007; Temple and Reynolds 2007). There have been relatively few benefit cost studies done with Extension programs (Willis, Montgomery, and Blake 2008) because few programs have the necessary data on outputs and outcomes to permit a careful analysis. In addition, the process of estimating monetary values is neither easy nor fast. Consequently, the definition used does not require benefit cost analysis.

Rather, the "best program" quality definition requires only the comparison of programs that have the same educational goals and the same audience, allowing comparisons of alternative outreach methods. This comparison is called cost effectiveness rather than benefit/cost analysis (Fitzpatrick, Sanders, and Worthen 2004). The drawback to cost effectiveness analysis is that it does not allow comparisons between programs or between Extension efforts and other types of publicly supported services. However, it is a practical first step.

Although the culture of Extension strives to be inclusive and sometimes avoids competition, the label "best program" is used intentionally. It is used in the spirit defined by Collins (2005) of selecting areas of work where "you can be the best in the world." When applied to Extension, this might be restricted to the "best in the state." Yet, with the internet, maybe even this is too restricting.

The above definition of quality focuses attention on the public and private value rather than on the long list criteria listed at the beginning of the chapter. With a list of 25 to 40 criteria for quality, it is nearly impossible for the public to understand. Further, it is easy for the program teams to focus on the output evaluations rather than outcome and public value impact evaluations. Some Extension critics might even suggest that having a long list of criteria allows program teams to dodge ultimate responsibility for whether or not their programs make any difference to society. A program team can continually focus on the great job they do in needs assessment, planning, organization, and attendance levels while sidestepping output, outcome, and impact questions.

In summary, there are two valid types of measures for program quality. First, the "regional program quality indicators" focuses on each phase of the program logic model and is primarily valuable as feedback to Extension Educators. Second, the best program quality definition focuses on the benefits to participants and to the public and is valuable to potential participants, taxpayers, and public officials.

Initial Results for Minnesota

The best program quality definition overlaps with the final phase of the program quality indicators. Hence, evidence on how the Minnesota quality indicators have changed after the move to the regional/county is examined in this section.

Phase I: Needs Assessment and Market Research

Target audience. Needs assessment cannot be done until you identify your target audience. As discussed in Chapter 7, each program team was asked to identify clearly their target audience as part of their program business plans. Over 70 percent of the regional educators and state specialists without tenure identified this as a benefit of the program business plans. Nearly half (47%) of the tenured faculty agreed it was a benefit. It is not surprising that fewer tenured state specialists saw this as a benefit since many have had more targeted audiences for years.

Learning about target audience. Both the regional extension educators and the state specialists reported that the Minnesota regional system helped REEs learn more about their target audiences, the essence of any needs assessment process (Table 10.1).

Adjust more quickly to new needs. Fifty-eight percent of REEs also reported they were able to adjust to new needs more quickly than before the change. This ability stems from the REEs' greater focus on both their area of expertise and from learning more about their target audience. Other factors, which probably reinforced this ability, are their greater opportunities to do scholarship on their programs, work as part of a team, and work with state specialists (Table 10.1).

Close relationships with audiences. The results on this were mixed. Thirty-nine percent reported fewer opportunities to develop close relationships with audiences but forty percent reported more opportunities. Adding to the puzzle, these results conflict with the REEs' perceptions that they can learn more about their audiences, adjust more easily to new needs, earn more respect from the audiences, and develop higher quality programs.

Table 10.1:

Needs Assessment Changes, MN, 2007 and 2009

Since 2004, to what extent has increased specialization resulted in increased opportunity for REEs to …?	Regional Extension Educators (% more)	Tenure-track State Specialists (% more)	Other State Specialists (% more)
Focus on my area of expertise	74	77	87
Focus on our program's target audience	71	59	87
Do scholarship on programs	69	70	60
Work as part of a team	63	60	93
Learn about our target audiences	62	41	60
Adjust to new needs	58	NA	NA
Earn respect from my audiences	54	59	60
Work with state specialists	53	67	80
Develop close relationship with audience	40	NA	NA
Respondents (N)	102	30	15

Source: Minnesota REE survey in 2007 and state specialist survey in 2009. NA = question not asked in the state specialist survey.

One possibility is that the wording on this item did not lead to reliable results. Another possibility for this inconsistency is that many educators developed social capital in the counties they lived through their personal and family connections. As the educators work statewide, this is not feasible. This hypothesis is reinforced when examining the differences between the established REEs, those working for Extension in 1999 or before, with the new REEs, those hired in 2004 or after. The new group sees much more opportunity (53%) compared to established REEs (39%).Ultimately, the question is whether the quality of the program suffers or improves as a result. By overwhelming majorities (62% to 6%), the REEs see greater opportunities for higher program quality.

Examples of market research and needs assessment. Shortly after the start of the new system, an informal team started exploring the potential of starting an equine program. They mailed surveys to a random sample of 1,008 Minnesota horse owners to learn about their interests in educational programs on equine issues. The high response rate (67%) demonstrated the interest among horse owners, even though at that time Extension was scored the lowest as the current source of information and education on horses. The survey results show the current sources of information, the topics on which they would like information or educational programs and the manner in which they would like the information or education delivered. The results of the survey were useful in forming a new University of Minnesota Horse Team, with 19 members from two campuses, three colleges, and eight departments. A series of five programs were done around the state in the winter of 2006, using Extension personnel, veterinarians, and local businesses (Martinson, Hathaway, Wilson, Gilkerson, Peterson, and Del Vecchio 2006). The program has evolved since then in multiple directions, with a major emphasis given to providing materials on the internet (www.extension.umn. edu/horse/index.html).

In youth development, the 70-page report entitled "Exploring the Supply and Demand for Community Learning Opportunities in Minnesota" on the needs for youth activities is another example of the new approach to needs assessment and market research (Lochner,

Allen, and Blyth 2008). This project did a telephone survey with a representative statewide random sample of 1,607 parents and 806 youth in the winter of 2007-2008. The purpose of the study was to identify the perceptions of youth and parents on the quality, availability, and impact of community learning opportunities. The authors organized their study and report around the following six questions.

1. How do Minnesota youth spend their time?
2. What is the perceived quality of Minnesota youth programs?
3. How satisfied are Minnesotans with their community efforts in youth programming?
4. What do Minnesota parents and youth want in programs?
5. What do Minnesota parents and youth value about youth programs?
6. How difficult is it for Minnesota families to find community learning opportunities?

The findings from this study were used to develop recommendations for all youth programming, whether done by Minnesota Extension or by other agencies.

The Master Naturalist Program provides another example of the type of market research. It uses a statewide focus group approach to determine the feasibility of adapting the Master Naturalist program from Texas and Florida to Minnesota (Savanick and Blair 2005).

In another area, the Community Economics Area of Expertise hired a marketing consultant to help them determine the fee that could be charged for their Retail Trade and Development Program. The results of the market research suggested the team was planning to charge too low a price for the program. When they increased the price, demand actually increased as communities took the program more seriously (Templin 2006).

In addition to the above examples, a study was done of the needs assessment/market research approaches done by all programs. Holli

Arp, one of the regional directors, studied the needs assessment/ market research techniques used by program teams in 2004. To do this, she was given special permission to examine each of the 2004 program business plans. Ninety-one percent of the programs used a mix of methods (Arp 2005). The most popular means of doing the needs assessment was using secondary data (95%), followed by informal input from participants and colleagues (89%), participant evaluations (66%), formal participant input methods (46%) and surveys (36%).

While the program teams appeared to have successfully implemented most aspects of short-run market research, most did not identify new or underserved audiences (Arp 2005). This is not surprising since the program teams were in the early stages of formation.

Conclusions on needs assessment/market research. Since the new system started, program teams are doing more market research. Both the 2007 survey of REEs and the 2009 survey of state specialists suggest that the new system is helping the teams do a better job on this phase of program quality.

Phase II: Capacity to Deliver

Has the new Minnesota model encouraged program teams to consider their capacity to deliver when planning programs?

Collaboration with state specialists. If the campus faculty and the field staff have worked together closely and developed trust and rapport, it is easier for them to address emerging problems. To measure the influence the new system had on collaboration, state specialists were asked, *"Overall, are Regional Extension Educators working more or less closely with you on Extension Programs than before 2004 and the shift to a regional system?"* The responses are shown in Table 10.2. Most state specialists (61%) responded that REEs were working more closely with them, with half of the tenure-track state specialists and 86% of the non-tenure track specialists reporting closer ties.

Over half of all tenured faculty reported that REEs worked more closely with them on planning, development, and delivering programs (Table 10.3). Over forty percent reported that REEs worked more closely with them on promotion of programs, educational material development, and evaluation of programs. While fewer reported increases in presentations at professional meetings, those reporting closer collaboration (36%) were twice those reporting less collaboration (16%). Only in the area of market research did tenured state specialists report less collaboration (27%) compared to more (20%), with over half (53%) reported the same. Further, over half the non-tenured state specialists reported more collaboration compared to 7% less.

Table 10.2:
Extension Program Collaboration, MN, 2009

REEs are working with state specialists on Extension programs…	Tenure-track State Specialists (%)	Non-tenured State Specialist (%)
Much less closely	7	0
Less closely	17	7
Same	27	7
More closely	43	50
Much more closely	7	36
Respondents (N)	30	14

Source: Survey of Minnesota state specialists in 2009 by G. Morse.

The non-tenured state specialist reported greater degrees of collaboration with REEs (Table 10.3), possibly because they can re-focus their own work more easily than can tenured faculty.

Other capacity factors. The program business plans helped program teams examine various other capacity factors. The primary benefits of the planning exercise was that it helped members identify who was on their team, identify their comparative advantage, better understand their program costs, and evaluate alternative delivery models (Table 7.4 in Chapter 7).

Table 10.3:
Areas of Collaboration in Programming, MN, 2009

Aspect of Extension Programming	Tenure-track State Specialists (% more closely or much more closely)	Non-tenured State Specialist (% more closely or much more closely)
Delivering programs	55	87
Program planning	55	73
Program development	55	73
Promotion of programs	48	67
Educational materials development	45	73
Evaluation of programs	45	60
Presentations at professional meetings	35	47
Market research and/or needs assessment	20	53
Respondents (N)	30	15

Source: Survey of Minnesota state specialists in winter 2009 by G. Morse.

Discontinuing programs. Discontinuing programs has always been very difficult to do in Extension, as it is in any public institution. However, because the program business planning process required the program teams to consider their capacity to deliver, a number of areas of expertise realized they simply did not have the capacity to address all of the critical needs in the state. For example, a program of ten online courses called Economic Development Online was terminated because of lack of resources. For similar resource reasons, programs were discontinued on aging and sheep production. More importantly, specific activities within many programs were modified or eliminated.

Conclusions on capacity to deliver. In the new regional/county system, Extension program teams are paying much closer attention to their capacity to develop a high quality program and to deliver it statewide. Furthermore, because of the increased collaboration, the teams have built greater capacity to implement programs statewide.

Phase III: Program Delivery

Each program team has a unique mode of operation, making it difficult to compare the effectiveness of their program delivery and implementation. However, the following data provide some clues on these questions.

Statewide teamwork. Statewide teamwork is one aspect of stronger implementation. Both field and campus faculty perceived their business plan as very successful in this respect (Table 7.4). Almost two-thirds (63%) of the REEs and over half of the state specialists reported the new system gave more opportunities for teamwork.

Statewide program leadership. In addition, the REEs reported they had much greater opportunities for statewide program leadership than before the change. Thirty percent reported many more statewide leadership opportunities and 47 percent reported more. Only five percent reported fewer statewide leadership opportunities (Morse and Ahmed 2008).

Frequency of use and updating business plans. Two-thirds of the REEs report using the program business plans annually or more often. When asked how often they would recommend their team update its program business plans, 91 percent of REEs said every three years or more often (Table 7.3). State specialists (64%) would recommend updating the plans every three years or more often.

Example of evaluation on program delivery. An evaluation on an aspect of program delivery was completed for Minnesota Extension's leadership programs (Scheffert 2007). The research question was, "What impact, if any, does the program duration have on participant outcomes?" Factor analysis was used to cluster 43 specific leadership development outcomes around five outcome concepts. Then the duration and focus of the programs was examined for each of these factors. The leadership programs in Minnesota ranged from five to 24 months. The study concludes,

> Program length matters. The longer the program, the more skill and knowledge outcomes can be expected. The long programs produced significant results on all five factors and improvements on 76% of the measurable impacts (Scheffert 2007).

Conclusions on program delivery. Program delivery has changed in several major ways because of the new regional/county system. Statewide teamwork has increased; REEs are providing more statewide leadership, and program plans are being used to guide the teamwork. Some program teams are doing evaluations to guide modifications in their delivery.

Outputs, Outcomes and Impacts

Very few program participants or taxpayers care about the evaluation details outlined above. The primary questions which program participants have about program evaluation are, "Will the program deliver what it promises? Will I learn something new? Will the time and costs be reasonable? Will the experience be pleasant or even fun?" Taxpayers, who often pay the majority of the costs for most Extension programs, have different questions. The taxpayers often ask, "How will I benefit if I do not participate in the program? Will the participants use their new skills or knowledge in ways that benefit me?" These questions require data on outputs, outcomes, and impacts.

Phase IV: Output Measures

Importance of output measures. Output measures document the educational activities completed and the level of participation by the target audience. These are building blocks in estimating the total private benefits and the total public value of Extension. Once a program has reliable measures of the private and public value per participant, the total benefits of the program equals the product of the value per participant times the number of participants.

Participation levels also provide an early indicator on whether the target audience sees high value in the program. Waiting lists for educational events signal high and growing public interest while low and falling participation suggests the program no longer is relevant.

Increasing participants per hour of time delivery of the program suggests potential economies of scale. However, these are only potential economies because participation is only an intermediate goal. The ultimate goal of an Extension program is to help as many people as possible learn new skills, make better decisions, and adopt new behaviors. If increased participation results in less effective educational outcomes and impacts, there are no economies of scale. This reinforces the partial nature of output measures. However, holding these constant, data on different promotional and delivery approaches can help program teams increase their productivity.

Data on output measures. There are numerous examples of increased program output in Minnesota. From 2004 through 2007, the author saw many examples that support the hypothesis that Minnesota Extension is doing more with less throughout Extension. Further, the articles in Extension *Source* magazine (www.extension.umn. edu) continue to provide graphic examples.

However, there are no reliable data on output levels by program both before and after the adoption of the new Minnesota model. Unfortunately, the pre-2004 data on participation was collected only at the end of the year and there were no ground rules on the unit of analysis. More recently, overall participation levels for face-to-face meetings grew from 310,000 to 446,000 from 2004 to 2007, an increase of 44 percent (University of Minnesota Extension 2007a).

Conclusions on output measures. The MyPrograms system is starting to collect high quality output data. However, a simple before and after examination of the changes in output per full time equivalent is not possible due to the lack of the earlier data. This data difficulty does not mean it is impossible to test the hypothesis that Minnesota Extension is doing more with less. Rather, it shows that testing it will be difficult. The best promise for exploring this hypothesis appears to be at the individual program level. Doing this type of work at a program level also would allow comparisons across states since the educational objectives and target audiences would remain the same.

Phase V: Outcome Evaluation

Outcome evaluations measure changes in program participants' aspirations, knowledge, attitudes, skills, or behavior. Common measurement techniques include pre-and post-tests, retrospective pre-post tests, and surveys several months after the event. The Minnesota Extension evaluation team is encouraging programs to do outcome evaluations. Many programs are doing retrospective pre-post tests at the end of educational events to measure knowledge gains and changes in attitudes (Davis 2003). There is growing interest in follow-up email, mail, and phone surveys several months after the events to measure changes in behavior. At this point, however, data does not exist on the percentage of programs doing different types of output evaluations.

Example on outcome evaluation. An excellent example of an outcome evaluation with implications for the program delivery is a study of the effectiveness of a program on farm transition and estate planning (Hachfeld, Bau, Holcomb, Kurtz, Craig, and Olson 2009). The first five authors are REEs in Agricultural Business Management and the sixth is the Area Program Leader who supervises this area of expertise. The article reports on both the learning and behavioral changes of 296 program participants who completed end-of-program evaluations and 152 participants who completed a mail survey six months after the workshop. The authors also shared eight lessons they learned, or had confirmed by the results, on how to teach this subject matter.

In the Family Development capacity area, members of the nutrition education team have evaluated the effectiveness of educational efforts on nutrition aimed at primary school children in the third and fifth grades. Using pre-post tests, students reported better choices in beverages (Roth-Yousey, Caskey, May, Reicks 2007). Another output evaluation in Family Development explored the changes in knowledge and behavior of participants (Dworkin and Karahan 2005).

Conclusions on outcome evaluations. The program teams are starting to do more outcome evaluations but relatively few of these have been published. This is not surprising, since the first year was focused on team building, the new scholarship requirements started in 2006, and the evaluation staff was not fully in place until 2007.

Phase VI: Impact Evaluations

Program participants often are interested in knowing that their new skills or knowledge will result in better health, better finances, or a stronger family, etc. While participants might be interested in whether the program really teaches them new skills (outcome evaluations), they also want to know if this new knowledge or skills help better their lives (impact evaluation).

Public value statements. If Extension was not publicly funded, behavioral change might not matter. However, taxpayers who are not program participants only receive public benefits if the participants make changes in their behavior and generate public value. For example, a taxpayer who does not participate in a program might ask, "Why should I pay taxes to support educational programs that I do not use?"

Dr. Laura Kalambokidis, a public finance state specialist from the Department of Applied Economics, provided training to program teams on how to identify the source of their program's public value (Kalambokidis 2004). The public value statements summarize the programs logic model and its impact on society. In particular, the public value statements describe the changes in behavior on the part of program participants leading to benefits for program non-participants. By 2006, every program had developed a public value statement. Here are two examples of public value statements.

Business Retention and Expansion Strategies (BR&E). Public support for the BR&E Program means community leaders will learn about the needs of local businesses and about how to help these local firms become more competitive. As these local firms become more profitable, they are more likely to stay and/or expand within the community, benefiting both the local and state economy (University of Minnesota Extension Service October 2006).

Nutrition Education Program. Public support for the Nutrition Education program means that families improve their healthy eating habits, preventing some nutrition-related disease, such as diabetes. In addition to benefiting the participants, this reduces public health costs, benefiting all taxpayers (University of Minnesota Extension Service October 2006).

These public value statements are short public relations messages to give a quick picture of the benefits to the public. However, many teams have realized that they need to verify the validity of these statements with research. Dr. Kalambokidis' training program provides initial suggestions on ways to approach this (Kalambokidis 2009). While these statements provide a framework, they must be followed by empirical studies on the impacts.

Domains of impact. To facilitate the measurement of public value, the Minnesota Extension evaluation team developed a framework of domains of impact (Table 10.4), based on the work in community capitals (Flora, Flora, Fey 2004; Emery and Flora 2006).

Table 10.4:
Domains of Impact Definitions

Domain of Outcome or Impact:	Description
Human capacity outcomes:	Individual knowledge, attitudes, skills, or aspirations
Human action outcomes	Individual behavior or action

Social Network Impacts	Networks based on trust and reciprocity among people and organizations, including bonding networks that provide security, bridging networks that expand opportunity, and linking networks that mobilize well-being.
Health Impacts	Ability of families, organizations, communities, or sectors to promote physical and mental well-being.
Political Impacts	Ability of families, organizations, communities, or sectors to access and mobilize public resources
Cultural Impacts	Ways that distinct worldviews are supported and celebrated within families, organizations, communities, or sectors, combined with limitations on the ability of privileged groups to maintain advantage.
Financial Impacts	Private wealth that is invested in the well-being of families, organizations, communities, or sectors
Building and Infrastructure Impacts	Structures and infrastructures that contribute to the well-being of families, organizations, communities, or sectors.
Natural Resource Impacts	Ability of families, organizations, communities, or sectors to protect landscape, air, water, soil, and biodiversity of both plants and animals.

Source: Chazdon, Bartholomay, Marczak, and Lochner 2007.

The changes were explained as follows:

The Community Capitals Framework was designed with rural communities of place in mind. As we moved to applying the framework to Extension impact evaluation, we discovered that much of Extension's programming targets social units other than communities of place. Programming targets families, organizations such as small businesses, communities of identity or interest such as the Latino community in a particular region of the state or statewide, and industry sectors such as corn growers. While impacts in these other social units may have crossover effects in rural communities of place, we felt it was important to include these other "levels" of impacts in our framework (Chazdon, Bartholomay, Marczak, and Lochner 2007).

Examples of impact evaluations. The domains of impact framework was used by Lott and Chazdon (2009) to examine the impacts of University of Minnesota Extension leadership program participants on their organizations and communities. The authors found that 43 percent of the participants gained new leadership skills, 59 percent reported their reputations as leaders was enhanced, and 88 percent had undertaken new leadership roles or new leadership positions since the program.

These new leadership roles were primarily at the local level, with 29 percent at the county level and 21 percent at the state level. The study then explored how these new leadership roles influenced social impacts, political impacts, financial impacts, build/natural resource impacts, and cultural impacts. In almost every case, over thirty percent of the respondents reported impacts on all of these areas with much higher levels on social networking impacts. This approach tracked both the private benefits to participants and the community impacts, which generate public value for Extension programs.

In agriculture, the public benefits have been studied for the popular Master Gardener program (Bartholomay 2007). Most discussions of public value assume that there is a logic model, which clearly identifies the nature of the public impacts generated by the program. Often this is not the case. For example, in this study of Master-Gardeners, 46 different public benefits were identified. The study examined the most valued benefits as seen by four constituent groups: Master-Gardeners, University Extension staff, the public and county decision-makers.

Conclusions on impact evaluations. By 2006, every program team understood the importance of describing and documenting their public value. All program teams had a short public value statement, which explained the benefits to non-participants. A number of teams are starting to do the empirical work related to measuring outputs, outcomes, and impacts to establish the validity of their public value statements. To date, however, the new regional/county system has not resulted in many new published impact evaluations. The next section explores whether this is likely to change.

Specialization's Impact on Evaluation

Does the Minnesota regional/county model encourage, discourage, or have no impact on the willingness and ability of program teams to do program evaluation? Three pieces of evidence will be used to explore this question: (1) data from the REE survey, (2) data from the state specialist survey, and (3) the opinions of the four evaluation specialists.

Regional Extension Educators (REEs) Views

Specialization by REEs appears to increase their willingness and ability to do evaluation projects. An average of 36% of their programs had written evaluations in 2001 and this increased to 47% in 2006 (Morse and Ahmed, 2008). While this still seems very low, recall that three of the four program evaluators were only hired after 2006 so it is likely that this understates the current level. Furthermore, there might be some confusion about the question. Some respondents might have interpreted "programs" to mean individual educational events rather than the entire set of activities aimed at the same audience and objectives. If this were true, then the percentage of programs evaluated would be higher than the set of events.

State Extension Specialists Views

The results from the state specialists' survey in 2009 also suggest that REEs are doing more on evaluation. Seventy percent of the tenure track faculty and 60% of the other state specialists perceived REEs as having more opportunity to do scholarship on programs. Further, as seen in Table 10.5, nearly half of the tenured-faculty and 60% of the non-tenure track faculty report REEs working more closely with them on evaluation of programs.

Additionally, the REEs are making more presentations at professional meetings and co-authoring more publications. Over one-third of the state specialists reported that REEs are working more closely with them on presentations for professional meetings and nearly one-third reported REEs are working with them more closely on publications.

Table 10.5:
Evaluation Measures, State Specialists Survey, MN, 2009

Are REEs working with you more or less closely on the following aspects of your Extension program...?	Tenure-track State Specialists (% more closely)	Other State Specialists (% more closely)
Evaluation of programs	45	60
Presentations at professional meetings	36	50
Co-authoring publications	32	31
Respondents (N)	30	15

Source: Minnesota state specialist survey in 2009.

Extension Evaluation Team's Views

The team of evaluation specialists reports that each capacity area has its own culture of evaluation practices (Chazdon, Bartholomay,

Marczak, and Lochner 2007). They observe greater focus on outputs and outcomes rather than public value impacts. At this stage, this is reasonable since without solid data on both participation levels and changes in behavior of participants, it is impossible to estimate the public value impacts.

The consensus among the evaluation team was that the Minnesota model of regionalization and specialization made evaluation at all levels more feasible (Bartholomay, Chazdon, and Marczak 2009). Further, the evaluators are starting to see greater evaluation efforts. They cited the following reasons for this. First, many more programs are being conducted statewide, providing sufficient replications that evaluation is more feasible. Second, the larger programs provide more incentives and opportunities for program teams to do the background research to develop logic models and to invest in formal evaluations at all levels. Third, the REEs now have much stronger promotion incentives to do program evaluations since these can count toward their scholarship requirements if they are peer-reviewed and shared with colleagues. Fourth, the increased focus of REEs and closer collaboration with campus faculty is leading to greater opportunities for doing evaluation research. Fifth, program teams are increasingly interested in being able to communicate their public value as a means of garnering more resources. To communicate meaningfully their public value, they must have data on the programs impacts for non-participants as well as participants.

Conclusions and Future Research

Conclusions

The hypothesis being investigated in this chapter is whether the Minnesota model of specialization by regional educators resulted in higher quality programming by Extension. The initial evidence suggests program quality has increased because of the new regional/ county model. Specifically, the quality of programs was improved from 2001 to 2006 in the following ways:

1. Program teams are investing more in program business plans and program implementation to enhance program quality, including the following:

   a. The explicit identification of the communities of interest and target audiences for each program;

   b. The formation of statewide program teams with both regional educators and campus faculty;

   c. The development of needs assessment of communities of interest rather than geographic areas;

   d. The clarification of program's capacity to delivery, comparative advantage, operational guidelines, costs, and financial potential prior to the selection of programs; and

   e. The ability to terminate programs, which no longer meet needs assessment and capacity criteria.

2. Program teams are investing more in program evaluation efforts to enhance program quality, including the following:

   a. An increased willingness by program teams to evaluate programs at both the process, outcome, and impact levels;

   b. An increased enthusiasm of REEs to share results with colleagues through professional meetings and publications; and

   c. An increased use of public value statements for each program.

Despite these very positive changes in Minnesota, there are continuing challenges in order to become the "best in the business" in each program.

Future Research

These rudimentary results leave many opportunities for additional research. Some of the questions on which future research are needed are:

1. How does the use of program business plans and market research influence the productivity of program teams?

2. What types of incentives are necessary for program teams to update their program business plans on a regular basis?

3. Would increased transparency of program business plans have more positive than negative effects?

4. What type of leadership is necessary to encourage a "best in the business" culture in Extension?

5. What incentives would encourage program teams to do empirical studies of their programs' public value impacts?

6. How does the specialization of programs teams influence their program quality?

7. Which of the Minnesota model policies have the greatest influence on program quality?

8. How do different systems of regionalization/specialization influence program quality and public value?

Chapter 11

Scholarship Results

George W. Morse

In my judgment, few if any issues are more important to the future of Extension than the issue of scholarship.

Theodore R. Alter, 2003

Cooperative Extension Service's comparative advantage as an outreach education unit stems from being located at research universities and having close ties to academic faculty and scholarship. The close ties between campus faculty and field educators are very important to Extension's mission of helping make university research practical to citizens around the state. However, in recent years, this partnership has broken down on many campuses. To address the broken partnership, a new promotion policy was introduced as part of the new Minnesota regional/county model.

This chapter discusses why campus faculty and Extension educator collaboration on scholarship is important and the obstacles to closer partnerships. The changes in collaboration and scholarship stimulated by the new system are explored. Data on these changes come from two surveys, one of Regional Extension Educators (REEs) and another of campus faculty. Since collaboration between REEs and campus faculty is central to improving REE scholarship, it is presented first.

Educator/Faculty Scholarship Collaboration

Importance of Collaboration

Scholarship efforts benefit from campus faculty having joint research/extension appointments and collaborating with Extension field staff in the following ways:

1. teaching extension audiences throughout the state enhances the Extension educator's awareness and knowledge of the state's concerns;
2. some participants already have an abundance of practical insights on the topics being taught, helping faculty deepen their expertise;
3. the Extension program's stakeholders gain confidence in the abilities of the Extension faculty, making the future funding of both extension and research efforts more likely;
4. field staff can assist in the implementation of some research; and
5. programs can encourage interdisciplinary research efforts.

The first three benefits to research, listed above, are more robust if there is strong social capital between the campus faculty and the field staff. When there is mutual respect and trust between these two groups, the field staff can provide feedback to faculty on new problems and concerns of Extension participants.

In some areas of research, the Extension Educators can facilitate the actual implementation of research projects. For example, in field trials for crops research, the Extension field staff can do the farm visits in their areas much more efficiently than a campus faculty member can.

Another benefit of strong social capital between field and campus is the development of interdisciplinary programs, also known as issue programming. As Professor Carole Bottom from Purdue University used to tell graduate students, "People don't have economic problems, technical problems, environmental problems, and sociological problems. They have problems with economic, technical, environmental, and sociological aspects." If faculty are working together closely on Extension programs and have developed strong bonds of social capital, the odds of interdisciplinary programs are likely to improve.

Obstacles to Faculty-Field Collaboration

Minnesota Extension Dean/Director Charles Casey initiated efforts to establish closer campus-field collaboration in Minnesota in 1999. A team investigated commonalities and differences in the working environment of campus-based faculty and field-based faculty (Ukaga, Reichenbach, Blinn, Zak, Hutchinson, and Hegland 2002). Not surprisingly, the team found major differences in all twelve areas they examined, even though both groups had a common goal of problem solving and translating research into useful and practical information for citizens around the state.

In the author's experience, the following obstacles to campus faculty-Extension field staff collaboration are the most common:

1. Extension educators are overextended on many topics, making it difficult for them to collaborate on statewide programs;
2. The promotion system for Extension educators has weak scholarship criteria;
3. The personality type of individuals hired for field positions are different than those hired for campus faculty positions;
4. The timeline for doing projects is usually shorter for field staff than for campus faculty; and
5. the selection criteria for new programs are often dissimilar for field staff and campus faculty.

Educators spread too thin. In Minnesota prior to 2004, collaboration between state and Extension Educators often was inhibited by the lack of focus by educators. At a 2000 campus seminar by four state Extension specialists, someone asked the question: "What would happen to your Extension program if there were no field staff at all?" The first specialist responded, "There are no Extension educators who specialize in our area so we don't work with educators. We would love it if there were three or four Extension educators who were specialized in our topic. It would really help us deliver much more." The other three state specialists echoed the same sentiment. One, however, went further. She said she tried to train the Extension educators, but their lack of focus often took time away from program delivery, rather than providing a multiplier effect. Many of the educators were unable to use the training provided because of the many other demands on their time.

Promotion lacks scholarship criteria. In Minnesota prior to restructuring in 2004, the scholarship criteria for field staff was very weak. If the field staff have no incentives to work on some applied research, they are unlikely to do so. Finding time for applied research and scholarship is very difficult to do, even for campus faculty on Extension appointments. Getting prepared for the presentation tomorrow night seems more urgent than writing a journal article that will be published in 18 months.

Type of individuals hired. In the traditional county delivery model or the county cluster model, the personality types of individuals hired for campus faculty positions and Extension field staff have tended to be dissimilar. Saunders and Gallagher (2003) found that campus faculty members tend to have different approaches to making decisions than do field staff. While 72% of the campus faculty made decisions based on impersonal and objective information, 60% of the field staff made decisions based on personal values and subjective information. While Saunders and Gallagher document this disparity, they do not speculate why it exists. Is this due to ingrained personality distinctions or is it a reflection of the relative costs of obtaining objective information in a timely fashion? Are the differences due to the inability of county or county cluster educators to focus as much as campus faculty? Alternatively, if it is true that there are personality differences, what leads to these? Does the traditional type of hiring system, which puts the final control in the hands of a local Extension committee, contribute to this dissimilarity? Does the supervision by District Directors, who have to supervise many different areas of expertise, contribute to an emphasis on the "feeling" style of decision-making?

Timeline differences. Extension educators often have shorter timelines than the campus faculty. For field staff, the timeline is driven by the needs of the target audience, who once they recognize the need for an educational program often want it almost immediately. However, for campus faculty, the timelines are driven not only by the needs of Extension audiences, but also by their research project cycle and by their classroom teaching. Some Extension Educators do not understand the time required to do the literature reviews, grant applications, graduate students hired and trained, data collected, data analyzed, articles written, and articles peer reviewed. Typically, a research project takes two or three years. Then, it often covers only a small piece of the total puzzle. Because of these differences in timeline, many extension educators feel that campus faculty members are non-responsive to their requests and the field staff stop suggesting ideas to campus faculty.

Selection criteria for programs. In the traditional county delivery model, county Extension educators tend to select projects and programs on a reactive basis (Loveridge, Parliament, Morse, Templin, Engelmann, and Elmstrand 1994). Campus faculty members tend to pick programs that will compliment their research and teaching agendas. While some would argue that campus faculty should be more flexible, there are limits on their flexibility imposed by the tenure system. If the campus faculty do not pick Extension programs which compliment their research and teaching programs, their overall productivity is likely to be lower and their odds of achieving tenure is likely to be less.

From a societal point of view, it is desirable for the campus faculty to focus their Extension programs on the topics they know the best, i.e. their areas of research and teaching. This ensures that they bring the latest research to the Extension program. From an Extension institutional point of view, it is also desirable for the campus faculty to coordinate their Extension and research programs for two reasons. First, without this possibility, it is very difficult to hire outstanding faculty. Second, if a new state extension specialists turns out to be an excellent outreach educator but does not receive tenure, not only has an excellent resource been lost, but also there is the danger that University budget freezes will result in the permanent loss of that state specialist position. The net result is that campus specialists have little choice but to tie their research, teaching, and extension programs together.

If field staff and campus faculty are to be on the same page, the field staff have to consider this as a given and adjust their menu of offerings accordingly. In the traditional county delivery model, this often does not happen.

Changes in Regional Educators' Scholarship

Does the Minnesota model lead to increases in the scholarship of REEs and greater collaboration between campus faculty and regional educators? Conversely, does the additional geographic area covered by regional educators lead to less collaboration? On the other hand, is there simply no difference?

State Specialists Survey Results

State specialists were surveyed in the spring of 2009 for reactions to the new regional/county system (Chapter 7). When state specialists were asked how the new regional/county model effected collaboration on research with REEs, the state specialists reported increases (Table 11.1). The gains in research collaboration with non-tenured faculty were much larger (67%) than the gains for tenured faculty (36%). These findings are not surprising since the nature of the research projects with non-tenured faculty are probably focused more on the scholarship of application and scholarship of integration, which have been the heart of past scholarship efforts by regional educators. The scholarship of discovery, which is the primary focus of campus faculty, takes a much longer time to implement, is not as practical, and is more difficult to integrate into Extension programs.

Table 11.1:
Faculty and REE Research Collaboration, MN, 2009

Overall, are Regional Extension Educators working more or less closely with you on *your research project* than before 2004 and the regional system?	Tenure -track State Specialists (%)	Non-tenure Track State Specialist (%)
Much less closely	11	0
Less closely	4	17
Same	50	17
More closely	29	50
Much more closely	7	17
N	28	12

Source: Survey of Minnesota state specialists by G. Morse, March 2009.

Some readers, especially Extension administrators and field educators, might object to the wording ("your research project") found in the questions for Tables 11.1 and 11.2. Possibly, some research projects are jointly developed to the degree that the project is co-owned by state specialists and regional educators. But this is very rare and most campus faculty have many years invested in specific projects, are the principal investigators, and see themselves as the owners of the project. To increase response rates, the survey did not attempt to debate this perception. In addition, the state specialists were asked, *"Since January 2004,*

*are Regional Extension Educators working with you more or
less closely on the following aspects of your research program?
(1) identifying research issues, (2) managing field trials, (3)
implementing surveys, (4) co-authoring publications, and (5) co-
authoring professional meeting presentations. "* The results are
shown in Table 11. 2.

Table 11.2:
Aspects of Research Collaboration, MN, 2009

"Since 2004, are Regional Extension Educators working with you more or less closely on the following aspects of your *research program?*	Tenure-track State Specialists (% more closely or much more closely)	Non-tenure Track State Specialist (% more closely or much more closely)
Identifying research issues	39	77
Co-authoring publications	32	31
Implementing surveys	30	62
Co-authoring professional meeting presentations	29	62
Managing field trials	23	30
N	31	13

Source: Survey of Minnesota state specialists by G. Morse, March
2009.

Almost forty percent of the tenured faculty reported REEs were
providing greater assistance in identifying potential research topics.
Further approximately 30 percent of the tenured faculty report
increased collaboration on co-authoring publications, implementing
surveys, and presentations at professional meetings. Since managing
field trials is likely to be only relevant in agricultural programs, it is
not surprising that this one has only 22 percent. Once again, the non-
tenured state specialists report greater increases, with the exception
of the publications. A possible reason for the publication exception

is that the non-tenured faculty members are probably not doing as many publications themselves so there are fewer opportunities for REEs to collaborate here.

Regional Educators Survey Results

Data from the Regional Extension Educator survey confirms the above picture of closer connections on research. The REEs were:

1. attending and participating more actively in national professional conferences;

2. doing more scholarship related to their programs;

3. participating in more applied research; and

4. providing more statewide leadership to programs.

Presentations at national professional conferences. As shown in Table 11.3, Regional Extension Educators became much more involved in national and regional professional meetings, with the average number attended increasing from 1.4 to 2.1 conferences, or a growth of 50 percent. Likewise, the percentage of REEs that attended at least one national or regional conference grew by 40 percent. This growth alone, however, might not indicate a qualitative change in the nature of their participation or their collaboration with campus faculty. However, the next two variables do.

The number of presentations done by REEs at regional or national professional meetings grew from an average of .69 per REE to an average 2.33 per REE, or by 238 percent. The percentage of REEs doing at least one presentation at these meetings doubled, growing from 35 percent to 72 percent. Likewise, the mean number of presentations prepared jointly with campus faculty grew from .38 per REE to 1.6 per REE, a growth of 321 percent. The percentage of REEs who worked jointly with campus faculty to prepare presentations more than doubled, going from 20 percent in 2001 to 44 percent in 2006. Further, the portion of total presentations done by REEs jointly with campus faculty went to slightly over one-quarter (27%) to three-quarters (76%).

Table 11.3:
REE Participation, Professional Conferences, 2001/2006

	2001	2006	Percent Gain
National or Regional Professional Conferences (mean # attended by REEs)	1.4	2.1	50
National or Regional Professional Conferences (percentage attending at least one)	63	88	40
Presentations Done by REEs at national or regional meetings (mean #)	.69	2.33	238
Presentations Done by REEs at national or regional meetings (percentage doing at least one)	35	72	106
Professional meeting presentations prepared jointly with campus faculty (mean # presentations)	.38	1.6	321
Professional meeting presentations prepared jointly with campus faculty (percent REEs doing at least one)	20	44	120
Percentage of all presentations done jointly with campus faculty	27	76	181
Respondents (N)	80	102	Na

Source: Survey of Minnesota REEs in 2007, Morse and Ahmed 2008

These joint presentations have a number of benefits, including building the following:

1. better understanding and respect between REEs and state specialists;
2. the REEs' knowledge and expertise in their specialty;
3. the REE's sense of purpose and ability to make a difference; and
4. the reputation of the state for having depth both on campus and in the field.

The first two benefits are well understood. The third is important to the recruiting of new REEs for new positions. A number of the REEs hired since 2004 have explicitly told us they would not have been interested in traditional county agent positions, which would have required them to work in many different areas of expertise, including youth development, rather than their area in which they received their M.S. or Ph.D. degree.

The way collaboration and specialization enhances a state's reputation became clear to the author at the 2006 National Association of Community Development Extension Professionals in Santa Fe, New Mexico during one of the presentations by a Minnesota REE in Community Economics. During the question and answer session there was an active, respectful, and professional exchange between five members of the audience and Bruce Schwartau, one of Minnesota's Community Economics REEs. The author knew all of the participants in the discussion, having been a state specialist in community economics for 25 years. The five audience members were all state specialist, discussing the issue with one of Minnesota's regional educators as a peer. It appeared that Bruce had had the opportunity to specialize just as much on retail trade analysis as many of the state specialists.

Doing scholarship related to programs. The results in Table 11.4 show some shift toward greater scholarship but not major ones. On average, each REE produced more bulletins and fact sheets as well as slightly more curriculum. Journal articles remained constant as an average per REE. However, the percentage of REEs with at least one journal article jumped from 8 percent to 27 percent. The average number of staff papers fell very slightly, but the percentage of REEs with at least one staff paper grew from 10 percent to 25 percent.

Table 11.4:
Scholarship Products by REEs, MN, 2001 and 2006

Scholarship Products	2001 (mean #)	2006 (mean #)
Bulletin or fact sheet	2.12	2.38
Curriculum for entire series of lessons	1.87	1.93
Journal Article	1.43	1.43
Staff Papers	1.83	1.81
Newspaper or magazine articles [a]	3.53	3.06
One time lesson [a]	3.57	3.06
Respondents (N) – those employed in both 2001 and 2006	74	74

Source: Survey of Minnesota REEs in 2007 by Morse and Ahmed, 2007.

a/ Newspaper articles and one-time lessons do not generally comply with the peer review portion of the Minnesota Extension scholarship definition.

Newspaper articles and one-time lessons per educator went down. The decline in number of newspaper articles reflects a new communications approach, which allowed articles written by one educator to be used throughout the state. The drop in one-time lessons was viewed as a positive development since the overhead costs of these are high. In fact, it is surprising that this did not drop more. Neither the newspaper articles nor the one-time lessons typically are peer reviewed. Hence, they would not qualify as a scholarship product.

This lack of growth in scholarship products is probably due to the long lead-time required for scholarship efforts to result in scholarship products. Further, the promotion policy, which provided greater emphasis on scholarship, only went into effect in 2006, although the importance of scholarship had been widely discussed for a year before this. A final factor for the slow increase might be the closer collaboration with campus faculty. If the type of scholarship shifted from scholarship of application and integration to discovery, this would slow the release of scholarship products.

Conducting more applied research. From 2001 to 2006, the average percentage time spent by Regional Extension Educators (REEs) jumped from 8 to 12 percent, the percentage that are doing no applied research dropping from 26 to 11 percent. Note that the data in Table 11.5 includes only those employed in 2001 or before. If the new educators had been included, the differences would have been larger. While the survey did not explicitly ask REEs if they were doing this applied research with campus faculty, it is a reasonable assumption that this is the case. Supporting evidence is that more REEs are doing joint presentations at national or regional professional meetings with campus faculty (Table 11.2).

Statewide leadership. As REEs moved to the regional positions and specialized, they assumed more statewide leadership. Over half of the REEs were providing statewide leadership on a program or an aspect of a program in 2006 compared to only 16 percent in 2001. As REEs assume greater roles in the leadership of programs, the state specialists have more time for the scholarship of application and scholarship of integration that directly benefits Extension programs. Furthermore, as the leadership is assumed more by REEs, the unexpected time demands on state specialists are likely to be reduced. This will help the state specialists protect their time for scholarship of discovery, which ultimately benefits Extension programs.

Table 11.5:
Applied Research Time by REEs, MN, 2001 and 2006

Percent time	2001	2006	Difference
None	26	11	-15
1 to 10	46	39	-7
11 to 20	17	28	11
21 to 30	5	16	11
31 or more	6	6	0
Estimated Mean[1/]	8	12	4
Respondents (N)[2/]	74	74	

Source: Survey of Minnesota REEs in 2007 by Morse and Ahmed, 2007.

1/ Assumed 35 percent for the "31 or more" category.

2/ Based on the 74 respondents employed in both 1999 and 2007.

Benefits of Specialization

The REEs were asked, *"Since 2004, to what extent has increased specialization resulted in increasing opportunities in the following areas?"* Sixty-nine percent of the REEs responded that the increased specialization gave them more opportunities to do scholarship compared to nine percent that reported fewer opportunities.

The state specialists as well as the REEs were asked a general question about collaboration. All three groups (REEs, tenured state specialists, and non-tenured state specialists) reported that REEs had greater opportunities to work with state specialists (Table 11.6). By wide margins, all three groups perceived the regional/county system leading to closer collaboration between REEs and state specialists.

Table 11.6:
Overall Collaboration, REEs and State Specialists, MN

Because of the regional system adopted in 2004, do the REEs have more or fewer opportunities to work with state specialists?	Regional Educators (%)	Tenure-track State Specialists (%)	Non-tenured State Specialists (%)
Much fewer	1	7	0
Fewer	19	3	7
Same	31	23	13
More	26	53	67
Many more	23	13	13
N	74	30	15

Source: Survey of Minnesota REEs in 2007 by Morse and Ahmed, 2007 and survey by G. Morse of Minnesota state specialists in March 2009.

Nearly half (49 %) of the REEs reported more opportunities to work with state specialists compared to under 20% reporting fewer. Interestingly the ratio for the tenured campus specialists was even higher, with 66% reporting more opportunities for REEs to work with state specialists compared to 10% reporting fewer opportunities. The non-tenured state specialists were even more positive with 80% reporting more collaboration opportunities compared to 7% reporting fewer.

REEs might have reported fewer opportunities for collaboration than state specialists did because the REEs were surveyed in 2007 while the state specialists were surveyed two years later. During these two years, the collaboration might have increased.

The state specialists were also asked: *"Overall, has the regional system (with increased REE specialization) been advantageous or disadvantageous to your work?"* This question came after a series of questions about Extension programming, research, and teaching so "work" captures all three. As shown in Table 11.7, the tenured (or tenure track) state specialists felt regionalization was advantageous to their work by nearly a three to one margin (54.8% advantageous to 19.4 disadvantageous). The non-tenured state specialists were even more positive. Seventy-three percent reported the new system as advantageous while none reported it as disadvantageous.

Table 11.7:
Regionalization's Impact on State Specialists, MN, 2009

Impact on State Specialist Work	Tenure-track State Specialists (%)	Non-tenure Track State Specialists (%)
Very Advantageous	13	20
Advantageous	42	53
Neutral	26	27
Disadvantageous	13	0
Very Disadvantageous	7	0
N	31	15

Source: Survey of state specialists in winter 2009 by G. Morse.

Conclusions and Future Research

Conclusions

Overall, the increased regionalization and specialization of the Minnesota Regional Extension Educators (REEs) has increased their levels of scholarship. The increased specialization also has increased the levels of collaboration between campus state specialists and REEs. Most state specialists now see the REEs as more capable of contributing both to their Extension programs and to their research. No one aspect of the new regional/county structure is likely to be responsible for these changes. Rather, the entire package of policies is responsible for the increased scholarship and collaboration.

Future Research

While these early results show promising possibilities that increased specialization and regionalization will lead to more scholarship and collaboration, the very nature of scholarship requires a longer-term view. Some of the questions, which need future investigation, are:

1. Will scholarship increase in significant ways as the Minnesota model becomes more mature?
2. Will the scholarship of regional educators shift from primarily scholarship of application and integration to include a greater portion of scholarship of discovery and scholarship of teaching?
3. Will the public value of Extension programs, particularly to federal taxpayers, be seen as primarily a function of the scholarship of teaching?
4. Will the increased specialization of regional educators lead to sufficient additional involvement and credibility with state specialists that the educators contribute to the research agenda?
5. How do different types of regional systems and Extension promotion systems compare in their ability to encourage all types of scholarship?

Chapter 12

Access to Extension

George Morse

*America is the most inventive country in the world
because everybody has access to information.*

Tom Clancy

One of the reservations about the new regional/county system and educator specialization was whether access to Extension would decline. In contrast, some stakeholders asserted specialization and regionalization would actually increase access. The impact of a regional delivery system depends on which definition of access is being used. At least five dimensions of "access to Extension" can be considered. They are access to:

1. Extension educators as civic leaders;
2. specialized educators;

3. Extension programs;

4. Extension information; and

5. programs for new underserved minority audiences.

This chapter explores changes in access in Minnesota as it shifted from a county cluster delivery model to the new regional/ county model.

Access to Extension Staff as Civic Leaders

In smaller rural communities, Extension staff members often are willing and able to work on any aspect of local problems. The organizational work of county-based educators has long been recognized as a valuable educational role for Extension (Peters, Jordon, Adamek, and Alter 2005). County-based extension educators often have the opportunity to play catalytic leadership roles on complex local problems (Flora, 2000; Morse, Brown, and Warning 2006). While the focus of Extension work is on delivering educational programs, Extension educators often have opportunities to contribute to many other community concerns in the towns in which they live.

The educators, many of whom have master's degrees and are civic minded, often build considerable social capital in their local communities outside their professional jobs (Putman 2000). Hence, the Extension educators become a valuable asset to a community beyond their area of expertise and beyond the number and quality of their programs.

The trust that Extension educators build with their local audiences helps to reduce the transaction costs and makes solving problems easier and quicker. Flora (2000) suggests that:

Uncertainty about the future or other-party actions leads to higher transaction costs. Given the rapid rate of change, the future is uncertain. We can never lay out all of the possible contingencies. Extension educators build social capital through helping different groups understand each other's actions better. This allows a better analysis of the impact of alternative actions on future conditions from a systems view (Flora 2000).

Conversely, in the regional/county system many regional educators work statewide, possibly reducing their level of civic participation (Slocum 1969). If so, this is a loss for both the educators and their residential communities.

The Minnesota Experience

For the communities in which the M.S. level Extension Educators lived prior to the 2004 restructuring, there probably was a loss of civic leadership access. Counties went from an average of 3.5 M.S. level educators per office to less than .4 FTE per county. The total number of employees in county offices dropped from an average of 6.7 to 3.5 total employees.

Recall from Chapter 6 that the total number of M.S. level educators in the field would have fallen even more if the old system was left in place. Without the change, there would have been only 138 M.S. level field staff (85 educators and 53 field administrators) compared to 188 M.S. level educators under the new system (34 county educators, 130 REEs, and 24 field administrators). Although there are more total M.S. level staff in the new system located somewhere in the state, total access, defined as civic engagement outside their area of expertise, might not have increased since the REEs have to spend much more time working outside the communities in which they reside.

A different picture emerges from the communities in which the educators originally lived. If the old system had been maintained, then 138 M.S. level educators probably would have remained in their original county offices (85 educators and 53 field administrators) compared to only 34 county educators in the new system.

In summary, it appears that access to well-educated citizens to participate in civic activities outside their area of expertise and programs probably declined with the adoption of the regional/county model. Some readers might question whether the typical state and federal taxpayer values this type of access or whether they see the role of Extension Educators in different ways. Answering this is beyond the scope of this book.

Geographic Access to Specialists

Access to specialized Extension Educators is a second type of access to Extension. This form of access depends on the depth of knowledge and expertise that the individual Extension staff member possesses. Prior to the 2004 adoption of the mixed regional/county model, nearly all of the state specialists were located at the University of Minnesota St. Paul campus. A few were located at Research and Outreach Centers around the state. The campus specialists were a mix of M.S. level specialists who worked full time for Extension and Ph.D. level specialists who had joint appointments in research and extension. In a few cases, the Ph.D. level specialists, who typically had tenure or tenure track appointments, had three-way joint appointments with campus teaching, research, and extension.

Table 12.1:
Specialists in Applied Economics, MN, 1967 to 2008

State Specialists with 50% time in Extension	1967	2003	2008
With Ph.D. degrees	8	8	9
With M.S. degrees on public funds	6	0	16 [a]
With M.S. degrees on earned income [b]	0	6	5
Total	14	14	31

a/ These sixteen regional extension educators are in the agribusiness management area of expertise and the community economics area of expertise and serve roles very similar to the 1967 M.S. level state specialists.

b/ This includes five extension economists in the Center for Farm Financial Management and, in 2003, one in the Business Retention and Expansion Program. While all of these are University of Minnesota employees, a large portion of their funding comes from earned income.

Prior to 1960, many of the state specialists held M.S. degrees and reported directly to Minnesota Extension. In the mid-1960s, when the University of Minnesota mandated that individuals with tenure must be located within academic departments and not within Extension, many of the existing Extension educators were shifted to departments. For example, in Applied Economics, fourteen new extension economists were added to the Department of Agriculture and Applied Economics in 1966 (Cochrane 1983). Of these, six (43%) held M.S. degrees (Table 12.1). As the M.S. level state specialists retired, they were replaced with Ph.D. level state specialists (Sundquist 2001).

This shift to Ph.D. extension state specialists changed the nature of access in three ways. First, due to the Ph.D. specialist's research responsibilities, their focus was much tighter than that of

M.S. level state specialists. A Ph.D. state specialist in community economics might focus on public finance or economic development but typically not both. Even within economic development, the state specialist is likely to focus on only one or two aspects of economic development. On the other hand, a specialized regional extension educator in community economics would cover all phases of local economic development and public finance. An analogy in medicine might be that the state specialists are playing the role of medical specialists while the regional educators play the role of general practitioners. However, in medicine, the general practitioners focus only on medicine and have a high degree of training.

Second, the total number of specialists in applied economics nearly doubled because of the move to regional centers. By 2008, there were 17 additional M.S. level specialists because of the shift to the regional system and one additional Ph.D. specialist. Third, by 2008 over half of the specialist positions were located in regional centers. In contrast, in 1967 and 2003, none of the specialists was located there.

In summary, under the new regional/county system, access to specialists increased in two ways. First, there more M.S. level specialists available. Second, these specialists are located throughout the state. The picture for other areas of expertise is similar.

Access to Extension Programs

Some county stakeholders equate access to programs as having the program delivered in their county rather than the program being available within a reasonable distance. In this case, the measure of access to the programs becomes the number of events held in the county and the number of county participants. In contrast, leaders of communities of interest are often most interested in providing access of high quality programs to as many individuals as possible without considering whether the program is offered in every county. To this group of stakeholders, the total number of participants in the state, or in large regions, is a more important measure of access.

Access by Communities of Interest

Historically, the programs available in a specific county often depended on the local staffing pattern. Very few programs have been available in every county. In order to reach large groups, programs provided by state specialists tended to be scheduled in several central locations, often in conjunction with meetings of industry organizations or other groups.

One way to measure the change in access for communities of interest is simply to monitor the total annual participation in educational programs. Minnesota Extension's overall participation levels for face-to-face program events grew from 310,000 to 446,000 from 2004 to 2007, or an increase of 44 percent (University of Minnesota Extension 2007a). These numbers suggest access has improved considerably from the community of interest perspective.

Access for Geographic Communities

Access to face-to-face programming. Some of the counties were concerned that their citizens would no longer have convenient access to some programs with the adoption of the regional system. In one respect, this concern is logical because program teams have an incentive to maximize the number of people they can reach, given the limits of their time and resources. In many cases, the program teams would contemplate providing programs in central locations that could draw large groups. On the other hand, the view that programs should be available in every county ignores the history of Extension. First, the reason Extension was organized at the county level originally was that travel and communications in the early 1900s was much more difficult. By 2004, individuals traveled much further for employment and other functions. Second, very few programs were available in every county under the old system.

Because of the historical importance of counties and their political importance to Extension, Minnesota Extension wanted to demonstrate that it was serving people in each county on an equitable basis. Consequently, as described in Chapter 8, Minnesota

Extension attempted to track participation by zip code, using the MyPrograms reporting system. Some teams collected this data as part of their end of meeting evaluations. Other teams used different ways to determine the zip code. However, the reporting aspect of this is not yet functional.

After five years of the new system, there is less apprehension about the location of programs. In part, this more relaxed attitude stems from the continued access to 4-H programs through the 4-H program coordinators and the 4-H REEs. In addition, many of the agricultural counties have contracted with Extension for a local agricultural Extension Educator or are sharing one with a neighboring county. Finally, the programs provided by the REEs and state specialists are being done statewide so communities of interest are no longer worried about access.

Table 12.2:

Sample of Online Programs, Minnesota Extension, 2008

Name	Who	What/ When/Format/Fee
FINPACK Online Training	Producers and agricultural professionals	Learn how to use every aspect of Web-based FINPACK // On-demand/ /self-learning// Fee = $300
Building Extension's Public value	Train-the-trainer for Extension professionals	Participants learn how their programs create public value and how to communicate this value to stakeholders//Specific dates// Two online seminars (two hours each)/ Fee = $100 per person with maximum of $500 per institution
Natural Resource Learning Modules	Landowners	Interactive learning modules cover forestry and wildlife topics//on-demand//Self-learning//No Fee
Parents Forever Online Train the Trainer Course	Professionals who want to use or teach the "Parents Forever" curriculum	Includes five modules. See website for details extension. umn.edu/LearnOnline/ On-demand//Self-learning//Fee = $200 ($100 for MN residents)
New Directions for Youth Development	Youth work professionals	Connects the newest knowledge with needed changes in practices ./Every two months//Webinars and on-demand recordings of past webinars// No Fee

Source: www.extension.umn.edu/LearnOnline/

Access to online courses. All counties have access to the online courses (Table 12.2). While online courses are a means of overcoming distance, they also can be done at any time, providing flexibility to the participants. In addition to the courses shown in Table 12.2, there were other courses (www.extension.umn.edu/LearnOnline/).

Some of the online web seminars, or webinars, are available at no charge but require registration. Other online courses can be used without registration. Finally, there are fees for some courses, ranging up to $300 per person.

Access to Information

Many Extension patrons, who do not participate in either face-to-face programs or online courses, use Extension's internet or phone services to gain objective, research based information.

Internet Information

The number of people accessing Minnesota Extension information via the Internet is climbing rapidly. In 2007, the Minnesota Extension website had over 39 million page views (University of Minnesota Extension 2007a). Although Minnesota Extension no longer tracks the number of unique individual users, usage is estimated to be over 5 million. When the term 'Extension Service' is put into a Google search, the University of Minnesota Extension is the first state program to be listed. However, for people who are uncomfortable with the internet, the telephone answering systems are used.

Telephone Answering Lines

The Farm Information Line and the Answer Line (described in Chapter 8) have provided access to those who cannot travel to a county office or do not have local agricultural or family development educators. From 2004 to 2007, over 125,000 answers were provided, averaging 31,000 per year.

Access by Diverse Audiences

To some stakeholders, "improved access" implies serving more minority or diverse audiences. Did the shift to a regional specialist delivery model increase or decrease access in this sense?

In 2007, Minnesota's minority population was 12.8 percent of the total. Seventeen percent of Minnesota Extension's participants are minorities, with this participation concentrated in programs in Family Development, Youth Development, and Community Vitality (University of Minnesota Extension 2007a).

The regional/county system allows Extension to focus on new minority audiences more than the traditional county or county cluster did. For example, one of the new REEs in Community Economics Area of Expertise started a major economic development project with four ethnic chambers of commerce located in four metropolitan counties in the Minneapolis – St. Paul metropolitan area. This would have been difficult to coordinate in the county cluster model.

There is no guarantee that the regional/county model will increase access for ethnic groups, new groups, and underserved audiences. Immediately after a major restructuring, established stakeholders vie for continued and even additional attention. In the short run, this competition for attention could reduce access for new audiences. It is hypothesized that this is a short-run problem and that in the long-run, greater attention can be focused on new audiences.

Conclusions and Future Research

Conclusions

"Access to Extension" has five dimensions. These include access to: (1) Extension educators as civic leaders, (2) specialized extension educators, (3) programs, (4) information, and (5) programs for diverse audiences. Although, smaller rural communities may have lost access on the first dimension, these same communities may now have higher access to specialized Extension Educators, Extension programs, and Extension information.

While access to programs by diverse audiences seems consistent with the percentage of the population, it varies widely with the type of program. It is not clear how the regional/county model changes access for minority populations.

Future Research

Additional research is needed on each of these dimensions of access. A few of the research questions are:

1. How do different forms of regionalization change access over time?
2. Which types of access are most valued by the different stakeholders and by taxpayers?
3. Can methods of tracking participation by zip code be developed which assist county leaders to understand new regional systems?

Chapter 13

Public Support Results

George Morse

*Double bottom line: The simultaneous pursuit
of financial and social returns on investment*

Jerr Boschee

No Money. No Mission

Conventional Wisdom

"No money, no mission." As this axiom asserts, any institution needs resources to achieve its mission. While volunteers are important to many aspects of Extension, the system could not run on volunteer labor alone. Hence, the level of funding is important, whether as a proxy for public satisfaction or a gauge of the feasibility of delivering programming.

The ultimate test of the success of any public innovation is whether it receives public support after its adoption. This is particularly true for services where the outcomes and impacts are difficult to measure objectively. Using an example from your personal life, consider dining at fine restaurants. While wait staff service is very difficult to measure objectively, every patron has an opinion on the quality of the service and tips accordingly. Likewise, whether the funding for Extension comes via public funding, grants, sponsorships, agency contracts, or user fees, this principle applies. Those paying the tab are more likely to provide greater funding when they find the service quality outstanding and want to encourage more of the same.

Public funding is often a lagging indicator of public support of Extension. Early indicators are the newspaper stories that are either positive or negative about changes in Extension. Major restructuring in Extension often results in legislative hearings, which are either positive or negative. Changes in funding at the county and state level often depend on the outcome of these public discussions.

This chapter first gives examples of the changes in tone of the media coverage and legislative hearings held during restructurings in 2002 and 2004. Second, it describes changes in national trends in Extension funding. Third, it reports on the changes in public funding for Minnesota Extension. Fourth, the changes in alternative revenues (user fees, grants, sponsorships, and contracts with other agencies) are reported. Fifth, the question of whether the regional/county model will insulate Minnesota Extension from needing to restructure in future during fiscal crises is explored.

Media Coverage and Legislative Hearings

While Extension administration had no idea in 2002 that it would need to restructure again in 2004, some legislators thought these two restructuring were part of an overall plan. This makes it useful to look at the reactions to both of these events.

The reaction to the 2002 restructuring was particularly strong and negative. The old saying goes, "When the oats are short, the horses bite each other." A few Extension educators, worried that funds might be inadequate to support everyone, urged their local legislators to cut Family Development programming. The initial legislative hearings in 2002, about a month after Minnesota Extension announced the first restructuring, were long and difficult. In fact, January 4, 2002 hearing in the Agricultural and Rural Development Finance Committee ran for four hours and three minutes. While Family Development was not eliminated, it was necessary for Extension to shift one group of Family Development from state funds to federal funds.

Just as the drama around the 2002 changes was settling down, Extension had to announce the second restructuring in April of 2003, to be effective on January 1, 2004. The media coverage immediately following the announcement of the new regional/county model was descriptive. However, within five months of the announcement, many articles, especially those aimed at production agriculture were voicing concern. An excellent example of the many media stories on the restructuring was the September 16, 2003 article in *Agri News*, which reported on the concerns of legislators (Wilmes 2003). By March 2004, some rural legislators were angry at Extension and expressed this in legislative hearings and in the press (Willette 2004). Some legislators suggested that Extension be taken away from the University of Minnesota and given to the Minnesota Department of Agriculture (MDA) or the Minnesota State Colleges and Universities system (MSCU). Among the specific concerns expressed were the potential cuts in production agriculture and the process for making the decisions. Extension argued against the proposals to move Extension to MDA or MSCU because neither of these had the research base to support a research-based outreach program. Nonetheless, these suggestions were threatening to all Extension employees.

By February 2005, the tone of the legislative hearings had changed dramatically. An officer in the Minnesota Soybean Growers Association told legislators that in eight years of growing soybeans, 2004 was the first year that Extension Service educators have provided meaningful educational programs. A leader from the dairy industry was asked if it was true that Extension educators were not getting out to farms as often since the restructuring. He responded that this was true, but that it was a good thing because their increased level of specialization allowed Extension to train the non-Extension professionals who were on farms every day.

By 2008, the media coverage on Minnesota Extension was almost entirely focused on programs and information provided by program teams, rather than discussions of the restructuring. While the public media became more positive, what happened to public financial support?

National Trends in Funding

To put the Minnesota Extension results in context, the national trends in funding of Extension are reviewed.

Public Funding

In fiscal year 2003, an average of nearly eighty percent (79.2%) of the funding for state Extension organizations came from appropriated federal, state, and local funds. Another 17 percent came from grants, many of which were from public agencies. State and local governments contributed the most, averaging 40 percent and 22 percent respectively. The federal government contributed 17 percent in FY2003 (JTF 2006).

Table 13.1:
Cooperative Extension Funding, 1972 and 2003

Source of Funding	FY 1972 (%)	FY2003 (%)
Federal	40.5	17.2
State	39.9	40.5
Local	17.6	21.8
Grants	2.0	17.2
Fees	0	3.6
Total	100	100

Source: Joint Task Force 2006

Nationally, the role of federal funding has declined significantly during the past thirty years, dropping from 41 percent to 17 percent of the total. While state and county funding have remained relatively constant as a percentage of the total, grants and fees have increased considerably. By 2004, grants and fees were greater than federal funding and almost as large as local funding (Table 13.1). While the total funding for Extension nationally grew by 72 percent ($325 million after adjusting for inflation) from 1970 to 2004, the federal contribution shrank by 27 percent ($35 million).

Alternative Revenues

Alternative revenues have been a major concern for many years (Barth, Stryker, Arrington, and Syed, 1999). At the national level, the Extension Committee on Organization and Policy (ECOP), a part of in the National Association of State Universities and Land-Grant Universities, has been exploring ways to increase alternative revenues for Extension. In 2006, an ECOP report titled "The Changing Portfolio of the CES," recommends a much greater emphasis on alternative revenue sources. This includes: (1) direct user fees charged to participants, (2) fees charged to local sponsors of programs, (3) grants, (4) contracts with other agencies, and (5) gifts.

The most recent national data available on grants and fees are shown in Table 13.1. Nationally, 20.8 percent of the average revenue for state Extension Services comes from grants and fees, making it larger than the amount from the federal government and almost equal to the amount from local governments. The alternative revenues are growing faster than any one of the other three public sources.

The amounts of grants and fees shown in Table 13.1 probably are understated because of the accounting systems in most universities. State specialists are the principal investigators on many grants and the accounting is done in their academic departments and colleges rather than in Extension. In many cases, there is no formal means for Extension to know the amount of the grants obtained by state specialists. The specialists tend to guard this information carefully to avoid any possibilities of some type of internal "tax" or "revenue sharing."

As of FY2003, direct user fees represented a very small portion of the total revenues for Extension Services. In part, this reflects the history of providing all Extension programs free of charge. While participants will only pay as much as they consider the program is worth, history matters. It is much easier to charge fees in new programs or with new audiences than in the traditional areas or with the traditional audiences.

Grants and Contracts

Two means of securing additional revenues are to subcontract with state or federal agencies to deliver educational programs and to win additional grants. While grants and contracts are slightly different from each other, both provide funding for the delivery of specific deliverables. Closely related are sponsorships of specific program events and programs by either public or private institutions.

The 2006 ECOP report recommended three steps to enhance the ability of Extension to secure contracts with federal agencies. Translated to a state level, these recommendations would be:

1. develop greater understanding among agencies of Extension's abilities;
2. establish a statewide approach to be more attractive to state agencies; and
3. develop the capacity to react to new possibilities quickly.

As the 2006 ECOP report emphasized, many state agencies do not understand how Extension could assist them in delivering educational programs. A weakness of the county-based system is the lack of uniform implementation and supervision, which reduces the potential for statewide impact. The county-based system also increases the transactions costs for coordination at the state level and slows the speed of decision-making. In the county cluster system, the process of putting together a reliable team to apply for contracts has been so difficult that most faculty and program leaders do not pursue this.

Public Funding of Minnesota Extension

The sources of funding in Minnesota in FY2007 were very similar to the national averages. Slightly more of Minnesota's funding came from public sources than was the case nationally, with 84.7 percent in Minnesota and 79.5 percent nationally. Grants were higher nationally but fees were higher in Minnesota.

Table 13.2:
Minnesota Extension Funding, 1998 and 2007

Source of Funding	FY 1998 (%)	FY2007 (%)
Federal	20.9	18.6
State	38.9	44.1
Local	21.4	22.0
Grants	9.4	10.2
Fees	6.9	6.8
Total (millions of dollars)	56.5	59.0
Inflation adjusted to 1998	56.5	47.5

Source: University of Minnesota Extension 1997 and 2007

Nationally, alternative revenues were 20.8 percent of the state's revenue compared to 17 percent in Minnesota. Minnesota's alternative revenues increased slightly from FY1998 to FY2007. While the total revenue increased by $2.5 million, the inflation-adjusted revenue fell by $9 million, or 15.9 percent.

County Funding Changes in Minnesota

When Minnesota Extension adopted the new regional/county model, one of the major concerns was that counties would not fund any local positions. Further, if the counties did cut back on their funding in significant ways, especially year after year, the state legislature might take that as a signal that Extension no longer had public value and also start cutting Extension's appropriations.

The level of local funding in Minnesota was about 26 percent of the total revenues compared to 22 percent nationally. Then, due to the state's 2004 fiscal crisis, the county contribution dropped to 20 percent. Ninety percent of counties cut their spending on Extension, (Table 13.3). Overall, this was a cut by 28.5 percent ($4.6 million) which counties had spent on Extension. All 87 counties put in some funding for Extension in 2004, paying all of the expenses of 114 county-based educators and 104 support staff (Chapter 6).

Table 13.3:
County Funding Changes, 2003 to 2004

Percent Change in County Funding from FY2003 to FY2004	Number of Counties	Percent of Counties
-81 to -100	0	0
-61 to -80	5	6
-41 to -60	10	11
-21 to -40	33	38
-1 to -20	30	34
No Change	4	5
+1 to +10	3	3
Greater than + 10	2	2
Total	87	100

Source: Morse and O'Brien 2006

The dire predictions on county funding did not come true (Table 13. 4). While there was a major cut by the counties in fiscal year 2004 because of the state reductions to counties, there have been increases every year since then. Counties have increased their spending an average of 6.9 percent per year (Werner 2009). By FY2008, counties provided 91.3 percent of the funding in FY2004.

Just before the major cut in FY2003, counties supported 26 percent of the total Minnesota Extension costs. The counties' share dropped to 20 percent in FY2004 but moved back to 22 percent by FY2008.

The county funding shown in Table 13.4 includes all of the county expenditures on Extension and not just the funds paid to the University of Minnesota Extension as fees for local positions. It includes the funds they retain at the county level for county Extension support staff, office supplies, and office rent. These funds are included since they are dedicated exclusively to the operation of Extension and including them gives a more accurate picture of the level of public support for Extension.

Table 13.4:
Public Funding for Minnesota Extension, 2003 to 2008

Fiscal Year	County Funding (millions)	State Funding (millions)	Federal Funding (millions)
2002-03	$16.1	$26.4	$10.4
2003-04	11.5	24.1	10.7
2004-05	12.4	24.8	10.6
2005-06	13.0	25.4	10.1
2006-07	14.0	26.6	10.5
2007-08	14.7	26.4	10.1

Source: Werner 2009.

State Funding in Minnesota

The second concern, that state funding would continue to fall after the 2004 restructuring, did not materialize either. The perilous decrease of 8.7 percent from fiscal year 2003 to fiscal year 2004 was the spark that caused the restructuring and that caused the reduction in county contributions. The FY2004 decline must be kept in context of the 13 percent decrease in most state funded agencies (Table 13.4). Each year after that, the state increased Minnesota Extension funding until fiscal year 2008. The slight decrease in FY2008 was followed by a 7.6 percent increase for FY2009.

As this book goes to press, there is uncertainty about the state's budget due to the 2008-09 recession and the federal fiscal stimulus package. Despite this uncertainty, the overall picture for the five years after the restructuring is that revenues from the state and counties have been stable and even growing.

Federal Funding for Minnesota

In fiscal year 2003, federal funding accounted for $10.4 million (or 16.6%) of the total Minnesota Extension budget. The federal funds shown (Table 13.4) includes the following federal allocations: (1) Smith-Lever base funding, (2) Renewable Resource Extension Act, (3) Integrated Pest Management, (4) Pesticide Safety Education Program, (5) Expanded Food and Nutrition Education Fund, (6) Civil Service Retirement System, (7) Federal Employee Retirement System, and (8) Farm Safety. Federal funding declined by 2.9 percent from FY2003 to FY2008.

Alternative Revenues in the Minnesota Model

Alternative revenues are essential for growth in Extension programs because the public funds have been declining. County funds, while rebounding well after the very large decline in FY2003, are still 8.7 percent lower in FY2008 than in FY2003. State funds are essentially the same in FY2007 as in FY2003, not adjusting for inflation. Federal funds are 2.8 percent lower in FY2007 than in FY2003. In total, the public funding from county, state and federal sources fell by 3.6 percent from FY2003 to FY2008. If there had been no change in alternative revenues, the purchasing power for Minnesota Extension would have declined by 15.9 percent.

Accurate estimates of earned income are difficult to track in any Extension Service due to the overlapping jurisdictions of colleges and state specialists. There are no official estimates from the Minnesota Extension on the total amounts of alternative income, which are available publicly. The author estimates the alternative revenues increased by 60 percent from 2003 to 2008. In fact, it appears that alternative revenues are now the second largest source of funds for Minnesota Extension. While the author is confident that the level of revenues has increased substantially, the estimate is an unofficial estimate. Most likely, the estimate is actually low because many of the grants for Extension programs have their accounting done in academic departments and are not considered part of Extension's budget.

Alternative revenue is defined as grants, gifts, program event sponsorships, and user fees. The Food Stamp Nutrition Education Program is Minnesota Extension's largest grant and accounts for the majority of the revenues shown under earned income.

Higher levels of alternative revenues not only diversify the funding sources for Extension but also provide a very direct means of doing needs assessment. Program teams that have waiting lists, even while charging fees that exceed their costs, know they are delivering a valuable program. Some programs should be supported because of their public value. Further, low-income individuals might not be able to access programs that charge fees. Both of these two types of programs need to be covered by public funding. Grants, which often fall between the direct fees and public funding, also provide a direct indication of the value of programs.

Did the Minnesota model increase the levels of alternative revenues over what had been generated by the county cluster model? It appears that it has but the data are weak on this question.

Fees in the Minnesota Model

Did the move to the new Minnesota regional/county model make it easier for programs to charge fees? Discussions with Minnesota Extension program leaders confirms that the regional/county model makes it easier than under a county cluster or county system for program teams to charge fees. The following reasons were mentioned most frequently in discussing this with the program leaders:

1. More of the programming is done with established curriculum which has been widely tested and established credibility with the target audiences;

2. The online registration system simplified the process of collecting the funds and having them deposited automatically into program accounts, while the county collection of funds often resulted in confusion on the accounting;

3. The statewide teams make it possible to deliver the program more widely, allowing the programs to be promoted in more parts of the state;

4. The centralized accounting and uniformity in pricing for a given program makes it easier to charge fees; and

5. The claim by participants that the county is already paying for Extension is not as frequently heard with regionally delivered programs as in county ones.

Grants/ Sponsorships in Minnesota Model

Has the move to the new regional/county model made it easier to secure grants? Due to the accounting and incentive problems mentioned earlier, there is little reliable data on the level of grants and contracts for Extension programs. However, the anecdotal evidence is that grants and contracts are increasing. The program leaders suggest the several reasons for this increase.

Increased credibility. As Extension educators focus and specialize, their programs become better, as well as better known. This encourages agencies to favorably review grant proposals and private firms to agree to sponsor individual events. For example, the Center for Farm Financial Management uses a sponsorship model for nearly all local educational events. A local agribusiness pays a meeting fee, about $600 in 2007, to cover the costs of the materials and time of the educators working with the Center. More importantly, the sponsor covers any costs for meals, meeting room, and publicity. Programs in Family Development are also starting to use this type of event sponsorship.

Economies of scale for sponsors. It is much simpler for a state agency to contract with one statewide Extension program than to contract with 87 different counties. Then the agencies only have to work with one accounting system and review one set of accounts and reports. Further, some agencies have more confidence in the University's accounting system than in county office systems. This is appealing to state agencies who might wish to contract with Extension to deliver educational programs.

Increased speed in responding. Program teams in Minnesota have established general priorities through their business planning efforts. This allows them to determine quickly which types of grants and contracts are consistent with their educational mission and focus.

One of the program leaders tells a story about the influence of specialization on the speed of decision-making. Before regionalization, a group inquired whether Extension could do a program for them and if so, what the cost would be and when it could happen. The program leader, who was new to the job, was shocked to see that the process of answering these questions took three weeks! The reason it took so long is that no one really "owned" the program and was responsible for making these decisions or for staffing it. As emails flew back and forth, it became clear that Extension needed to be able to make decisions much more quickly. With the regional/

county model, statewide program teams have discussed most of these issues in advance and know how to respond quickly.

State specialists' grant experience. State specialists have considerable experience in securing grants and ongoing relationships with the agencies that provide grants. Under the new Minnesota model, state specialists are either members of program teams or the direct supervisors of REEs. In either role, they can assist in the preparation of grant applications.

Bottlenecks. There are some negatives, however. Many Extension grants come through state agencies or small local foundations. When these entities do not provide any overhead funding, the grants are less appealing to the University. If the funding is a local foundation or government entity, sometimes these groups prefer to have the funds stay within the county rather than go to Extension. This varies widely by program, depending on the prior history of the program and the attitudes of the educators.

While grants are generally much easier to implement in the new regional/county model, there is a new consideration for small grants. When grants are run through the University of Minnesota Extension rather than through county offices, the University sets priorities on the grants that can be requested, especially from major foundations.

Regionalization's Impact on Future Restructuring

Since 1982, Minnesota Extension has restructured five times, with four of the five caused by budget deficits. Will future cuts in state funding require a new organizational structure? On the other hand, can the Minnesota model survive with adjustments to the level of staffing in different programs?

Avoiding a system wide restructuring is very important because the level of programming declines for a period. This reduces Extension's public value and threatens future cuts in public resources, creating a downward spiral.

The author's hypothesis is that if there are major cuts in the future for either state or county funding, a whole system restructuring will not be needed (The analysis that follows is the author's alone).

If the county funds are cut, then there will be fewer local positions, probably concentrated in 4-H because over 70 percent of the local positions funded by counties are for 4-H program coordinators. Theoretically, other groups or organizations could cover some of the local positions. In May 2009, a group in Washington County, Minnesota is exploring alternatives to county funding since the county has announced it cannot continue after September 2009 (Mohr 2009).

If there are deep cuts in state funding, it probably will be necessary for Extension to make non-renewals of some personnel since a large percentage of the total budget covers people. There are difficult choices that could be made by Extension administration. For example, if 16 regional educator positions had to be cut, the choices could be: (1) eliminate one regional educator from each of the 16 areas of expertise, (2) eliminate two of the areas of expertise, (3) eliminate 16 administrative and support positions, or (4) some combination of the first three. Regardless of the choice made, none of these would require a complete restructuring. The earlier restructurings appear to have been partially driven by the need to include 87 autonomous county partners in the decision-making.

Balancing the budget after public funding cuts requires either lower expenditures or higher alternative revenues. If the new regional/county model increases the amount of alternative revenue sufficiently, this can offset reductions in public funding.

Conclusions and Future Research

Conclusions

The Minnesota regional/county model has not lost all county funding. Funding from counties dropped significantly the first year due to the state budget cuts but has grown every year from 2004 through 2008. Overall public revenue declined by 3.6 percent from

FY 2003 to FY2008 and the adjusted inflation purchasing power of the public funding fell by 15.9 percent.

Alternative revenues from fees, grants, and sponsorships appear to be growing rapidly because of the new regional/county model. However, the data is too incomplete for a full picture on this.

It seems unlikely that Minnesota Extension will need to restructure again due to changes in county or state funding. This does not mean that major budget cuts will not result in reductions in employees but it will not force a complete restructuring as in the past.

Future Research

The hypothesis that a regional/county delivery system with greater specialization of Extension Educators will lead to a more sustainable financial future needs further investigation. Some of the questions that need to be examined are:

1. How does the degree of regionalization and specialization of extension educators influence the amount of alternative revenue generated?

2. Do program teams that actively do market research and program business plans produce more alternative revenue per regional educator than those that do not use these tools?

3. What type of incentive systems can be used to encourage state specialist to report their grants and earned income on Extension programs to Extension administration?

4. What are the pros and cons of different forms of alternative revenues in support of the outreach mission of Extension?

5. How does active use of public value statements and evidence by a program impact affect the level of public funding and grant funding secured by programs?

Chapter 14

And In My State?

George Morse and Jeanne Markell

Luck is what happens when preparation meets opportunity.

Seneca, Circa AD 55

This final chapter was written for those readers who wonder if the "Minnesota regional/county model" could work in their states. To do that justice, you will see a writing style switch, a "first person" message from two of the authors who experienced this Minnesota transformation "up close and personal."

Over the past five years, we have had many questions about how replicable and viable Minnesota's model really is: from county commissioners, campus faculty, county Extension educators, state legislators, federal agencies, representatives from many communities of interest, and Extension administrators across the country and in Washington D.C. Questions come in various forms. Some are seeking evidence that flaws in the Minnesota regional/county model would disqualify it for their state. Others are looking for the strongest evidence that the model works in Minnesota and would have potential for other states.

This chapter addresses some of those questions. We wrote this book to document the "whys," to share some of the "hows," and to provide preliminary results on the "so whats." For our state, the changes meant more rigor in educational programming, a more flexible staffing plan, and a better business model to address fiscal challenges. We believe the evidence supports that without this change, Extension in Minnesota would be less effective and less sustainable for the future. Many states face similar economic challenges and administrators are looking for new options to meet those challenges. We hope this portrayal of the Minnesota's new regional/county delivery model helps others consider new options for their organizations. Others may want to replicate parts or all of what Minnesota did, but clearly, this is not about advocating any one particular structure or system as a "one size fits all" solution. We acknowledge the importance of context and we know each state is unique. Differing aspects of history, politics, and demographics should drive your change efforts, just as they did in Minnesota.

This chapter will be less helpful to you if you have not read the previous chapters in the book. This chapter assumes your understanding of the policies and practices that define the Minnesota regional/county model (Chapters 3 to 9), and the preliminary evidence on the impacts of the new model (Chapters 10 to 13).

Is the Minnesota Model Working?

Yes, the initial evidence at the five-year point indicates the Minnesota regional/county model is working well. The changes made in the first half of this decade resulted in increased program quality, more field/campus collaboration, greater scholarship, more public access to specialized Extension educators, and continued public support. Extension faculty and staff feel good about their opportunity to focus and sharpen skills and delivery methods in their areas of expertise. In addition, the changes have resulted in more successful branding and organizational marketing for Extension as a system and for its many parts. Data from surveys of regional Extension educators and state specialists support these claims. Certainly, there is room for improvement, as in any system. For example, the gains in scholarship, while very impressive for the short time span tested, are still small. Moreover, program evaluation is still more focused on outputs and outcomes than societal impacts and public value. Even that, however, is changing. The University of Minnesota Extension professional evaluation team reports more new efforts in outcome evaluation of statewide programs than prior to the changes.

Many who watched the changes take place predicted a widespread decrease in county support. This has not occurred; in fact, county funding has increased every year since the restructuring. Current economic conditions certainly could change that situation, but indicators tell us that our county partners like the idea of the choice and flexibility that this model created. The overall good will toward Extension and its partnership with counties has not diminished and the flexibility may indeed serve us well in the economic downturn. The current business model means University of Minnesota Extension can make adjustments without a complete restructuring in order to maintain a portfolio in important areas of expertise.

Alternative revenues (fees, grants, contracts with state agencies or foundations) have increased because of the Minnesota regional model. This largely stems from the shift in supervision to campus faculty by area of expertise, making it possible for teams to respond much more quickly.

The evidence on whether the Minnesota regional/county model is working is preliminary with the REE results only reflecting the first three and half years and the state specialists data only reflecting the first five and half years. Further, much more analysis could still be done to understand the relationships between the variables even in these data sets. Other types of data could be used to measure program quality, scholarship, and public value. However, the current data says it is working and working well.

Would This Work in My State?

'This', in the title immediately above, could relate to the regional/county delivery model, the program business plans, the promotion system, or the support systems. We will deal with each, starting with the regional/county system.

Minnesota's Regional/County System

Would the Minnesota regional/county model, as described in Chapters 3, 5, and 6, work in my state? We recognize that the characteristics, history, and politics of states vary greatly; meaning Extension delivery systems and funding models look different across the country. Minnesota had to consider many variables in deliberation of a changed system, and any state looking at our model should do the same. If you are considering the regional/county aspects of the Minnesota model (Chapters 3, 5, and 6), here are six strategic questions we think are important in weighing the merits of our model for your state:

1. *Do current economic conditions demand a new way to fund Extension?* The public understands you have to do things differently if there are major budget cuts at state and local levels. They see the cuts and restructuring happening in other segments of the economy and will have more tolerance of changes in how Extension's services are delivered.

2. *Does my state have enough field educators to establish a critical mass of educators in ten to 20 areas of expertise?* The success of moving to a model with specialization of regional educators depends on having a *critical mass* of educators in each area of expertise. Critical mass in a specialization is determined as much by the complexity of a knowledge base (i.e. dairy science) as it is by the state size or program priorities. In Minnesota, we decided that having seven to nine educators per area of expertise (i.e. crops,

nutrition, and community economics) was necessary for this critical mass. Using that criterion, your state would need at least 70 county agents or field educators to have ten or more areas of expertise. Thirty-five states have over seventy field educators. Other states might be able to operate fewer areas of expertise or have fewer people per area of expertise by collaborating with other states.

3. *Is it possible for your state to fund a sufficient number of areas of expertise using state and federal funds, independent of local dollars?* Once your state determines the minimum number of areas of expertise needed and the critical mass of educators per area of expertise, is there sufficient base funding from state and federal sources to sustain these areas of expertise teams' core team? Funding these teams independent of local dollars is essential to the specialization of the regional educators.

4. *Is there current funding from counties to support local facilities/offices throughout the state and totally funding some compliment of local educators?* States in which the counties provide funding for local positions and office support staff will find it easier to adopt the Minnesota regional/county model than those in which counties pay nothing toward positions housed in counties. Essentially, this allowed Extension to continue a local, grassroots presence throughout rural and non-rural Minnesota (locally funded positions) while still building more specialized capacity at the regional level (federal and state funded positions). The local funding leverages state and federal funding and continues the historic tri-parte arrangement but in a new way.

5. *Are there other agencies or communities of interest who wish to fund local Extension positions?* While counties are the largest purchaser of local positions in Minnesota, several other agencies and groups are sponsoring local educational positions. All of these are employees of the University of

Minnesota and are educational rather than advocacy or administrative positions.

6. *Do you sense support for making sweeping change from at least some stakeholders at all levels?* Large-scale organizational change is very hard work, frequently impossible work. It is more likely that people inside the organization want to hunker down and live with the limping status quo than to embrace the challenges that come with change. External stakeholders may resist change for other reasons. That is why you ought not to expect overwhelming consensus to move forward with large-scale change. Yet, if your state is to consider something as monumental in scope as Minnesota, you must know that at least some support exists in each stakeholder group. Top administrators need the buy in of some of the staff up, down, and across the system. Some key university officials and colleagues must understand and be on board. Finally, it is essential that you work with a small team of supporters from external constituent circles: clientele, advisory groups, elected officials, other funders/ donors, etc.

The devil is in the detail with all strategic plans and change efforts. The Minnesota details may or may not be yours, but if you explore these six central questions, you will be on your way to a wise conclusion about the "fit" of the Minnesota regional/county aspect of the model for your state.

Minnesota's Business Plan Approach

Would the Minnesota Extension's program business plan model, with its associated market research and definition of public values, work in my state? Here are the questions that you will need to ask to evaluate the applicability of this approach to your state:

1. *How many statewide program teams can be assembled to do the market research, the program planning, the identification of public value, the program delivery, and the program evaluation?* We know that this approach requires a statewide program team, which can commit to carrying out the plans once they are developed. Further, we know the transaction costs are much lower when the supervision of all of the Regional Extension Educators is done by one individual for each area of expertise for the entire state. We are certain you can do this in states without the full Minnesota regional/ county model. However, the more statewide program teams, who report to one individual, the more easily this will go.

2. *Do you have any professionals who can assist the program teams in market research, public value identification, business planning, and evaluation?* Some program teams can do all of this with no assistance; some cannot do any of it. Most teams can so some of it but not all. If you want rapid progress, you need to provide some assistance and lots of transparency so teams can learn from each other. For some aspects of this work, your staff can get training online. For example, there are online workshops on public value (Kalambokidis 2009).

3. *What incentives can you provide to the administrators who supervise the program teams?* Our experience in Minnesota was that most program teams would go along with these efforts if their supervisors are enthusiastic about them and assist the teams in implementing them. State faculty are often more reluctant than Regional Extension Educators, at least initially. Minnesota had 54 of 56 teams complete their market research and program business plans within six months by linking funds to the capacity areas to the completion of the plans. Without some tangible incentives to encourage active participation, we doubt that these will be widely used in a state.

Minnesota's Promotion System

Would Minnesota Extension's promotion system for Regional Extension Educators (Chapters 9 and 11) work in my state? We think the Minnesota promotion model for REEs is unlikely to work well in states that have a county delivery model or a county cluster delivery model. When educators have some of their funding from county or other local agencies, it is difficult for them to focus sufficiently on topics to develop either the scholarship or program leadership necessary to be successful in the Minnesota system. For this reason, the local educators in Minnesota are not included in Minnesota's promotion system for the regional educators.

Strongest Reason to Adopt Minnesota Model

Occasionally, we are asked, *"What is the strongest reason for adopting the Minnesota regional/county model?"* In the long run, we believe the increased program delivery efficiency, increased program quality, and greater scholarship are the primary benefits to both Extension and the public. All three of these contribute value not only to the people who directly participate in the programs but create public value for non-participating taxpayers. Unless Extension is able to demonstrate increased public value to taxpayers, the funding from federal, state, and county sources is likely to continue to be uncertain or declining.

In the short-run, the primary benefit of the Minnesota regional/county model is the increased flexibility it gives to both county partners and to the state Extension administration. The Minnesota model allows counties to pay for those services that fit their perceived needs the best while giving state Extension the ability to deliver high quality programs throughout the state on many topics that could not be resourced at a county level. The flexibility in staffing and programming is particularly important to both the state Extension office and the counties during times of fiscal instability. Minnesota Extension is unlikely to have to restructure with the next major cut in state funding.

Yet, we know that each state is unique and the fit of the Minnesota regional/county model to other states is unlikely without a considerable number of modifications. In some cases, it simply will not be applicable at all.

Next Steps in Exploring Regionalization/ Specialization

Does regionalization/specialization of Regional Extension Educators increase their productivity? In this book, preliminary data from surveys of the Regional Extension Educators and state specialists was used to examine this question. Specifically, data were presented on how the changes from a county cluster model in Minnesota to a more highly specialized regional/county model changed outcomes in program quality, scholarship, collaboration with campus faculty, access, and public support. These initial results tentatively support the idea that regionalization/specialization can increase productivity. Yet, there is much more research which needs to be done to fully understand the consequences of regionalization and specialization. Some of this is addressed now.

National Research Agenda

So far, the literature on the consequences of regionalization and specialization is limited, with only eight articles in the *Journal of Extension,* one in the *Journal of Higher Education Outreach and Engagement,* and three additional staff papers. As of May 2009, there were no empirical studies in research journals analyzing the outcomes of Extension efforts adopted by states to encourage greater specialization. Yet, there are many unanswered questions about regionalization and specialization in Extension, as outlined at the end of each chapter. Five of the major questions are:

1. How do different regional systems influence the degree of specialization possible by regional educators?
2. How do variations in specialization by regional educators affect the state's program quality, scholarship by regional

educators, collaboration between educators and state specialists, access to programming, public value, and public support?

3. Do distinctions in the promotion systems for Regional Extension Educators change the quality of programming and the level of public value?

4. Can program business planning, market research, public value identification, and documentation be widely done in states with county or county cluster deliver models?

5. How do the outcomes of new regional systems and levels of specialization change over time?

Some of these research questions can be answered by research within states, such as Minnesota, Alabama, Illinois, Michigan, Nebraska, Iowa, and Wyoming, which have implemented regional systems with greater specialization. However, cross-sectional analysis of different regional systems and different degrees of specialization are likely to be more useful than analysis of an individual state. Some questions simply cannot be explored without the variation provided by systems in different states. The intellectual exchanges between researchers from different states and different disciplines would result in greater rigor and credibility for the research.

There are a number of disincentives for states to do extensive research about their own restructuring. First, during the early phases of the new system, nearly all talent is focused on making the new system work. It is difficult to set aside the resources to do in-depth research early in the process. Second, given the uncertainty in any major restructuring, administrators need to take a positive attitude, making it hard for them to guide evaluation research on the effort. Third, few individuals within the states are immune from a point of view about fundamental changes, making it difficult to design and implement unbiased research.

Another reason that states seldom do in-depth research on structural changes is that other states benefit more from the research than the state being studied. If a state's Extension stakeholders perceive the new system is working well, there is very little incentive for that state to study the system further. If aspects of the new system are not working, there is even less incentive for administrators in a state to share this with a national audience. In many cases, studying structural change causes the stakeholders to linger on debates that have been resolved rather than moving on to focus on maximizing the public value within the new structure.

In summary, the benefits of studying restructuring fall to those outside the state being studied while the costs and risks fall to those inside. This suggests that the funding for studying regionalization and specialization over the long-term needs to come from federal sources, even when the studies focus on individual states. Extension prides itself as a learning organization and continually encourages others to use research to learn how to operate more efficiently and effectively. Doing more organizational research on how to deliver programs, more effectively and efficiently, would provide an excellent example to all stakeholders.

Professional Exchanges

Research proceeds at a snail's pace because it is complex and expensive. Results need to be replicated several times to establish validity and reliability. The peer review process, so essential to establishing high quality research, simply takes a long time. While we strongly encourage more research, more immediate ways to encourage professional exchanges exist. We have established a blog "Economics in Cooperative Extension" to explore alternative types of regionalization and specialization in Extension. (http://www. apec.umn.edu/George_Morse2.html)

We assume that some readers will identify omissions in our discussion of the Minnesota regional/county model or will take exception to our interpretation of the data. We welcome their reactions on the blog. Some readers will want more detail than the book provides. While the authors cannot promise to provide this, they will forward the questions to Minnesota leaders. In some cases, the questions might be answerable right away. In other cases, the questions might suggest research, which needs to be done. As time passes, we expect there will be more research available from other states on regionalization and specialization. We will welcome citations to this being posted on the blog.

In addition, we encourage the exploration of other avenues to discuss regionalization and specialization, including webinars, community of interest, etc. Finally, the authors welcome comments sent to us directly at the email addresses shown on the blog.

A Final Word of Optimism

We are optimistic about the future of the Cooperative Extension System. Unlike those who despair that Extension will become extinct in the near future, we see a very bright future for it. However, we expect that Extension will need to learn to do more with less, just as other institutions in both the private and public sector have. If Extension studies state experiences with regionalization and specialization, Extension could provide leadership for the other public institutions that are looking at the same issues. Further, if Extension demonstrates improved public value and improved efficiency in delivering public value, the public might even decide that it is such a good investment that more should be invested in it.

Appendix A
Cooperative Extension System Overview

George Morse

This short overview of Cooperative Extension System (Extension) is intended for readers who are unfamiliar with this educational institution in the United States. For much detail, see books by Warner and Christenson (1984), Rasmussen (1989), Seevers, Graham, Gamon, and Conklin (1997), and McDowell (2001). Each of these earlier books assumes the county or cluster-county system is a permanent aspect of Extension.

Origins of Cooperative Extension System

The Cooperative Extension System (Extension) is the largest adult education system in the nation (Peters and Jarvis 1991), with nearly 17,000 full-time equivalent (FTE) employees in 97 universities and 3,154 counties. Extension is also one of the most admired informal educational efforts. Everett Rogers (1995), the foremost scholar on the diffusion of innovations, writes:

> The agricultural extension service of the United States is reported to be the world's most successful change agency. Certainly, it is the most admired and most widely copied.... The main evidence for the success of the agricultural extension model is the agricultural revolution, a dramatic increase in U.S. farm productivity in the decades following World War II (Rogers 1995).

Extension is part of the land-grant university system, which includes university classroom teaching, agricultural experiment stations for applied research, and noncredit outreach educational efforts. While Maine and Pennsylvania established agricultural colleges in 1823 and 1855 respectively, most early U.S. colleges were focused on the classics, preparing students for medicine, law, and the ministry (Seevers, Graham, Gamon, and Conklin 1997). Federal support for colleges that covered agriculture, mechanic arts, and other practical aspects of life was sought since the early 1800s, but it took the Civil War to achieve it. Many southern representatives were opposed to federal assistance for such colleges as an invasion of state's rights. The exit from the Union by the Southern states in 1861 allowed the passage of the Morrill Land-Grant College Act (Rasmussen 1989). Signed by President Lincoln in 1862, the act provided federal land to each state and territory for an endowment to set up:

> at least one college in each state where the leading object shall be, without excluding other scientific or classical studies, to teach such branches of learning as are related to agriculture and the mechanic arts, as the legislatures of the states may respectively prescribe, in order to promote the liberal and practical education of the industrial classes in the several pursuits and professions of life (Eddy 1957).

However, agricultural colleges were a hard sell. They had very little to teach, since they had no research base that went beyond the practical skills already known by most farmers. After 10 years, there were only 27 agricultural colleges, and only three served more than 150 students (Rasmussen 1989). This led to a push for the development of agricultural experiment stations to develop a stronger research base that could enhance college courses. Twenty-five years after the Morrill Act started the colleges, the 1887 Hatch Act provided funding to states for agricultural experiment stations.

While experiment stations generated much-needed research, farmers often did not see the benefits of this work, endangering its long-term public support. Bulletins for farmers on new research attempted to make the research more useful and practical. Special outreach education efforts also included "a trainload of college professors who would tour the state to stump in favor of some agricultural innovation" (Rogers 1995). In 1911, the Binghamton, New York chamber of commerce's "Farm Bureau," with financial backing of the Delaware and Lackawanna Railroad, hired a Cornell University agricultural graduate as its first "county agent" to work with farmers (Rogers 1995). By 1914, the federal government had passed the Smith-Lever Act, providing funding for each state to establish an extension service. Since the funding ultimately came from federal, state, and county sources, it was called the Cooperative Extension System.

Program Staffing and Priorities

Extension started work almost exclusively with agriculture, but quickly expanded to include youth development and home economics (now often called family development). Since the 1950s, efforts in community development and natural resources have increased. In 1992, the agriculture and natural resources program area was the largest area, with almost half (45 percent) of the full time equivalents. The home economics area and the youth development area each had 26 percent and 23 percent of the staff. Finally, the community resource development accounted for 6 percent of the employees (Ahearn, Yee, and Bottom 2003).

The 2007 distribution of Extension staff remains essentially the same as in 1992. Agriculture and natural resources areas have grown from 45 percent to 46 percent. The category called "Quality of Life in Rural Areas" accounts for 35 percent of the total full time equivalents. This category includes the areas of health, safety, biosecurity, resource management, technology and sociology, human development and family well-being, families and youth at risk, 4-H youth development, housing and indoor environments, and community planning and development, with youth development accounting for about half of the expenditures in the quality of life category. Nutrition and food safety have 10 percent of the total Extension staff nationally. The community and economic development program area has 7 percent of the total (Hewitt 2008).

Rates of Return to Extension

Since the 1950s, there have been 125 estimates of the social rate of return (SRR) for Extension and 1,225 estimates of the SRR for Extension and research. These estimates are based on gains in agricultural productivity (Alston, Chan-Kang, Marra, Pardey, and Wyatt 2000). The estimated SRR on public investment is based on estimates of the net benefits (benefits minus costs) to all parts of society, while private rates of return are based only on the benefits accruing to those making the investment (Organization for Economic Co-operation and Development 2002).

The median rate of return for the 125 estimates for Extension is 63 percent, while the median rate of the 1,225 estimates for both Extension and research is 37 percent. The median rate for research alone is 48 percent. The joint extension/research estimate is lower because it is impossible to separate gains in productivity from each of these sources. Hence, when individual estimates are made, the benefits estimate is the same for both, but the cost estimate is lower. The joint estimates, which are the most reasonable, are very impressive. They clearly indicate the public would benefit from additional investment in agricultural research and extension.

A very important point is that there is "no evidence to support the view that the rate of return to research has declined over time" (Alston, Chan-Kang, Marra, Pardey, and Wyatt 2000). However, it is unclear how the rate of return for Extension alone has changed over time.

Politicians might not invest public funds based on these social rate of return estimates because they must compete for votes in the political arena and many interest groups are less interested in maximizing the overall societal benefits from a policy than in maximizing the benefits that flow to their own group. This is particularly true if the public does not understand the nature of the public value of the publicly supported programs that is the spillover benefits to non-participants (Kalambokidis 2004). In addition, limits on the amount of funds available may restrict decision makers' ability to invest based on SRR estimates, even if they believe the estimates are correct (Alston, Chan-Kang, Marra, Pardey, and Wyatt 2000).

Research on the payoff for nonagricultural programs is much more recent and the research base is much smaller. This reflects in part the differences in the size and history of the work of Extension, and in part, the differences in research approaches that can be used for educational programs around an entire industry (agriculture) and specific educational objectives related to youth, families, and communities. However, there are some initial efforts. For example, several benefit-cost studies have been completed for Extension's Expanded Food and Nutrition Program, which is aimed at low-income families. The benefits per dollar invested in Extension's Expanded Food and Nutrition Program ranges from $2.66 to $17.04 (Willis, Montgomery, Blake, 2008). Outside these efforts, few states have undertaken systematic benefit-cost studies of their programs. However, there is growing interest; Texas Extension, for example, has hired a full-time extension economist to do benefit-cost work (McCorkle, Waller, Amosson, Bevers, and Smith 2009).

Appendix B
Labels for Minnesota Extension Positions/Structures

The original labels, shown below, were used in the Minnesota model from 2004 until 2008. The new labels have the benefit of encouraging stakeholders to focus on the private and public value of Extension programs rather than Extension's structure. A secondary benefit is that some of the terms are more consistent with university terminology. A third benefit of the new labels is that some of the new labels are more consistent with the work being done. For example, over half of the REEs work statewide rather than in smaller regions.

In this book, the original titles are used for two reasons. First, the book is about structure. The original title for REEs is more descriptive of that class of workers than the new title. Second, the survey of regional educators was done when the original labels were being used.

Readers are encouraged to contact their counterparts in Minnesota to explore the ideas in this book. If a reader does this, it probably will be easier to exchange ideas if the discussion used the same labels.

The roles and responsibilities of these positions and structures did not change with this change in labels.

Original Label (New label). Description is provided.

Area Program Leader (new label: Program Leader): In 2008, there are 16 area program leaders in Minnesota. They directly supervise all of the regional extension educators throughout the state in a given area of expertise. Each area program leader reports to one of four Associate Deans in charge of a capacity area. See Chapter 5 for their roles and responsibilities.

Area of Expertise (new label: Program Area): An area of expertise is roughly parallel to an academic department but often includes individuals from several different academic disciplines. Nationally, several other states use the term "area of expertise" in the same way as Minnesota did from 2002 to 2007. Michigan and Ohio are two examples.

Capacity Area (new label: Extension Center): Capacity Areas was the name used for the following five broad areas of work:

1. Agriculture, Food and Environment
2. Natural Resources and Environment
3. Youth Development
4. Family Development
5. Community Vitality

The new name for these is Extension Centers. The first two have been combined. Now there are the following centers:

1. Extension Center for Food, Agriculture, and Natural Resource Sciences
2. Extension Center for Youth Development
3. Extension Center for Family Development
4. Extension Center for Community Vitality

In some states, these Centers or Capacity Areas are called program areas.

Capacity Area Leaders (new label: Associate Deans for (name of Extension Center): The Capacity Area Leaders are the highest-level administrative position in each of the capacity areas and report to the Dean/Director of Extension. In the Minnesota model, they are the equivalent of department heads in academic departments. They make the final decisions on hiring, on annual salary adjustments, and on promotions. While program teams and area program leaders make most program decisions, the capacity area leaders are the public voice for the capacity area for central administration and the legislature. They set the vision for the capacity area and supervise the area program leaders.

Regional Extension Educators (new label: Extension Educators in (name of area of expertise): The new label shifts the emphasis to the nature of the work rather than the structure. The new name recognizes that the regions vary widely by area of expertise and capacity area. Nearly half of the REEs have a "region" equal to the state. Others have only 3 or 4 counties. Almost none have the same regions as covered by the Regional Director. The original title is still used in official documents related to promotion because a term is needed for the class of educators. The new Iowa system, adopted in April 2009, went directly to "program specialists," probably for similar reasons. For details on the roles of REEs, see Chapter 5.

Local Extension Educator (new label: Extension Educator for (name of funding partner or agreed upon work description): Local educators are nearly the same as the CSREES definition of a County Extension Educator. Most cover only one county, with some covering two. For details on their roles, see Chapter 6.

Regional Centers (new label: Regional Offices): The 18 regional centers provide offices for the regional Extension educators. Generally, the Regional Centers are not centers of educational activities. Most of the educational events are done in venues in other communities.

Regional Directors (no change): The Regional Directors' roles are described in Chapters 4 and 6.

Appendix C
Leadership for the
Minnesota Regional/County Model,
2003 to 2007

George Morse

Hundreds of people shaped the new Minnesota model. It will be impossible to mention all by name, in part because the 2004 model was developed on the foundation of work done by several decades of work by previous Minnesota Extension administrations and by the experiences of other states. However, this appendix will venture to name those directly involved in the design and implementation of the Minnesota regional model for three reasons. First, these individuals risked a great deal as they provided leadership to this new system. They deserve recognition and gratitude. Second, this demonstrates that system wide changes like those that are described in this book require the commitment and input of many people at many different levels of the organization, demonstrating the importance of an overall vision to guide their independent actions. Third, readers from other states who have additional questions might wish to communicate with individuals in roles similar to their own. By naming the actors involved in Minnesota, we hope to facilitate direct contacts. While this increases the risk that some of these individuals will disagree with our conclusions, we are confident that those who talk with a number of Minnesota participants will confirm our results. Yet, differences due to additional data and detail will help readers, and maybe others, evaluate the Minnesota model and consider new ways to increase productivity within their own states.

A couple of my colleagues cautioned me that naming names had the risk of omitting key people. While I fully recognize this risk, I concluded the benefits far exceeded the risks. Further, I will add names as I discover these omissions. Now to a discussion of roles. For ease of review, I start with those in administration and end with the support staff. However, maybe this should have been reversed since every single role was essential to the transition to the new model.

Minnesota Extension Administration

While the system adopted in 2004 was radically different from the earlier delivery model, earlier administrations had laid some of the groundwork for these changes. Dean Patrick Borich stressed the need for outstanding educational skills in addition to specialization in a subject matter. Interim-director Gail Skinner-West started an exploration of pricing for Extension program fees. Katherine Fennelly encouraged greater evaluation efforts and explored ways to broaden the focus of Extension, particularly in urban areas. All of these prior Deans/Directors stressed the importance of program quality. The work done during this period helped prepare staff attitudes for the more radical changes adopted in 2004.

Dr. Charles Casey, who was the Dean/Director of University of Minnesota Extension Service from 1999 to 2005, did a skillful job of leading the organization through two difficult restructurings (2002 and 2004). He encouraged teamwork, sought and listened to advice from all stakeholders, and showed great courage and patience in promoting these changes. Throughout his term, he stressed both program quality and financial sustainability. This dual emphasis became known as the "mission and money" double-bottom line. Almost immediately after he was appointed, he sponsored an "E-Summit," a two-day conference for program teams on program entrepreneurship. His primary role, especially during the second change in 2003/2004 was in working with the state legislature, county commissioners, stakeholder groups, and University administration. I doubt the Minnesota model would exist without his leadership during this period.

Diane Flynn was the Interim Associate Dean/Director from 1999 to 2002 and provided leadership to the organizational restructuring efforts in 2001-2002. As my immediate predecessor, she provided invaluable coaching and assistance as I started in July 2002. For the month that we worked together nearly daily, she told me at least once a day, "Remember, once you have seen one Capacity Area, you have seen one capacity area." There was not a day in the next five years that that statement did not ring true. However, especially in the new system, this diversity and decentralization of decision-making was a good thing, a source of richness of ideas and energy.

The administrative team that made the initial decision to adopt the unique Minnesota model had passion for Extension's long-term mission of taking the University to the people (and vice versa), were creative about new approaches, and displayed courage in hard and unpopular decisions. The original team that developed the model included: Charles Casey, Dean and Director; George Morse, Associate Dean for Programs; Jeanne Markell, Assistant Dean for External Relations; Calvin Walker, Assistant Dean for Human Resources; David Nelson, Assistant Director for Technology; Philip O'Brien, Assistant Director for Finance; Aimee Viniard-Weideman, Director of Communications; District Directors: Terry Anderson, Sheila Barbetta, Rod Hamer, LuAnn Hiniker, Lee Raeth, Kay Stanek, David Werner, and Deborah Zak; Associate Deans and Capacity Area Leaders: Dale Blyth, Pat Huelman, Michael Schmitt, Richard Senese, Catherine Solheim. This team had a passion for the Extension's mission and for the people they supervised. While the group had an abundance of conflicting ideas and approaches for solving the 2003 crisis, they worked together respectively and honestly. In the end, they approved the new Minnesota regional/ county model unanimously.

Jeanne Markell, Associate Dean for External Relations, Aimee Viniard-Weideman, Director of Communications, and Toni Smith, Liaison with the Association for Minnesota Counties, provided leadership for the external relations strategy and efforts. As described in Chapter 4, they guided the efforts of everyone from support staff to the Dean/Director. Jeanne Markell and I worked very closely together, meeting several times a week to work on issues that overlapped the programming teams that I had responsibility for and the external relations work she coordinated. Two Directors of Field Operation, Lee Raeth and David Werner, who reported to

Jeanne Markell, Assistant Director for External Relations, directly supervised the Regional Directors.

Minnesota Extension has done an excellent job at branding, developing internal and external communications tools under the leadership of Aimee Viniard-Weideman, now Assistant Dean and Director for Communications. For a sample of their work, see the Source magazine at http://www.extension.umn.edu/Source/

The Capacity Area Leaders, now called Associate Deans for Extension Centers, were the team I was responsible for coordinating and supporting. Their roles evolved into one akin to department heads, with major supervisory and program leadership responsibilities. This group had to wrestle with some very complex decisions and approached each with creativity, passion and a positive manner. Their "can do" attitude was a major factor in helping REEs adjust to their new positions. One of the most important first tasks of this the Capacity Area Leaders was the selection of the Area Program Leaders and REEs for regional positions. They did it well. This group included Dale Blyth, Beth Emshoff, Patrick Huelman, Patricia Olson, Michael Schmitt, Richard Senese, Karen Shirer, Catherine Solheim, and Robert Stine.

The Area Program Leaders, now called Program Leaders, supervise the Regional Extension Educators within the sixteen areas of expertise. The individuals who accepted these key leadership roles had to devote a lot of additional time initially simply because the details on the roles were being worked out as they started their roles. As the article by Schmitt and Bartholomay (2009) reports, the field staff is very pleased with this new supervisory structure. Individuals who have served as Area Program Leaders are Timothy Arlt, Melvin Baughman, Tamara Bremseth, Michael Darger, Joellen Feirtag, Dorothy McCargo Freeman, Jeffrey Gunsolus, Nancy Hegland, Mary Ann Hennen, Nathan Johnson, Sue Letourneau, Barbara Liukkonen, David Moen, Kent Olson, Patricia Olson, Renee Pardello, Jeffrey Reneau, Carl Rosen, Eli Sagor, Donna Rae Scheffert, Brenda Shafer, Minnell Tralle, and Thomas Wagner.

The Regional Directors had one of the most difficult jobs in the organization during the early transition to the new system. They had to bridge the gap between the tradition county stakeholders and the program teams that now were focusing on communities of interest. The longer I worked with this group, the more respect I developed for their dedication to the mission of Extension and their skill with people. The Regional Directors during the early years included: Timothy Arlt, Holli Arp, Robert Byrnes, James Carlson, Sarah Chur, Nathan Crane, Jayne Hager Dee, Tom Hovde, Rodney Elmstrand, Deanna Himango, Nancy Forsaker Johnson, Kelly Kunkel, Martha Harder, LuAnn Hiniker, Nathan Johnson, Patricia Morreim, Dawn Newman, Connie Nygard, David Resch, Kay Stanek, Duane Starkey, and Deborah Zak.

The Human Resources Department, under the direction of Leslee Mason, processed hundreds of change of assignments and other personnel papers. In addition, they had to work on many unique personnel issues that follow a major restructuring. This team was also instrumental in the smooth operation of the new promotion system.

Philip O'Brien, with the help of the new Regional Directors, had the responsibility for finding eighteen regional office spaces and equipping them in less than six months. One office had to be built from scratch. Only after the job had been successfully completed did we learn that experts in this area felt the job could not be done in this short of time.

Larry Coyle, and the IT team, set up the technology infrastructure in the 18 centers in the same time, including broadband Internet with standard authentication, standardized local computer networks in all regional offices, web conferencing, and laptop computers and cell phones for all educators in the field and on campus.

Diana Martenson, Organization and Program Development Specialist, was an invaluable asset to Extension as she provided leadership on many projects related to both the regional directors, the capacity area leaders, and the area program leaders. She assisted me on a wide variety of projects ranging from needs assessment, annual conference, staff participation, promotion policy, and much more.

Richard Senese and Joyce Hoelting, in addition to their roles as Capacity Area Leader and Associate Capacity Area Leader for the Community Vitality Capacity Area, provided leadership to the MyPrograms web tracking system and the data collection and development of the annual federal report.

The team in the Minnesota Extension's Resource Development Unit (RDU) made important contributions to the changes in skills and culture on program business plans. Thomas Klein led the RDU in early 2004 when the program teams were asked to do this. Kudos to Tom Klein, Neil Anderson, Anita Dincesen, Catherine Dehashti, Karen Lilly, Sonja Brown, and Karen Sorensen. Robert Craven, Kevin Klair, and Wynn Richardson of The Center for Farm Financial Management in the Department of Applied Economics, developed the template and hints for the program business plans.

The team of program evaluators (Thomas Bartholomay, Scott Chazdon, Ann Lochner, and Mary Marczak) are helping program teams document the impacts of their programs.

In September of 2005, Beverly Durgan became the Dean/ Director of Minnesota Extension, moving from an Associate Dean position in the College of Agriculture, Food and Environment as Charles Casey became Chancellor of the University of Minnesota-Crookston. In January 2006, Dean Durgan also became the Director of the Minnesota Agricultural Experiment Station. These dual leadership positions have encouraged closer working relationships between outreach and research. Program evaluation has been a key area of emphasis, together with administrative efficiency.

University of Minnesota Administration

The University of Minnesota Extension Service received excellent support from the University President, Dr. Robert Bruininks and the Provost, Dr. Christine Maziar. After Extension's reporting line shifted from the Provost to the Senior Vice President for System Administration, Dr. Robert Jones provided continuing support to Extension. Many additional administrative leaders assisted in the implementation of the new model. The Board of Regents, and in particular, Dallas Bohnsack, provided encouragement and support to the restructuring efforts.

Dr. Charles Muscoplat, who was dean of the College of Agricultural, Food, and Environmental Sciences, vice president for agricultural policy and director of the Minnesota Agricultural Experiment Station, assisted Extension in working with the agricultural committees in the legislature and with agricultural stakeholders. Dean Muscoplat was also instrumental in encouraging the adoption of program business planning by tenured state specialists. Dr. Susan Stafford, dean of the College of Natural Resources; Dr. Shirley Baugher, dean of the College of Human Ecology; and Dr. Jeffrey Klausner, dean of the College of Veterinary Medicine, were also instrumental in building support among their faculty and stakeholders.

Citizen Advisory Boards

The Dean's Citizen Advisory Committee helped the administrative team explore general options prior to the final decision, provided feedback on the concerns about specific implementation issues, and helped legislators understand the new system. During this transition period, the group actively gave us their frank opinions and asked uncomfortable questions and the new system evolved in better ways as a result. Members during the initial transition included: Kim Anderson, Janet Bosch, Jean Burkhardt, Mary Callier, Lori Carter, Darroll Englemann, Jon Evert, Rick Failing, Andy Favorite, Janice Fransen, Sheri Freiderichs, Ben Hawkins, Dennis Hegberg, Nitaya Jandragholica, Bob Lefebvre, Evans Mbuka, Chris Moldan, Mark Norman, Patrick O'Connor, Steven Renquist, Vikki Sanders, Doug Sandstrom, Kati Sasseville, George Thompson, and Don Timmer.

Nine individuals served on the "Extension Regional Center Selection Criteria Committee" to develop criteria for the location of regional centers. This group did not suggest specific cities for the offices but rather a set of criteria to be used in the selection process. After their meeting, the criteria were distributed widely and counties and cities invited to submit proposals. Over 100 proposals were received for the centers. Extension administration recommended three different sets of communities, based on 16, 18 and 20 centers. University of Minnesota President Robert Bruininks made the final decision, selecting the 18-center option. The members of the selection criteria committee included: Three members of the Dean's Citizen's Advisory Committee (Jan Fransen, Theresa Pesch, and Steven Renquist), two county commissioners (Sharon Bring and Joanne Fay), a county auditor (Sharon Anderson), and three non-Extension university administrators (Steve Cawley, Associate VP and CIO; Beverly Durgan, Associate Dean in College of Agriculture, Food and Environment: and Al Sullivan, Vice Provost).

The Association of Minnesota Counties (AMC) was very helpful in working with Extension on the transition to the new regional/county model. The AMC Extension Committee provided considerable feedback during the transition. The AMC Executive Director, Jim Mulder also provided ongoing reactions and advice. Toni Smith served as the Minnesota Extension Fellow with the Association of Minnesota Counties since 2002. Since Toni knew practically every county commissioner across the state and worked closely with Jim Mulder, this facilitated close communications.

Applied Economics Colleagues

Several of my Minnesota colleagues, especially in the Department of Applied Economics, participated in many hours of discussion about the role of specialization and regionalization of Extension field staff for over a decade before the 2003 budget crisis made this necessary for Minnesota Extension. In particular, Michael Boehlje, Brian Buhr, Robert Craven, Vernon Eidman, James Houck, Laura Kalambokidis, Kevin Klair, Scott Loveridge, William Lazarus, Dale Nordquist, Kent Olson, and Claudia Parliament.

Several Extension Educators, with close ties to the Department, often participated in these discussions, including Rodney Elmstrand, Susan Engelmann, Robert Koehler, Toni Smith, and Elizabeth Templin. These discussions had an influence on the book as well as the development of the new model.

During the early days of the 2003 fiscal crisis, I asked the Department of Applied Economics to suggest ideas since the problem had a public finance component to it. As described in Chapter 3, Dr. Vernon Eidman provided the overall framework for the Minnesota regional/county model based on an economic theory called "club theory" or "the theory of clubs."

Another Department of Applied Economics faculty member, Dr. Laura Kalambokidis, also made central contributions to the new model. While doing a program review of some of our best programs, Jeanne Markell asked the teams how they would explain their value to legislators who had no connection to their program. All of the teams could do a great job in explaining their value to their participants but many had difficulty explaining why non-participating taxpayers should willingly pay taxes to support their work. I recognized this as a public finance question and asked Laura Kalambokidis to develop a training program for these teams. Over the following five years, her program on public value not only trained all 56 of our program teams, the Regional Directors, all Extension administrators, and many of our citizen advisory members, she provided training in many other states. For more information, see: http://www.extension. umn.edu/community/publicvalue.html

Support Staff

Support staff, in different types of professional positions, played a very important role in the transition to the new system. While I only list those staff who either worked directly for me, or who assisted me on major projects during this transition, they represent the many others who played important roles. My special thanks to Laura Bipes, Erik Bremer, Peggy Buckley, Ellen Carlson, Catherine Dehdashti, Georgia Dunlevy, Gwendolyn Gmeinder, Tim Ha, Jo Ann Hardy, Cheryl Hays, Patrice Johnson, Sharon Kill, Cynthia Kommers, Louise Letnes, Karen Lilly, Debra Madison, Karen Matthes, Elaine Reber, Willa Reed, Barbara Roberts, Thomas Stanoch, Michelle Tschida, Phay Vang, and Judith Wirebaugh.

Extension Educators, State Specialists, Program Coordinators, and Nutrition Education Assistants

Ultimately, impacts of the new Minnesota regional/county are due to the work of state specialists, regional extension educators, the local educators, the program coordinators, the nutrition education assistants, and the clerical staff. While it is not possible to name all of these people, the current staff is listed at the University of Minnesota website at: http://www.extension.umn.edu/staffdirectory/. The changes in Minnesota were the results of teamwork from many different people at many different levels.

Ongoing Contributions

This list of contributions does not extend beyond July 2007 when the author retired and moved to the coast of Maine. Naturally, many additional people have contributed to the implementation of the new model since then. The transition was not over in July 2007. My hunch is it will never be completely over. The changes in the societal needs, the knowledge base, educational technology, and funding options will all drive continual change in Extension, in both Minnesota and elsewhere.

Appendix D
Program Business Plan Outline

Thomas K. Klein and George Morse

1. Executive Summary
2. Program Description
    a. Program Summary
    b. Capacity Area
    c. Program History
    d. Location
3. Strategic Plan
    a. Mission Statement
    b. Goals
    c. Expected Outcomes
    d. Competitive Position
    e. Research Basis
4. Marketing Plan
    a. Target Market
    b. Pricing Strategy
    c. Promotion
    d. Distribution
5. Operations and Implementation Plan
    a. Program Development Plan
    b. Timeline
    c. Logistical Support
    d. Risk Management Plan
    e. Evaluation Plan
6. Management Plan
    a. Team Leaders

b. Team Members

c. Partners

d. Consultants

7. Financial Plan

   a. Budget Summary

   b. Budget Narrative

   c. Source of Funds

   d. Financial Sustainability

   e. Net Revenue Distribution and Accounting

Comments on Outline

For each of the above topics, there was a set of suggested questions to guide the discussion of the program teams. None of these items were required by central Extension administration, but strong encouragement was put on item #6 (management plan). Without knowing who is on the team and who has leadership roles for various parts of the program, it is impossible to do the rest. Likewise, strong emphasis was put on identifying the target market (#4 a.).

The initial template was web-based. Later, it proved to be easier for teams to use a word-based template and share drafts in that format.

A Complementary Tool

Another useful tool, especially for program teams who are reluctant to do "business" plans, is Jim Collins' *Good to Great and the Social Sectors* (2005). This 35-page monograph is aimed at those in mission driven organizations such as non-profits, religious institutions, and education. It stimulates similar types of discussions as the development of a program business plan. Collins' monograph (2005) is not really a substitute for the items listed above. However, it is an excellent preliminary exercise for a team.

Sample Program Business Plan

The program business plan for "Retail Analysis & Development" in Appendix E has all of the above elements except for #7 (Financial Plan), which is addressed in their annual Program Implementation Plan. Most plans cover several years and are not revised in major ways every year. Adjustments are made, however, in the annual implementation plans.

As this example demonstrates, a program business plan can cover several different but related "programs," including:

1. Retail trade analysis program
2. Small stores success strategies program
3. Market area profile
4. Road side advertising in a digital age

Key contacts are noted in the plan, making it easier for those in Extension to contact someone in the program. This program business plan is not a marketing tool, however. For promotion, the team relies on the approaches outlined in their plan.

Note the sections on their strategic plan. In particular, review the statement of private and public value.

Appendix E
Program Business Plan
For
Retail Analysis & Development

Developed by Program Managers
Sherri Gahring, Extension Specialist
Bruce Schwartau, Ryan Pesch, Adeel Ahmed

Updated December 2, 2008

Reprinted with Permission

1. Executive Summary

The retail trade sector of the state of Minnesota contributes a significant amount to the state's economy. In 2001, the retailing sector contributed $18,358 million dollars to the gross state product (www.bea.doc.gov, 2004). In addition, the Minnesota Workforce Center reported that retailers employ approximately 308,572 individuals ("Minnesota Current Employment" 2003). That retail trade as an industry is important to the state is also evidenced by the location of the first enclosed mall (Southdale) and the largest enclosed mall (Mall of America) within the state. Minnesota is also home to some of the most successful retailers-Target Corporation and Best Buy-within the United States. However, the large majority of retail stores are small businesses.

One of the economic and social changes facing citizens of the state of Minnesota is the changing environment of retailing. Over the past decade, retailing practices and channels have changed dramatically. Paramount among these changes is the development of the large discount retail format (e.g., Wal-Mart) and the use of the Internet to source and sell merchandise. Target, Wal-Mart, or Kmart stores are located in more than half of Minnesota cities with populations between 5,000 and 10,000 ("Changing places" 2001) and nearly all cities with populations over 50,000. As retailing formats continue to evolve, there is concern about the survival of the small-sized retailer. One third of new retailers do not survive the first year of business and two thirds do not continue beyond three years. Most failures involve small-sized retailers (U.S. Department of Commerce, 2002).

Especially at risk of closure are retailers located in small cities within the state. These retailers may lose or close their businesses for a number of reasons. Paramount among these reasons is the increasing competition from discount retailers. Small business owners believe that they operate in highly competitive environments that are becoming increasingly aggressive. Big box stores can present a significant competitive threat to small firms. Twelve percent of small business owners indicated that big box stores were significant competitors and another 13% said that big box stores were marginal competitors (Dennis, 2003). Kenneth Stone (Iowa State University retail economist) identified big box retailers as the single largest threat to the survival of small-town retailers.

A technology change is also affecting our retailers. It is estimated that by 2010, fifty million people will be using GPS devices, while 40 million people are already using mobile internet phones (blackberries, iphones, etc.), to help them find their way to businesses, services and other points of interest. The impact of this for retail businesses is to almost literally drive traffic to the point of transaction. Because not only can GPS and handheld internet devices tell you how to get there, they can tell you where to go. Companies like Google, Mapquest, Garmin, Magellan Tom Tom, Navteq, TeleAtlas, and Telenav are busy adding content to their products to enrich the experience of their customers. These companies are adding content on a daily basis and especially content from major metropolitan areas. Left out are small towns and rural areas. Rural retailers have lacked the assistance to bridge the gap on the digital divide in regards to placement of retail businesses on digital maps and GPS devices.

The Retail Analysis and Development Program encompasses four outreach programs that help small independent retailers in Greater Minnesota improve their business practices to more competitively co-exist with mass discount merchandisers within their communities. Ultimately, these improved business practices will not only provide jobs and income to owners and employees, but will also provide access to vital products for residents, thus increasing the quality of life in a community.

1. Retail Trade Analysis Program

- The goal of this program is to aid the economic entities within communities in assessing their capture of their retail trade market potential.
- Communities receive a customized 16-31 page report for their community and a 2-hour workshop.

2. Small Store Success Strategies Program (program will not be offered 2/1/2009 to 7/1/2009 while under review for reformatting)

- The goal of this program is to help independent retailers improve their practices concerning marketing, merchandising, customer service, and business operations and to gain a better understanding of their customers' expectations and satisfactions.
- Primary target audiences include Chamber of Commerce members, downtown business organizations, city officials, financial institutions, and economic development entities.

3. Market Area Profile

- The goal of this program is to aid communities by organizing market data into a format that can be used by business and government entities. It will teach communities how to use this information along with their local knowledge to improve the retail economy within their area, especially in the area of identifying potential businesses to fill gaps in the community

4. Road Side Advertising in a Digital Age

- The goal of this program is to increase the visibility of organizations and businesses on the internet through helping community and business leaders, residents, small businesses, local governments and non-profit agencies get their communities on the map by utilizing web 2.0 technologies.

Team members and key contact: Sherri Gahring and Bruce Schwartau are the key contacts. Ryan Pesch and Adeel Ahmed are taking key roles in developing new RAD curriculum, teaching other team members, and managing financial decisions in RAD components. Other team members are the CV – Community Economics educators. The Program Leader is Michael Darger.

Website: www.extension.umn.edu/retail

2. Program Description

2. a. Program Summary

This Retail Analysis & Development program will aid independent retail stores to more competitively co-exist with mass merchandisers by improving practices in their assessment of retail trade, marketing, merchandising, customer service, and business operations. In addition, small retailers will learn about consumer expectations and satisfaction with small stores. Ultimately, these improved business practices will not only lead to providing jobs and income to owners and employees but will also provide access to vital products for residents, thus increasing the quality of life in the community.

The following four related workshop categories are available from the Community Economics Extension Educators:

o   Product 1 is the Small Store Success Strategies program for independent retail stores. This fee-based program will be delivered face to face in workshops sponsored by organizations such as Chambers of Commerce. It is expected that participants will implement at least one of the best practices within six months following the program.

o   Product 2 is the Retail Trade Analysis program for use by retail businesses, financial institutions, developers, and local government officials.

o   Product 3 is the Market Area Profile program for use by retail businesses, financial institutions, developers, local government officials, and entrepreneurs. The program has a second tier of consumer research to better serve communities that have seasonal residents.

o   Product 4 is the Road Side Advertising in a Digital Age set of 3 workshops that teach participants how to take advantage of GPS devices and digital maps to help guide shoppers to businesses and tourists to Points of Interest (POIs). The workshops also aim to create awareness about how people are using GPS devices and digital maps to find where they want to go.

All of the products are delivered in 90 to 120 minute workshops by specialists or extension educators in local communities. The Small Store Success Strategies workshop is targeted to independent retailers and retailer organizations. The Retail Trade Analysis, Market Area Profile, and Road Side Advertising in a Digital Age programs are designed for retailers, planners, developers, financial organizations, government officials, newspapers, entrepreneurs, and interested members of the public. RADA will also have audiences in the tourism and non-profit organizations because of the map creation projects. Additionally, Communities that conduct the RTA or MAP workshop receive a customized report for their community.

The expected outcomes are for community members is to use the information to create a healthier local retail climate, guiding retailers to provide products and services, and assisting local retailers to retain more of their operating income within the local community.

The four products have been recovering a majority of the development and delivery expenses. A goal has been to create a price that conveys value to the participants but is affordable for even smaller budgets.

2. b. Extension Center

This program has been identified as a program priority area of the Community Economics Area of Expertise within the University of Minnesota Extension Center for Community Vitality. This program is associated with retail merchandising research conducted in the Department of Design, Housing, and Apparel.

2. c. Program History

Over the past 20 years, Dr. Kenneth Stone, Extension Economist from Iowa State University, has observed and researched the impact of mass merchandisers on small stores in rural communities throughout Iowa. Through his research, he developed a community retail trade analysis tool called "Pull Factor" analysis using Iowa retail sales data. This tool aided communities in assessing their capture of their market potential. In addition, Dr. Stone compiled recommendations from the retail merchandising literature which he shared with retail owners in presentations not only throughout Iowa, but throughout the country.

In 2002, Dr. Stone provided training to the Minnesota REE's (economic development) on his "Pull Factor Analysis" and his recommended (though not researched) retail business strategies for small stores. At that time, he and Dept. of Design, Housing and Apparel retail merchandising faculty began to explore possible future research studies that could be conducted in Minnesota to see if successful retailers were using any of his recommended retail strategies, as well as a consumer survey to learn more about customer expectations and satisfactions with their local retailers. That research was conducted in 2003 and is the basis for the Small Store Success Strategies program.

Dr. Stone was contracted to adapt the Iowa Retail Sales Analysis (Pull Factor) website for Minnesota. Funding for the Retail Trade Analysis programming was provided by the Blandin Foundation ($12,000) and the University of

Minnesota Extension Service—Community Vitality. Market research conducted in Minnesota found that cities needed more help in interpreting the pull factor data. The program team made a decision to conduct workshops instead of using the Iowa method of disseminating information over the website.

Funding for the Small Store Success Strategies pilot study conducted in 2003 was provided by the University of Minnesota Extension Service – Community Vitality Capacity Area ($6,400), University of Minnesota Dept. of Design, Housing, and Apparel ($1,400), and the University of Minnesota Center for Small Towns ($1,000) In addition, the 9-month appointment non-extension retail merchandising faculty provided significant in-kind (unpaid) contributions of their expertise in data collection over the summer of 2003. Funding for the Retail Trade Analysis was supplemented by a grant from the Blandin Foundation. It was agreed that we would provide some basic retail information at no charge on our web site and rural communities would have access to their RTA reports at a lower cost.

In 2005, Kim Johnson, Seung-Eun Lee, and Sherri Gahring received approval from the Minnesota Agriculture Experiment Station to conduct a study, "Business Environments and Strategies of Small-town Retailers." The overall research and outreach goals of this study are:

- to identify the business environments of small towns in Minnesota
- to identify what and how business strategies are creatively construed and conveyed by small-town retailers in varying business environments within Minnesota

- to differentiate successful small-town retailers on the basis of their business strategies and business environments
- to support existing Retail Analysis and Development outreach programming in the University of Minnesota Extension Service

In 2006 and 2007, Ryan Pesch, Bruce Schwartau, and Kent Gustafson visited with Wisconsin Extension Specialist Bill Ryan about his work with the ESRI Business Analyst program. Bill Ryan has been doing some intensive outreach with some communities but it was not being delivered by the local educators. During 2007, Ryan developed and tested a deliverable program with the city of Perham that can now be replicated by a trained Extension Educator.

In 2007 and 2008, Adeel Ahmed shared how the use of new handheld devices that utilize the global positioning system might provide private benefits to small business in rural communities by attracting potential customers that are increasingly tech savvy. Public benefits are generated when a local government participates in the RADA program and then makes it more convenient for residents to locate government services online. The team is currently searching for academic confirmation of the impacts.

2. d. Location, Delivery, and Technology Enhanced Learning
All RAD offerings will be delivered statewide in face-to-face workshop formats and RTA updates may be delivered by distance education methods such as UMConnect. Greater Minnesota communities were the primary marketing areas during the first year. The RTA, RADA, and MAP offerings can be conducted in the metropolitan areas but the Small

Store Success Strategies research was conducted in rural areas so caution needs to be used in large cities.

Product 1: Small Store Success Strategies

(Program will not be offered 2/1/2009 to 7/1/2009 while under review for reformatting)
3. Strategic Plan

3. a. Mission Statement

Aid independent rural retail stores to competitively co-exist with mass merchandisers by improving their practices in marketing, merchandising, customer service and business operations.

3. b. Goals

- o Small retailers will learn "best practices" related to merchandising, marketing, customer relations, and business operations based on a 2003 University of Minnesota study.
- o Small retailers will learn customers' satisfaction and expectations of small retailers based on a 2003 University of Minnesota study.

3. c. Expected Outcomes

Small retailers will implement at least one of the above-mentioned "best practices" within six months after attending the program.

3. d. Private Value and Public Value of Outcomes

The improved business practices for small retailers will ultimately lead to providing jobs and income for owners and employees but also will provide access to vital products for local residents, thus increasing the quality of life in the community.

3. e. Program Competitive Position

There is limited research on small stores, especially stores located in the same town as mass merchandisers. No one else is presenting this information to small store owners. This program is unique in that it is based on current and continuing research conducted at the University of Minnesota.

3. f. Program Strategy

Due to the increasing numbers of big box retail stores throughout Minnesota, many main street businesses in Greater Minnesota are struggling to survive. Consequently, there is moderately good demand for this program offering statewide.

3. g. Research Basis

The research basis for the Small Store Success Strategies program is a pilot study, "Successful Independent Retailers Versus Big Box Retailers: How to Survive", conducted by U of M Department of Design, Housing, and Apparel faculty Kim Johnson, Seung-Eun Lee, and Sherri Gahring. Seahee Lee, graduate student from DHA, and Extension Educators Elizabeth Templin and Lisa Hinz were also members of the research team.

More recently, Kim Johnson, Seung-Eun Lee, Sherri Gahring, and DHA graduate student Jaeha Lee have begun working on an Agriculture Experiment Station study (for 2005-2007), "Business Environments and Strategies for Small-town Retailers, to provide additional research basis for Small Store Success Strategies program.

In following section, we will overview the literature review conducted prior to the development of Small Store Success Strategies program implemented in 2005.

Over the last several decades, small-town retailers have suffered economic losses to "big box" merchandisers (Ryan, 2002). More than half of Minnesota cities with populations between 5,000 and 10,000 have a Target, Wal-Mart, or Kmart store ("Changing places" 2001). This phenomenon coupled with population out-migration and out-shopping has made it increasingly difficult for small-town retailers to survive (Ayres, Leistritz, & Stone, 1992).

Kenneth Stone, Iowa State University Extension Economist and author of *Competing with the Retail Giants,* identified big box retailers as the single largest threat to the survival of small-town retailers today (Stone, personal communication January 2003). Stone suggests that small-town retailers do not have to end up as casualties of mass merchandising if they take advantage of the positive effects that the arrival of a Wal-Mart or Target can have (1995). These effects include keeping shoppers from leaving town to shop in other communities ("Big box versus small business," April 29, 2002), increasing trade area, and generating increased traffic (Stone, 1995). In order to be successful Stone did recommend specific strategies be followed by small-town retailers though he did not conduct research to determine the success of his recommendations. In addition, very few researchers (Achua & Lussier, 2001; McGee & Finney, 1997) have investigated across communities whether any strategies recommended by Stone or others have resulted in success for small-town retailers.

Since the early 1990s, dramatic changes have occurred in the retail environment. Paramount among these changes is computer applications to retailing and the use of the Internet to source and sell merchandise. Unknown is to what extent small-town retailers have incorporated these new technologies to compete successfully with big box retailers. In addition, there is little empirical research addressing small-town consumers' expectations and satisfaction with these same small-town retailers.

4. Marketing Plan

4a.   Market Research and Needs Assessment

In 2004, forty-two Minnesota counties indicated an interest in the Retail Analysis and Development Program (either RTA and/or SSSS) with over 463 participants of whom about 80 served a formal role of county government (commissioner, Extension committee member, auditor and/or administrator). Of those forty-two counties, thirty-six indicated that the program would address issues that are currently of very high importance to citizens, and five indicated it would address issues they anticipate will be of very high importance to citizens within the next two years.

4. b. Target Market

   a.   Chambers of Commerce
   a.   Business Organizations
   b.   Downtown Business Associations

c.

4. c. Pricing Strategy

Market research was conducted by outside consultant, Sonya Brown, and it was determined that a fee of $500 was a reasonable price for the Small Store Success Strategies program for most cities in Greater Minnesota and the 7 county metro area. It has been most successful when marketed with the Retail Trade Analysis at a combined fee.

4. d. Promotion

1. We have a prepared 30-minute "teaser" presentation on this product. This presentation was used at the "U and Your Economy" sessions. It can also be used at other venues with audiences who would purchase / pay for Extension to deliver the full program to retail businesses in their community. Specific targeted groups are:

o Minnesota State Chamber of Commerce Executive Directors (done in 2005)
o Minnesota Bankers Association

2. A web-based joint program brochure, "Retaining Retail Store and Customers in the Community" has been developed and is on-line at www.extension.umn.edu/retail

3. Yearly updates to the promotion and marketing will occur in the annual Program Implementation Plan.

4. e. Distribution

Extension Educators in Community Economics will make the presentations to community organizations in their respective regions.

5. Operations and Implementation

5. a & b. Program Development Plan and Timeline
Updated annually in the Program Implementation Plan.

The Extension Educator will follow the existing protocol for confirming community programs, evaluation, and billing. The contact person is responsible for handling local publicity, registrations, collecting fees, and meeting arrangements.

5. d. Risk Management Plan

o The risk is not meeting our financial goals. Expenses have been below revenues.

5. e. Evaluation Plan

Continue to follow evaluation plans established in combination with our evaluation specialist.

6. Management Plan

6. a. Team Leaders

Sherri Gahring with assistance of Ryan Pesch, Bruce Schwartau, and Adeel Ahmed.

6. b. Team Members

Extension Educators in Community Economics

6. c. Partners

    Center for Small Towns
6. d. Consultants

    Dr. Kim Johnson, Department of Design, Housing and
    Apparel
    Dr. Seung-Eun Lee, Department of Design, Housing, and
    Apparel
    Dr. Ken Stone, Professor Emeritus, Iowa State University
    Bill Ryan, Retail Trade Specialists, University of Wisconsin
    Retail Faculty at St. Thomas University, Twin Cities
    Other -TBD

7. Financial Plan

    Addressed in the annual Program Implementation Plan

Product 2: Retail Trade Analysis

3. Strategic Plan

3. a. Mission Statement
    Program purpose: To aid communities in maintaining a
    healthy retail marketplace by organizing sales information
    into a format that can be used by business and government
    entities within a community.

    The Retail Trade Analysis Program will also teach
    communities how to use this information along with their
    local knowledge to improve the retail economy within their
    area.

3. b. Goals

The main purpose is to educate business people, community officials, developers, and other citizens about the history and current status of their retail and service sectors. Specific program goals are:

    a. Update the RTA computer program to generate reports for all communities that have Revenue Department data for latest sales data.

    b. Work with community partners to cumulatively present RTA reports in 40% of the rural cities with sales tax data and 7 county-only reports.

    c. Through the Retail Trade Analysis, communities will have documentation of how much existing stores have captured their potential retail sales of city population.

    d. Through facilitated sessions, retail businesses will understand where their business fits within the community's pull factors and use the information to make better business decisions.

    e. Local government officials and businesses thinking of locating in the community will have data to support their decision-making on expansion of retail in the community (e.g.: zoning, financing, etc.)

3. c. Expected Outcomes

    o By knowing the relative strengths and weaknesses of an area's business sector, it is hoped that merchants and community leaders will be able to capitalize on areas of opportunity. This can lead to increased use of available buildings and more employment.

o Trade statistics, business numbers, and sales data can provide insight for a variety of purposes, including decisions concerning expansion, relocation, marketing, government finance, and community development.

o Communities will develop business recruitment and expansion strategies that are appropriate for their goals.

3. d. Private Value and Public Value

There are private benefits that encourage participation in the Retail Trade Analysis program. Local organizers have seen the program as one that shows they support their local businesses and are trying to provide useful information to them. Local businesses can use the data to see how well they compete with other stores.

The public value is shown when economic entities are then gathering and reviewing the information for further action. One community told us it will help them determine the right mix of retail businesses that they desire for their future. Others have said it will keep more taxpaying businesses in the downtown area. Local residents benefit from having local stores as compared to having to travel to adjacent towns.

3. e. Competitive Position

No one else does a community-level retail sales analysis using this data. Individual consultants may do a market analysis using retail square-footage but at a very high cost. This square-footage option is greatest in the metropolitan area.

3. f. Research Basis

The pull factor tool was developed by Dr. Kenneth Stone, retired Iowa State Extension Economist. He developed the on-line pull factor analysis for Iowa communities and Extension Specialist Georgeanne Artz modified their computer program for Minnesota data.

4. a. Target Market

- o *City officials (City Council, City Administrator, Economic Development Authorities) who are seeing the local businesses are meeting the retail needs of their citizens.*
- o *Small independent retailers in rural Minnesota communities can use pull factors as one tool in evaluating their effectiveness in capturing retail sales potential*
- o Entrepreneurs starting businesses or businesses considering re-location to the community can use pull factors in determining market potential.
- o Newspapers, chambers of commerce, and financial institutions who want to support the livelihood of their local retail market.

4. b. Pricing Strategy

- o Retail Trade Analysis presentation in a community at a price that allows most towns to find a sponsor very easily. Started originally at $650.
- o For the all areas, there is a combined RTA-SSSS price of $1,000.
- o For previous RTA purchasers who want updated pages without a new in-person presentation – Approximately $100

4. c. Promotion

- o To Chambers:
  - o Brochure marketing the following Extension programs: At Your Service, Small Store Success Strategies, Access E-commerce
- o To Cities:
  - o Article in the League of Minnesota Cities magazine (reaches the city staff)
  - o Workshop at the League of Minnesota Cities Annual Meeting (reaches elected officials)
  - o Workshop at the Minnesota Planning Association Conference (reaches the city planners)
- o To Economic Development Professionals
  - o Newsletter article for EDAM
  - o Minnesota Planning Association
  - o Economic Development Association of Minnesota summer meeting
  - o Minnesota Association of Development Organizations (the statewide entity of Regional Development Commissions)
  - o Minnesota Bankers Association
- o Extension Public Web site
  - o Update web page with new information
- o Update promotion plan annually in the Program Implementation Plan.

4. d. Distribution

- o The Retail Trade Analysis presentation will be made by the Extension Educators. The use of UMConnect technology will allow the review of the preliminary data without traveling to every community before the public presentation. Communities purchasing updates may have that presentation done by distance technology.

5. Operations and Implementation

5. a. & b. Program Development Plan and Timeline

Task	Start Date	End Date	Person Responsible
Gather updated State of Minnesota Sales Tax Data	As available	ongoing	Bruce Schwartau
Recreate MN map of surplus/deficit counties	Annually	ongoing	Bruce Schwartau
Update RAD website	January	ongoing	Karen Lilley
Explore addition products that fit well with the retail audience Such as trade area mapping, consumer survey research, business succession issues, and customer lifestyle analysis	December	Ongoing	Team Members

5. c. Logistical Support

o   Web site updates with Karen Lilly.

5. d. Risk Management Plan
Potential risks are:

o *Not enough revenue to meet expenses although to date revenues have exceeded expenses.*

o Extension could be asked to "weigh in" on a community debate over whether or not the city council should allow a mass merchandiser to locate into the community.
   o Extension's role will be to present existing pull factor data for the community and the results of Ken Stone's research on the impact of a mass merchandiser on a community.

5. e. Evaluation Plan

o Evaluations conducted at the presentations by Extension Educators.

o Discussion with community purchasers to list how the data was used.

6. Management Plan

6. a. Team Leaders

Sherri Gahring and Bruce Schwartau with assistance from Ryan Pesch and Adeel Ahmed

6. b. Team Members

Extension Educators in Community Economics

6. c. Partners

State of Minnesota Department of Revenue (source of sales tax data), Blandin Foundation (provided startup funding for computer programming)

6. d. Consultants

Ken Stone, Retired from Iowa State – Georgeanne Artz, University of Missouri, Columbia)

7. Financial Plan

Updated in the annual program Implementation Plan.

Product 3: Market Area Profile

3. Strategic Plan

3. a. Mission Statement

Program purpose: To aid communities in maintaining a healthy retail marketplace by organizing market data into a format that can be used by business and government entities within a community.

The Market Area Profile Program will also teach communities how to use this information along with their local knowledge to improve the retail economy within their area, especially in the area of identifying potential businesses to fill gaps in the community.

3. b. Goals

- To teach participants how to apply the Market Area Profile information in their businesses and communities.
- To identify, together with participants, business opportunities to fill community gaps
-

3. c. Expected Outcomes and Impacts

o By knowing more about the factors of their local market, it is hoped that merchants and community leaders will be able to capitalize on areas of opportunity. This can lead to increased use of available buildings, more employment, and main street vitality.

o Trade statistics, business numbers, and sales data can provide insight for a variety of purposes, including decisions concerning expansion, relocation, marketing, government finance, and community development.

o Communities will develop business recruitment and expansion strategies that are appropriate for their goals.

3. d. Private Value and Public Value

The public value of the Market Area Profile derives from the positive externalities of community economic vitality. A vital main street not only provides goods and services for local residents, but also has spillover effects like business development and community pride.

3. e. Competitive Position

There are a number of individual consultants which perform market analysis for communities. This is typically at a high cost which is prohibitive for many small communities and neighborhood organizations. Also, the standard approach of consultants is to supply recommendations based on their outside knowledge.

The Market Area Profile is competitive because we provide a service to small communities and neighborhoods (which typically cannot afford service from private consultants) and we collaborate with local organizations to develop their own recommendations. This is in keeping with Extension's niche of building local capacity.

3. f. Research Basis

The tools we currently use in MAP directly derive from the work of Bill Ryan, retail specialist at University of Wisconsin Extension. Ryan has utilized trade area mapping, market potential calculations, and the Business Analyst software as part of the Downtown and Business District Market Analysis program to help communities improve their downtown business districts.

4. Marketing Plan

4. a. Target Market

- o *Government authorities (City Councils, County Commissions, Economic Development Authorities) which are concerned about local business districts meeting the needs of their citizens.*
- o Non-governmental organizations (chambers of commerce, neighborhood NGOs, CVBs, or other economic development, business development, or tourism organizations) which want to support the livelihood of their members.

o Financial institutions which want to play an active role in supporting their communities' business districts both for public relations and service to their account holders.

4. b. Pricing Strategy

We developed pricing for MAP products based on our experience selling Retail Trade Analysis, a comparable product. Prices were adjusted upward considering the level of time investment.

o A standard MAP including report and presentation is $750. A standard product uses any simple trade area identified by a local study group.
o A customized MAP including report and presentation is $1,500. A customized MAP is one where local data sources like property tax records or customer lists are utilized to more accurately define the trade area or create a profile.

Prices are highly reasonable considering the value we provide. Private consultants supply greater value though greater customization, experienced analysis, and additional information through interviews and intercept surveys. Communities typically pay $10,000-$50,000 for these in-depth studies. Comparable raw data is available in many forms online through a number of sources like Claritas and ESRI for $50-$500, but without any of the relational value we bring through application.

4. c. Promotion

o To tourism-related entities:

- o Roundtable at Explore Minnesota Conference
- o Communications and mailings through the Tourism Center

o To Cities:

- o Article in the League of Minnesota Cities magazine (reaches the city staff)
- o Workshop at the League of Minnesota Cities Annual Meeting (reaches elected officials)
- o Workshop at the Minnesota Planning Association Conference (reaches the city planners)

- o To Economic Development Professionals
  - o Newsletter article for EDAM
  - o Minnesota Planning Association
  - o Economic Development Association of Minnesota summer meeting
  - o Minnesota Association of Development Organizations (the statewide entity of Regional Development Commissions)
  - o Minnesota Bankers Association
- o Extension Public Web site
  - o Update web page with new information
- o Update the promotion plan annually in the Program Implementation Plan

4. d. Distribution

The Market Area Profile report will be compiled by Ryan Pesch or Art Nash will compile the Market Area Profile report. The local Community Economics Extension Educator will lead the Market Area Profile presentation as well as any pre-meetings in the creation of the profile.

5. Operations and Implementation

5. a. & b. Program Development Plan and Timeline

Updated in the annual program Implementation Plan.

5. e. Evaluation Plan

An end-of-workshop evaluation will be used to measure learning objectives, although a long-term assessment will be necessary to measure impacts due to the program.

6. Management Plan

6. a. Team Leaders

Ryan Pesch, Extension Educator, is primary contact and manager for the Market Area Profile product. Art Nash, Extension Educator, supports Ryan in conducting Business Analyst to compile community reports.

6. b. Team Members

Extension Educators in Community Economics and Tourism Center Staff

6. c. Partners

Bill Ryan, Retail Specialist, University of Wisconsin Extension

7. Financial Plan

Updated in the annual program Implementation Plan.

Product 4: Road Side Advertising in a Digital Age

1. **Strategic Plan**

    a. **Mission Statement**
        To help community and business leaders, residents, small businesses, local governments and nonprofit agencies get their communities on online digital maps by leveraging web 2.0 technologies.

    b. Goals
        The main goal is to give organizations the knowledge, skills, and tools to maximize their online presence by teaching them how to:

        1. utilize mash up features of sites like Windows Live, Yahoo Maps, Google Maps, MapQuest
        2. add enriched content to maps
        3. transfer created content to their current websites

    c. Expected Outcomes

        By knowing how tech savvy customers are using online maps on PCs and handheld devices:

        1. Business owners will be better able to market their goods and services.

2. Governments will make it more convenient for customers to find services

3. Tourism Associations will be better enable tourists in finding Points of Interest

d. Private and Public Value

    i. There are private benefits that encourage participation in the RADA programs. Local organizers have seen the program as one that shows they support their local businesses and organizations and are trying to provide useful information to them. Local businesses and organization can use the skills and tools they learn in the RADA program to better market their goods and services to customers.

    ii. The public value of the RADA program is that better marketing will increase customer traffic in a community. The increased traffic to businesses will thereby increase tax revenue which benefits the public. Additionally, when governments utilize the tools taught in the RADA program they will make it easier for the public to find government resources.

e. Competitive Position

Apart from online resources, such as blogs, no one teaches face-to-face classes on how to leverage electronic map technologies to market goods and services online.

f. Research Basis

    i. The RADA program was developed in house by Adeel Ahmed who is an avid electronic map user. The need to teach RADA stems from industry figures of how many people are using handheld internet devices and handheld devices. The main sources for these numbers are Neilsen Media, Marketing Charts.com, and other trade publications. But this does not mean that we cannot have an academic research basis for the RADA programs.

    ii. Our main objective in the RADA program is to enlarge a community's presence on mapping sites on the web, like on Google Maps and MapQuest. So our hypotheses could be that communities that participate in RADA see a higher growth rate of presence on online maps as compared to communities that do not participate in RADA.

    iii. We can gather data to prove our hypothesis by measuring the presence, before and after, of organizations in a particular community in Google's local business center.

        1. We could possibly obtain from Google the number of businesses in a particular are who are registered in the local business center.

        2. Take this number from before the delivery of RADA 1.0 and 2.0 and compare it to the number of businesses registered a period of time after program delivery.

        3. Repeat this several times to arrive at the rate of growth of business to the local business center.

        4. Compare these rates to towns that have not participated in RADA.

5. Then we have evidence for our hypothesis to show that the rate of growth of the local business presence in the Google's local business center is higher for communities that participate in RADA than in communities that do not.

iv. A lingering question remains though - what is the importance or impact of being on Google's local business center?

2. Marketing Plan

   a. Target Market

      i. Tourism associations & Chambers of Commerce – can offer as a valuable service the placement of their clients on online maps.
      ii. City Councils, City Administrators, County Administrators – can make it easier find and locate services for the their customers
      iii. Individual businesses – can have an online presence without having to maintain a website.

   b. Pricing Strategy

      i. **Introduction to RADA** – A 15-minute presentation to small groups such as Chamber of Commerce meetings that introduce our RADA programs and capacities.
      ii. **RADA – 1.0 Show & Tell** – One hour class that teaches people the value of having a presence on online maps and GPS devices and creates awareness among business owners and those who represent them about how people are using online

maps and GPS devices to find where they want to go. This workshop aims to create excitement among the target audience to undertake efforts to increase and enhance their online presence. $200

iii. **RADA 2.0 - Put your POI on the Map** – two-hour hands on workshop walks attendees through the steps needed to assess, edit, and place their organization and add enhanced content to various online maps. $300

iv. **RADA 3.0 - Map Making** – Two hour hands on workshop walks attendees through the steps needed to make content rich online maps and place the map on their organization's website. $300

1. A key additional feature the RADA 3.0 workshop is that Extension can take basic maps of various categories of points of interest created through the mash up process and layer it onto one map. This map can then be transplanted to an already existing website adding tremendous content. The community or organization is responsible for collecting the data and creating the single category maps, Extension then combines all the category maps created onto a single map. The delivered product to the client then is a snippet of code that they can copy onto their website. This work is technical and falls in the realm of consulting time. The cost for a community to get this product varies and starts from $1000.

    c. Promotion

        i. Present the "Show and Tell" workshop during meetings with partners and stakeholders

        ii. Currently we are distributing a marketing flyer to the audiences in our target market and receive good response

        iii. We need to add further info under http://www.extension.umn.edu/Retail/

        iv. And create a webpage under http://www.extension.umn.edu/Retail/digital marketing

        v. Write articles about it to
           1. Journal of Extension
           2. MPR – Jon Gordon – Technology news, "Future Tense"

        vi. Blog about it on community blogs and professional blogs

        vii. Present at various conferences

           1. Tourism Conference
           2. EDAM Conference
           3. NACDEP Conference

    d. Distribution

        i. The RADA workshops will be conducted by the Extension Educators.

        ii. There is always the option of using UMConnect to make the presentation also.

3. Operations and Implementation

    a. Program Development Plan and Timeline

Task	Start Date	End Date	Person Responsible
Develop manual for RADA 2.0 for educators	In Progress	Dec 1, 2008	Neil Lindschied
Develop manual for RADA 3.0 for educators	Dec 2, 2008	March 1, 2009	Adeel Ahmed
Create RADA portion on the Extension website	Nov 10, 2008	Jan 1, 2009	Adeel Ahmed
Develop a research basis for the RADA program	In progress	Ongoing	Team Members
Write JOE article	Feb 1, 2009	Feb 28, 2009	Adeel Ahmed
Write a newspaper article about impacts of online mapping	Jan 1, 2009	Jan 30, 2009	Adeel Ahmed

   b. Logistical Support

   c. Risk Management Plan

       1. Not recovering costs associated in delivering the program

   d. Evaluation Plan

       1. We have evaluation forms for RADA 1.0 and 2.0
       2. Need to develop for RADA 3.0
       3. Six month follow up with clients to see if they have made any progress on putting points of interest online

4. Management Plan

    a. Team Leaders
        i. Adeel Ahmed and Neil Linscheid
    b. Team Members
        i. Extension Educators in Community Economics
    c. Partners

5. Financial Plan

Fee Structure
The fee structure was developed in order to deliver the maximum possible while also fully recovering the expense of the educator and recovering some income to further develop the program. These have third party sponsors.

- RADA 1.0 is a one hour presentation and we are charging $200 for it
- RADA 2.0 is a two hour workshop and we are charging $300 for it
- RADA 3.0 is a two hour workshop and we are charging $300 for it
- A customized map snippet provided to the client is an additional $1000

Product 5: Products to Explore

There is a need to explore new products that fit under the heading Retail Analysis & Development. Several ideas that have been discussed by the Community Economics team include the following:

- o Consumer research tools
- o Training on business ownership succession decisions.

Glossary

Area of Expertise. An area of expertise is roughly parallel to an academic department but often includes individuals from several different academic disciplines. Nationally, several other states use the term "area of expertise" in the same way as Minnesota did from 2002 to 2007. Michigan and Ohio are two examples. The areas of expertise are described in more detail in Chapter 5. In 2008, Minnesota Extension changed this term to "program areas."

Area Program Leaders. In 2008, there are 16 area program leaders in Minnesota. They directly supervise all of the regional extension educators throughout the state in a given area of expertise. Each area program leader reports to one of four Associate Deans in charge of a capacity area. This term was changed to "program leader" in 2008.

Area Specialist. See District/Area Specialist

Associate Dean for Capacity Areas. See Capacity Area Leaders.

Associate Dean for Extension Centers. See Capacity Area Leaders.

Benefit-Cost Analysis. A method of examining the advantages and disadvantages of public projects by estimating monetary values for all stakeholders of all the advantages and all the disadvantages of the project. Estimates are made of the monetary value of environmental values, the value of life, and other items that are not traded in the market and have market value.

Capacity Area. Capacity Areas was the name used for the following five broad areas of work: (1) Agriculture, Food and Environment, (2) Natural Resources and Environment, (3) Youth Development, (4) Family Development, and (5) Community Vitality. In some states, these are called program areas. Starting in 2008, Minnesota calls these Extension Centers.

Capacity Area Leaders. The Capacity Area Leaders are the highest-level administrative position in each of the capacity areas and report to the Dean/Director of Extension. In the Minnesota model, they are the equivalent of department heads in academic departments. They make the final decisions on hiring, on annual salary adjustments, and on promotions. While program teams and area program leaders make most program decisions, the capacity area leaders are the public voice for the capacity area for central administration and the legislature. They set the vision for the capacity area and supervise the area program leaders. In 2008, this term was shifted to Associate Deans for Extension Center (name of center).

CES. See Cooperative Extension System

Communities of Interest. The collection of individuals who have related programming interests, regardless of their location in the state. Some of the communities of interest are statewide, particularly in Youth Development, Family Development, and Community Vitality. In agriculture and natural resources, the communities of interest depend on the zones that cover certain types of agriculture or natural resources.

Cooperative Extension. See Cooperative Extension System.

Cooperative Extension System (CES). This is the outreach education system that operates from the land-grant universities and is funded jointly by the U.S. Department of Agriculture, the states, and counties. Each state Cooperative Extension Service is an independent operation, working in collaboration with the other 97 units. Appendix A provides a brief overview of CES.

Cooperative State Research, Education, and Extension Service (CSREES). This is the unit within the U.S. Department of Agriculture, which administers the federal funds for CES. The unit also provides national program leadership on a variety of Extension efforts.

Cost Effectiveness Analysis. This is a form of economic analysis that estimates the ratio of measures of the outcome of a project in quantitative terms to the financial cost of the project. Benefit/cost analysis takes this one-step further by converting the estimates of outcomes or benefits to monetary terms so that both benefits and costs are in the same units.

County. CSREES defines a county as "That county of a district considered an administrative unit. The county director administratively reports through the District Director. The staff is involved in program only within the county boundary" (USDA

2007). After 2004, almost none of this applies to Minnesota. In Minnesota, there are 87 counties, which started as administrative units of state government but have many local functions. For details on Minnesota counties, see the Association of Minnesota Counties website: www.mncounties.org

County Agents. CSREES defines a "County Extension Agent" as "the person(s) who is/are responsible for a segment of a program and issue in one county. He/she provides leadership in planning, organizing, implementing, and is accountable for a segment of a program or issue. He/she reports to the county director/county coordinator/leader" (USDA 2007). Minnesota has county-based educators or local educators, but they report to area program leaders who cover large regions.

County-based Extension Educator. See Local Extension Educator.

County Clustering. A program delivery model that relies on multicounty teams of Extension educators to work major, multifaceted educational programs. The educators are located in county offices and each educator is asked to serve as a specialist in a particular area of expertise for the cluster of counties. Sometimes "clustering" is used for this concept. In this book, the term county-cluster model is used for this concept.

County Educators. See Local Extension Educator.

County Extension Director (CED). A county level administrative role in the county-cluster model. The CED worked with county commissioners and county Extension advisory boards, supervised the support staff, and even had some role in the evaluation of county educators.

District. CSREES definition is "That area of a State designated as an administrative unit, consisting of counties whose Multi-County Director or County Director reports through the District Director on administrative matters and in some states on program matters too" (USDA 2007). Minnesota has no districts under the new model.

District/Area Specialist. CSREES defines this as "that/those person(s) who is/are responsible for a highly specialized segment of a subject matter for a district of the State" (USDA 2007).

District Directors. In the cluster-county model, the District Directors were the mid-level administrators who supervised all the Extension Educators in their district. In Minnesota, prior to 2004, a district included about eleven counties. Their roles shifted to the Regional Directors (external relations) and the Area Program Leaders (supervision of the REEs and other educational staff).

Double-bottom Line. The concept that mission driven organizations must pay attention to both their mission and their financial sustainability (i.e. "money"). Neither is more important than the other since without financial sustainability the mission cannot continue in future years. However, most organizations, including Minnesota Extension, stressed the importance of getting the mission right first since the money is unlikely to follow if there is no private or public value.

Extension. Another term for Cooperative Extension System. Also used for the individual state units.

eXtension. eXtension is a partnership between the land-grant universities to provide information and learning opportunities via the internet. See. http://about.extension.org

Extension Centers. See Capacity Areas.

Extension Educator for (name of local funding partner). See Local Educator. For example, this might be Extension Educator for Stearns County if the county funded it.

Extension Educator in (name of area of expertise). See Regional Extension Educator. For example, this could be Extension Educator in Community Economics or Extension Educator in Crops.

Extension Committee on Organization and Policy (ECOP). ECOP is a standing committee with the Association of Public and Land-Grant Universities (APLU). The 18-person committee provides national leadership for the Cooperative Extension System. Membership includes dean/directors state Extension units, administrators from CSREES-USDA, and committee chairpersons.

Face Validity. A survey has face validity if it "looks like" it is going to measure the concepts it is intended to measure.

Fiscal Year. The period of time over which a unit does its accounting.

Full-time equivalent (FTE). One full-time equivalent position is equal to one full-time job for a year. Two people, each working half time for one year would be one FTE.

Geographic Communities. These are collections of people in a given geographic area. In Extension, this area has often been counties, but could be cities, town, and multi-county regions.

Linkage Agents or Educator. See spanner agent or educator.

Local Extension Educator (LEE). The University of Minnesota Extension Educators located in county offices or in the offices of other funding partners rather than in a regional office. The work of these educators is described in Chapter 6. The terms county-based Extension Educator or county educators are also used for this position. Starting in 2008, the working titles changed to "Extension Educator for (name of funding partner or agreed upon work description). See "county agents."

Local Positions. Local positions include local educators, 4-H program coordinators, Master Gardener program coordinators, Nutrition Education Assistants and support staff.

Mission and Money. The slogan is used in social entrepreneurship to signify that education and other mission driven organizations need to maximize a double bottom line, their mission, and their funding to support the mission.

Minnesota Extension. The official name of the Cooperative Extension System unit in Minnesota is *University of Minnesota Extension.* For brevity, Minnesota Extension will be used synonymously with University of Minnesota Extension. Before 2007, the official name was the University of Minnesota Extension Service.

Multi-County Agents. CSREES defines these as "That/those person(s) who is/are responsible for a highly specialized segment of subject matter for two or three counties. He/she provides leadership in the planning, organizing, implementing, and controlling a segment of that program. He/she reports to a Multi-County Program Leader or Director" (USDA 2007). In Minnesota, the 4-H REEs are close to this type of position since they each cover 3 or 4 counties. However, they do not report to Multi-County Program Leaders but to Area Program Leaders which cover about 30 counties each for 4-H but not for other programs.

Program. An Extension program is defined as all the educational activities aimed at the same educational objectives and the same target audience. A program is likely to consist of a number of different educational events and activities, such as workshops, popular press releases, applied demonstrations, websites, webinars, and field days.

Program Areas. See areas of expertise.

Program Centers. There currently are four program centers in Minnesota Extension, including the Extension Center for Youth Development, the Extension Center for Family Development, the Extension Center for Food, Agriculture, and Natural Resource Sciences, and the Extension Center for Community Vitality. In many states, these program centers are called program areas. This book reports results for five centers since agriculture and natural resources were separate from 2004 to 2008.

Program Leaders. See Area Program Leaders.

REEs. See Regional Extension Educators.

Regional Extension Educators (REEs). The REEs are specialized Extension Educators who are located at one of 18 regional centers around the state. Most work statewide or in regions of 7 to 8 counties. As a result, their position is closer to the "state specialist" position as defined by CSREES (USDA 2007). The 4-H educators work in 3 or 4 counties and supervise local 4-H program coordinators. Details on the nature of their specialization are provided in Chapter 5. Starting in 2008, their working titles became "Extension Educator in (name of their area of expertise).

Regional Extension Educators, Established. This term is used in this book to indicate the REEs who worked for Extension in 1999 or before and still worked for Extension in the year of the survey, 2007.

Regional Extension Educators, New. This term is used in this book to indicate the REEs who were hired by Minnesota Extension in 2004 or after.

Retrospective Pre-Post Tests. In a standard pre- and post-test evaluation, two surveys are administered, one before the educational event and one after. In the retrospective pre-post test, only one survey is administered, after the educational program. However, respondents are asked to indicate how much they knew before the educational experience as well as how much they know after the experience.

Regional Directors. The regional directors manage Minnesota's regional centers and supervise their staff. One of their major roles is external relations with county commissioners and county Extension committees. They play the lead role in promoting new positions with counties. However, they do not supervise the REEs or other program staff.

Smith-Lever Funds. Funds provided by the federal government on a formula basis for base programming in Extension as outlined in the Smith-Lever Act. See Appendix A.

Smith-Level Act. The federal legislation, originally passed in 1914, which established the national Cooperative Extension System.

Spanner Agents or Educators. An Extension educator who bridges the differences between generalist county agents, or other professionals with a generalist background, and highly specialized state specialists or researches. Rogers (1995) identifies this gap as differences in professionalism, formal education, technical expertise, and specialization. Rogers writes that the original "state specialists were created as spanner or linkage agents." See Chapter 2 for further discussion of how this changed.

State Specialists. CSREES defines these as "That/those person (s) who is/are responsible for a segment of a total program within a State. He/she normally has specific responsibilities in agronomy, computer specialists, 4-H, dairy, nutrition, clothing, or other segments of programs or subject-matter" (USDA 2007). Using this definition, all of the campus specialists in Minnesota and two-thirds of the Minnesota Regional Educators (outside 4-H) are state specialists. This is a part of the reason the term REE was changed to Extension Educator in (name of area of expertise).

State Specialist, Associate. CSREES defines these as "That/those person(s) who provides support to the State Specialist working on a special project or grant. He or she reports to the State Specialists" (USDA 2007). While Minnesota has few individuals that would fit this definition, the REEs do not because the REEs and the Minnesota state specialists are co-equal members of program teams, with different responsibilities. The REEs report to an Area Program Leader in their area of expertise, but not to a specific state specialist on a special project or grant.

Technical Assistance. Technical assistance is defined as answering specific questions and providing consulting on specific applications of the principles and practices taught in educational programs.

Transaction Costs. Transaction costs refer to the costs and time required to make decisions, to negotiate new projects or programs, or oversee the implementation of programs.

References

Abraham, R. H. 1986. *Helping People Help Themselves: Agricultural Extension in Minnesota, 1879-1979,* St. Paul: Minnesota Extension Service, University of Minnesota.

Ahmed, A., and G. W. Morse. (forthcoming). "Opportunities and Threats Created by Extension Field Specialization." *Journal of Extension.* See: www.joe.org

Agnew, D. M. 1991. "Extension Program Delivery Trends." *Journal of Extension 29(2).* See: www.joe.org

Ahearn, M. and T. Parker. 2009. "Farm Household Economics and Well-being: Beginning Farmers, Demographics and Labor Allocations." *Briefing Rooms,* Economic Research Service, USDA. Available online at: http://www.ers.usda.gov/Briefing/WellBeing/demographics.htm (accessed April 14, 2009)

Ahearn, M.; J. Yee; and J. Bottom. 2003. "Regional Trends in Extension System Resources." Electronic Report from the Economic Research Service, USDA, *Agricultural Information Bulletin* Number *781.*

Alston, D. G. and Reding, M.E. 1998. "Factors Influencing Adoption and Educational Outreach of Integrated Pest Management." *Journal of Extension 36(3).* Available: www.joe.org

Alston, J. M.; C. Chan-Kang; M. C. Marra; P. G. Pardey; and T.J. Wyatt. 2000. *A Meta-Analysis of Rates of Return to Agricultural R&D: Ex Pede Herculem?* Washington, D.C., International Food Policy Research Institute Research Report 113

Alter, T. R. 2003. "Where Is Extension Scholarship Falling Short, and What Can We Do About It?" *Journal of Extension 41(6).* See: www.joe.org

Alves, J. L. 1993. "Reaching Native Americans." *Journal of Extension 31(1)*. See www.joe.org

Anderson, N. 2009. Director of Resource Development Unit, University of Minnesota, *Personal Correspondence,* 2009

Archer, T. M.; P. D. Warner; W. Miller; C. D. Clark; S. James; S.R. Cummings; and U. Adamu. 2007. "Can We Define and Measure Excellence in Extension?" *Journal of Extension 45(1).,* See: www.joe.org

Aronson, B. 2003 "Marketing Your Ideas Though the News Media." December 29, 2003. The Aronson Partnership, Inc. Eagan, MN.

Arp, H. 2005. "Needs Assessment in the University of Minnesota Extension Service." Masters of Education Thesis, College of Education and Human Service Professions, University of Minnesota, Duluth.

Barth, J. A.; B. W. Stryker; L. R. Arrington; and S. Syed. 1999. "The Implications of Increased Alternative Revenue for the Cooperative Extension System: Present and Future Strategies for Success." *Journal of Extension 37(4)* See: www.joe.org

Bartholomay T. 2007. "University of Minnesota Extension's Master Gardener Program: Public Benefits Highly Valued by Minnesotans and Vital Program Constituents: Summary of Evaluation Findings." College of Food, Agricultural and Natural Resource Sciences, University of Minnesota. http://www. mg.umn.edu/pdfs/2007ConfHandouts/Moen_PublicBenefits. pdf (accessed, April 14, 2009)

Bartholomay, T., S. Chazdon, and M. Marczak. 2009. Conference Call with the George Morse.

Bartholomew, M. and K. L. Smith. 1990. "Stresses of Multicounty Agent Positions." *Journal of Extension 28(4)* See: www.joe. org/

Batte, M. T.; E. Jones, and G. Schnitkey. 1990. "Farm Information Use: An Analysis of Production and Weather Information for Midwestern Cash Grain Farmers." *Journal of Production Agriculture, 3(1).*

Batte, M. T.; G. Schnitkey; and E. Jones. 1990. "Sources, Uses and Adequacy of Marketing Information for Commercial Midwestern Cash Grain Farmers." *North Central Journal of Agricultural Economics 12(2).*

Bergstrom, C. T. and T. C. Bergstrom. 2006. "The Economics of Ecology Journals." *Frontiers in Ecology and the Environment* 4(9).

Borich, T. O. 2001. "The Department of Housing and Urban Development and Cooperative Extension: A Case for Urban Collaboration." *Journal of Extension 39(6),* See www.joe.org

Borich, P. J. 1988. "Clients Face Uncertainty, Too." *Journal of Extension 26(4)* See www.joe.org

Boschee, J. 2009. The Institute for Social Entrepreneurs, See: http://www.socialent.org/beta/index.htm

Boyer, E. L. 1990. *Scholarship Reconsidered: Priorities of the Professorate.* The Carnegie Foundation for the Advancement of Teaching San Francisco: Jossey-Bass.

Boyer, E. L. 1996. "The Scholarship of Engagement." *Journal of Public Service & Outreach 1(1).*

Brent, R. J. 2006. *Applied Cost-Benefit Analysis.* Northhampton. Edward Elgar Publishing

Bridges, W. and Associates. 1992. *Managing Organizational Transitions.* Mill City, C. A.

Buchanan, J. J. 1985. "An Economic Theory of Clubs." *Economica* 32(125)

Bull N; H. Cote; P. Warner; and R. McKinnie. 2004. "Is Extension Relevant for the 21st Century?" *Journal of Extension 42(6)* See: www.joe.org

Casey, C. H.; Morse, G. W.; and Markell, J. 2004. *Strategic planning framing concepts.* St. Paul, MN: University of Minnesota Extension Service. See: http://www.extension.umn.edu/jump/ compact05/summary.html (accessed April 10, 2009).

Caravella, J. 2006. "A Needs Assessment Method for Extension Educators." *Journal of Extension* 44(1). See: www.joe.org

Center for Rural Policy and Development. 2009. *Atlas of Minnesota Online Edition.* See: www.ruralmn.org (accessed April 10, 2009) .

Center for Rural Policy and Development. 2008. *The 2007 Minnesota Internet Study: Tracking the progress of broadband. St. Peter. Seewww.ruralmn.org/ (accessed April 10, 2009) .*

Chazdon, S; T. Bartholomay; M. Marczak; and A. Lochner. 2007. "Using the Community Capitals Framework for Extension Impact Evaluation." Paper presented at the Fourth Annual Community Capitals Framework Institute, Ames, Iowa.

Cochrane, W. W. 1983. "Agricultural Economics at the University of Minnesota: 1886-1979." Department of Agricultural and Applied Economics, University of Minnesota. *Miscellaneous Publication 21.* See http://ageconsearch.umn.edu

Collins, J. 2001. *Good to Great: Why Some Companies Make the Leap...and Others Don't.* New York, Harper Collins.

Collins, J. 2005. *Good to Great and the Social Sectors.* Boulder, Co. Jim Collins Publishing.

Collins, J., and J. I. Porras. 2002. *Built to Last: Successful Habits of Visionary Companies.* Harper Collins.

Committee on the Future of Agriculture in the Land Grant University System. National Research Council (U.S.) 1995. *Colleges of Agriculture at the Land Grant Universities: A Profile.* National Academies Press.

Cooperative Extension Section, NASLGC. 2007. *Strategic Opportunities for Cooperative Extension Service.* See: http://www.aplu.org/NetCommunity/Page.aspx?pid=649&srcid=758

Council on Public Engagement. 2006. http://www1.umn.edu/civic/reports/index.html

Cropper, R. J. and R. F. Merkowitz. 1998. "Cluster a Great Way to Work." *Journal of Extension 36 (1).* See: www.joe.org

Cuomo, Gregory, 2008. Extension Associate Dean; Food , Agriculture and Natural Resources, University of Minnesota Extension, St. Paul, *Personal Communication,* November 2008.

Davis, G. A. 2003. "Using a Retrospective Pre-Post Questionnaire to Determine Program Impact." *Journal of Extension 41(4),* See: www.joe.org

Deming, W. E. 1992. "Four-Day Seminars." The W. Edwards Deming Institute. Washington, D.C. http://deming.org/index. cfm?content=72

Dillman, D. A. 1978. *Mail and Telephone Surveys: The Total Design Method.* New York: John Wiley & Sons.

Dillman, D. A. 2000. *Mail and Internet Surveys: The Tailored Design Method, 2nd Edition.* New York John Wiley.

Dworkin, J. and A. R. Karahan. 2005. "Parents Forever: Evaluation of a Divorce Education Curriculum." *Journal of Extension 43(1).* See: www.joe.org

ECOP Personnel and Organizational Development Committee. Revised 10/2001. 1998. "The Implications of Increased Alternative Revenue in the Cooperative Extension System: Present and Future Strategies for Success." Extension Committee on Organization and Policy, Association of Public and and Land-grant Universities, Washington, D.C. See: http://podc.unl.edu/revenue.pdf (accessed April 16, 2009)

Eddy, E. D. Jr. 1957. *Colleges for Our Land and Time: The Land-Grant Idea in American Education.* New York, NY. Harper and Brothers.

Eidman, V. R. 1995. "The Continuing Search for Relevance in Agricultural Economics." *American Journal of Agricultural Economics 77(5).*

Emery, M. and C. Flora. 2006. "Spiraling Up: Mapping Community Transformation with Community Capitals Framework." *Community Development 37(1).*

Excellence in Extension Task Force. 2006. *Measuring Excellence in Cooperative Extension*. Extension Committee on Organization and Policy, Available online at: http://www.ca.uky.edu/ECOP/index.htm (accessed April 9, 2009)

Farner, S; M.E. Rhoads; G. Cutz; B. and Farner. 2005. "Assessing the Educational Needs and Interests of the Hispanic Population: The Role of Extension." *Journal of Extension 43(4),* Available at www.joe.org

Fehlis, C. P. 2005. "A Call for Visionary Leadership." *Journal of Extension 43(1).* See: www.joe.org

Fernandez-Cornejo, J. 2007. "Off-Farm Income, Technology Adoption, and Farm Economic Performance." *Economic Research Report No. ERR-36.* Available online at: http://www.ers.usda.gov/Publications/ERR36/ (accessed on April 8, 2009)

Fitzpatrick, J. L.; J. R. Sanders; and B. R. Worthen. 2004. *Program Evaluation: Alternative Approaches and Practical Guidelines, Third Edition.* Boston. Pearson Education, Inc.

Flora, C. B. 2000. "Extension and Place: Reducing Transaction Costs for Better Communities." *Rural Development News 24(3.)*

Flora, C. B.; J. L. Flora; and S. Fey. 2004. *Rural Communities: Legacy and Change, Second Edition.* Boulder, Colorado: Westview.

Ford, S.A. and E. M. Babb. 1989. "Farmer Sources and Uses of Information." *Agribusiness 5(5).*

Gillmor, D. 2006. *We the Media: Grassroots Journalism by the People, for the People.* O'Reilly Midea. Inc.

Gloy, B. A.; J. T. Akridge; and L. Whipker. 2000. "Sources of Information for Commercial Farms: Usefulness of Media and Personal Sources." *International Food and Agribusiness Management Review 3(2).*

Ha, T. 2008. Accountant for Minnesota Extension Food and Nutrition Program, *Personal Correspondence*, 2008.

Hachfeld, G. A.; D. B. Bau; C. R. Holcomb; J. N. Kurtz; J. W. Craig; and K. D. Olson. 2009. "Farm Transition and Estate Planning: Farmers' Evaluations and Behavioral Changes Due to Attending Workshops." Journal of Extension 47(2). See: www.joe.org.

Haines, A. L. 2002. "Blended teaching: Land Use Planning Education in Wisconsin and Lessons Learned." *Journal of Extension 40(5).* See: http://www.joe.org

Harding, P.A. and L.C. Vining. 1997. "Guest Editoral:The Impact of Knowledge Explosion on Science Education." *Journal of Research on Science Teaching. 34(10)*

Harriman, L. C. and R. Daugherty. 1992. "Staffing Extension for the 21st Century." *Journal of Extension 30(4). See*: www.joe.org.

Hewitt, B. 2008. "2007 Annual Report Statistical Summary." Cooperative State Research Education and Extension Service, United State Department of Agriculture, See; www.csrees.uisda.gov. (Accessed May 14, 2009).

Hildreth, R.J. and W. J. Armbruster. 1981. "Extension Program Delivery – Past, Present and Future: An Overview." *American Journal of Agricultural Economics 63(5).*

Hoag, D. L. 2005. "Economic Principles for Saving the Cooperative Extension Service." *Journal of Agricultural and Resource Economics 30(3).*

Hutchins, G. K. 1990. "Agent Specialization and the 4-H PRK Model." *Journal of Extension 28(4). See* www.joe.org

Hutchins, G. K. 1992. "Evaluating County Clustering." *Journal of Extension 30(1).* See www.joe.org

Hyde, A. C. 1992. "Implications of Total Quality Management for the Public Sector." *Public Productivity & Management Review 16(1).*

Ison, R. and D. Russell. 2000. *Agricultural Extension and Rural Development: Breaking Out of Traditions.* Cambridge: Cambridge University Press.

Iverson, S. V. 2008 "Now Is the Time for Change: Reframing Diversity Planning at Land-Grant Universities." *Journal of Extension 46(1).* See www.joe.org

Johnsrud, M. D. and Rauschkolb, R. S. 1989. "Extension in Transition: Review and Renewal." *Journal of Extension 27(1).* See: www.joe.org

Joint Task Force on Managing the Changing Portfolio of the Cooperative Extension System (JTF). 2006. "Final Report." Submitted to Extension Committee on Organization and Policy, APLU . Available on line at: http://www.csrees.usda.gov/qlinks/pdfs/portfolio_report.pdf (accessed April 7, 2009)

Kalambokidis, L. 2004. "Identifying the Public Value in Extension Programs." *Journal of Extension 42(2). See* www.joe.org

Kalambokidis, L. 2009. "Help Build Extension's Public Value!" University of Minnesota Extension, St. Paul, MN. See: http://www.extension.umn.edu/community/publicvalue.html (Accessed May 9, 2009)

Kellogg Commission on the Future of State and Land-Grant Universities. 1999. *Returning to Our Roots: The Engaged Institution*, National Association of State Universities and Land-Grant Colleges, Washington, D.C.

King. D.A. and M. D. Boehlje. 2000. "Extension: On the Brink of Extinction or Distinction?" *Journal of Extension 38(5)*. See www.joe.org

King, R.N. and Rollins, T.J. 1995. "Factors influencing the adoption of a nitrogen testing program." *Journal of Extension 33(4)*. See www.joe.org

Klein, T. K and G. W. Morse. 2007. "The Role of Business Planning Concepts in Balancing Mission and Financial Sustainability Responsibilities in Extension Programming." University of Minnesota, Department of Applied Economics, *Staff Paper No. 07-2*. See: http://ageconsearch.umn.edu/

Kotval, Z. 2003. "University Extension and Urban Planning Programs: An Efficient Partnership." *Journal of Extension 41(1)*. See www.joe.org

Krone, R. M. 1991. "Symposium Introduction: Total Quality Management: (TQM): Achievements, Potentials, and Pitfalls." *Journal of Management Science & Policy Analysis Vol. 8.*

Laughlin, K. M. and J. L. Schmitt. 1995. "Maximizing Program Delivery in Extension: Lessons from Leadership for Transformation." *Journal of Extension 33(4)*. See www.joe.org

Leeuwis, C. 2004. *Communication for Rural Innovation: Rethinking Agricultural Extension*. Wiley-Blackwell,

Leholm, A: L. Hamm; M. Suvedi; I Gray; and F. Poston. 1999. "Area of Expertise Teams: The Michigan Approach to Applied Research and Extension." *Journal of Extension 37(3).* See: www.joe.org

Leholm, A. G. and R.D. Vlasin 2006. *Increasing the Odds for High-Performing Teams: Lessons Learned.* Michigan State University Press.

Lochner, A; G. Allen; and D. Blyth. 2008. *Exploring the Supply and Demand for Community Learning Opportunities in Minnesota. University of Minnesota Extension.* Available online at: http://www.extension.umn.edu/distribution/youthdevelopment/00093.html.

Lott, S. and S. Chazdon. 2009. "The Effects of Leadership Development: Individual Outcomes and Community Impacts." *A U-Lead Impact Study*, Extension Center for Community Vitality, University of Minnesota Extension, St. Paul, MN.

Loveridge, S; C. Parliament; G. W. Morse; E. Templin; S. Engelmann; and R. Elmstrand. 1994. "Revitalizing Specialist-Agent Collaboration in Extension Education." *Choices 9(2).*

Martenson, D. 2002. "Creating the Base for Extension Priority Issues." *Journal of Extension 40(5).* See: www.joe.org

Martenson, D. 2005. *Vitality Task Force Report.* University of Minnesota Extension Service

Martin, M. V. (2002). "The roles of extension in agricultural economics departments." *Journal of Extension 40(5).* See: www.joe.org

Martinson, K.; M. Hathaway; J. H. Wilson; B. Gilkerson; P. R. Peterson; and R. Del Vecchio. 2006. "University of Minnesota Horse Owner Survey: Building an Equine Extension Program." *Journal of Extension 44(6)*. See: www.joe.org

McCorkle, D. A.; Waller, M. L.; Amosson, S. H.; Bevers, S. J.; and. Smith, J. G. 2009. "The Economic Impact of Intensive Commodity Price Risk Management Education." *Journal of Extension 47(2)*. See: www.joe.org

McDowell, G. R. 1985. "The Political Economy of Extension Program Design: Institutional Maintenance Issues in the Organization and Delivery of Extension Programs." *American Journal of Agricultural Economics* 67(4).

McDowell, G. R. 2001. *Land-Grant Universities and Extension into the 21st Century: Renegotiating or Abandoning a Social Contract.* Iowa State University Press, Ames, IA.

McDowell, George. 2004. "Is Extension an Idea Whose Time Has Come—and Gone?" *Journal of Extension. 42(6)*. See www.joe. org.

McGrath, D. M. 2006. "The Scholarship of Application." *Journal of Extension 44(2)*. See: www.joe.org

McGrath, D. M.; F. D. L. Conway; and S. Johnson. 2007. "The Extension Hedgehog." *Journal of Extension 45(2)*. See www. joe.org.

McKinsey Global Institute. 2008. *Accounting for the cost of US health care: A new look at why Americans pay more.* McKinsey & Company. See: http://www.mckinsey.com/mgi/publications/

Meyer, M. H. 1999. "Native Americans' Interest in Horticulture." *Journal of Extension 37(1)*. See www.joe.org

Miao, J. and W. Haney. 2004. "High School Graduate Rates: Alternative Methods and Implications." Boston College, See: www.bc.edu/research/nbetpp/statements/nbr5.pdf (accessed April 16, 2009)

Minnesota Extension Service, 1992. "Re-inventing the Minnesota Extension Service for the 21st Century: A Working Blueprint." University of Minnesota Extension Service, St. Paul, MN.

Mishra, Ashok K., and T. Park (2005). "An Empirical Analysis of Internet Use by U.S. Farmers." *Agricultural and Resource Economics Review* 34(2).

Mohr, E. 2009. "Groups rally to save Washington County 4-H funding." *Pioneer Press*, St. Paul, MN (May 20, 2009) See: http://www.twincities.com/localnews/ci_12416550 (Accessed on May 22, 2009)

Moore, M. H. 1995. *Creating Public Value: Strategic Management in Government.* Boston: Harvard University Press.

Morse, G. (ed.) 1990. *The Retention and Expansion of Existing Businesses: Theory and Practice in Business Visitation Programs.* Iowa State University Press, Ames.

Morse, G. 2005. "Scholarship and Promotions Task Force Charge." University of Minnesota Extension

Morse, G. 2006. "Minnesota Extension's Regional and County Delivery System: Myths and Reality." *Journal of Extension 44(4).* See: www.joe.org

Morse, G. and A. Ahmed. 2007. "Specialized Field Specialists" Believable Label or Oxymoron." *AAEA 2007 Selected Poster Paper*, American Agricultural Economics Association, See: http://ageconsearch. umn.edu/

Morse, G. and A. Ahmed. 2008. "Regional Extension Educator's Perception of University of Minnesota Extension's Regional/ County Model." Department of Applied Economics, University of Minnesota

Morse, G. and T. K. Klein. 2006. "Economic Concepts Guiding Minnesota Extension's New Regional and County Delivery Model." *Journal of Higher Education Outreach and Engagement 11 (4).*

Morse, G., and S. Loveridge, 1998. "Is It for Our Community?" in *Implementing Local Business Retention and Expansion Visitation Programs.* Northeast Regional Center for Rural Development, No. 72.

Morse, G. W., and D. Martenson. 2005. "'Best in the Business' Concept: Does this Apply to Extension?" University of Minnesota Extension Service, St. Paul, MN

Morse, G., and P. O'Brien. 2006. "Minnesota Extension's Mixed Regional/County Model: Greater Impacts Follow Changes in Structure." *Staff Paper PO6–7*, Dept. of Applied Econ., University of Minnesota.

Morse, G. W., and T. Smith. 1999. "What is Extension Entrepreneurship?" University of Minnesota Extension Service, See www.extension.umn.edu/ (accessed April 16, 2009)

Morse, R. S.; P. W. Brown; and J. E. Warning. 2006. "Catalytic Leadership: Reconsidering the Nature of Extension's Leadership Role." *Journal of Extension 44(2).* See: www.joe.org

Mueller, M. R. 1991. "Quality Means Results." *Journal of Extension, 29(1)*. See: www.joe.org

National Agricultural Statistical Service. 2007. *Farm Computer Usage and Ownership.* Sp Sy 9 (07), U.S. Department of Agriculture.

National Center for Social Entrepreneurs, 2006 http://www.missionmoneymatters.org/aboutus.html

NEP (Nutrition Education Programs). 2007. "Nutrition Education Programs: Fact Sheet." University of Minnesota Extension, http://www.extension.umn.edu/nutrition/ (accessed April 10, 2009)

Olson, K. D.; J. A. Skuza; and C. R. Blinn. 2007. "Extension Educators' Views of Scholarship and Performance Evaluation Criteria." *Journal of Extension 45(4)*. See: www.joe.org

Olson, M. 1971. *The Logic of Collective Action: Public Goods and the Theory of Groups.* Harvard University Press, Cambridge, Mass.

Organization for Economic Co-operation and Development, *Education at a Glance*. Paris, 2002.

Ortmann, G. F.; G. F. Patrick; W. N Musser; and D. H. Doster. 1993. "Use of Private Consultants and Other Sources of Information by Large Cornbelt Farmers." *Agribusiness 9(4)*.

Osborne, D. and T. Gaebler. 1992. *Reinventing Government: How the Entrepreneurial Spirit is Transforming the Public Sector.* Reading, MA, Addison-Wesley Publishing Co.

Osborne, D. and P. Hutchinson. 2004. *The Price of Government: Getting Results We Need in an Age of Permanent Fiscal Crisis.* New York, Basic Books.

Pardello, Renee, 2008. Area Program Leader in Natural Resources, Extension Center for Food, Agriculture and Natural Resources, University of Minnesota, November, 2008

Patrick, G. F. and S. Ullerich. 1996. "Information Sources and Risk Attitudes of Large Scale Farmers, Farm Managers and Agricultural Bankers." *Agribusiness 12(5).*

Patton, M. Q. 1985. "Extension Excellence in the Information Age." *Journal of Extension 23(2).* See: www.joe.org

Peters, J. and Jarvis, P. (Eds.). 1991. *Adult education: Evolution and Achievements in a Developing Field of Study.* San Francisco: Jossey-Bass

Peters, S. J. 2002. "Rousing the People on the Land: The Roots of the Educational Organizing Tradition in Extension Work." *Journal of Extension* 40(3). See: www.joe.org

Peters, S. J.; N. R. Jordan; M. Adamek; and T. R. Alter. (Eds.).2005. *Engaging Campus and Community: The Practice of Public Scholarship in the State and Land-Grant University System.* Dayton, OH: Kettering Foundation Press.

Poister, T. H. and G. T. Henry. 1994. "Citizen Ratings of Public and Private Service Quality: A Comparative Perspective." *Public Administration Review 54(2).*

Poister, T. H. and R. H. Harris. 1996. "Service Delivery Impacts of TQM: A Preliminary Investigation." *Public Productivity & Management Review 20(1).*

Putnam, R. D. 2000. *Bowling Alone: The Collapse and Revival of American Community.* Simon and Schuster, New York

Ratchford, C, B. 1984. "Extension, Unchanging, but Changing." *Journal of Extension 22 (5).* See: www.joe.org.

Rasmussen, W. D. 1989. *Taking the University to the People, Seventy-five Years of Cooperative Extension.* Ames, IA; Iowa State University Press.

Reynolds, C.R. and E. Fletcher-Janzen. 2007. *Encyclopedia of Special Education: Third Edition.* John Wiley and Sons.

Rockwell, S. K., J. Furgason; C. Jacobson; D. Schmidt; and L. Tooker. 1993. "From Single to Multicounty Programming Units." *Journal of Extension 31 (3).* See: www.joe.org

Rogers, E. M. 1995. *Diffusion of Innovations (Fourth Edition).* New York, NY. The Free Press.

Roling, N. G. 1988. *Extension Science: Information Systems in Agricultural Development.* Cambridge University Press

Roseler, D. K.; Chase, L. E; and McLaughlin, E.W. 1994. "Information Dissemination in Dairy Nutrition." *Journal of Extension 32(1).* See www.joe.org

Roth-Yousey, L; M. Caskey; J. May; and M. Reicks. 2007. "Modifying Beverage Choices of Preadolescents Through School-Based Nutrition Education." *Journal of Extension 45(3).* See: www. joe.org

Russell, T. L. 2008. *No Significant Difference Website.* http://www. nosignificantdifference.org/ (accessed April 9, 2009)

Russell, T. L. 2001. *The No Significant Difference Phenomenon. (Fifth Edition).* International Distance Education Certification Center.

Saunders, K. and T. Gallagher. 2003. "Decision-Making Styles: An Exploration of Preferences of On-and Off-Campus Faculty." *Journal of Extension 41(3).* See: www.joe.org

Savanick, M.A., and R. B. Blair. 2005. "Assessing the Need for Master Naturalist Programs." *Journal of Extension 43(3).* See: www.joe.org

Schafer, S.R. 2006. "Clientele Perceptions of the University of Wyoming Cooperative Extension Service Livestock Program." *Journal of Extension 44 (2).* See: www.joe.org

Schauber, A. 2001. "Talk Around the Coffeepot: A Key to Cultural Change toward Diversity." *Journal of Extension 39(6).* See: www.joe.org

Scheffert, D. R. 2007. "Community Leadership: What Does it Take to See Results?" *Journal of Leadership Education 6(1).*See: http://www.extension.umn.edu/community/00012.pdf

Schmitt, M. A. and T. Bartholomay. 2009. "Organizational Restructuring and Its Effect on Agricultural Extension Educator Satisfaction and Effectiveness." *Journal of Extension 47(2).* See: www.joe.org

Schnitkey, G.; M. Batte; E. Jones; and J. Botomogno. 1992. "Information Preferences of Ohio Commercial Farmers: Implications for Extension." *American Journal of Agricultural Economics* 74(2).

Seevers, B.; Graham, D.; Gamon, J.; and Conklin, N. 1997. *Education through Cooperative Extension.* New York: Delmar.

Senese, Richard, 2008. Extension Associate Dean, Extension Center for Community Vitality, University of Minnesota, November 2008.

Sensenbrenner, J. 1991. "Quality Comes to City Hall." *Harvard Business Review 69(2).*

Shonkoff, J. P. and S. J. Meisels. 2000. *Handbook of Early Childhood Intervention. Second Edition.* Cambridge. Cambridge University Press.

Slocum, W. L. 1969. "Specialization and Change in Extension." *Journal of Extension 7(3)* . See: www.joe.org

Smith, A . 1776. *An Inquiry into the Nature and Causes of the Wealth of Nations.* London: Methuen and Co. Ltd. Ed. Edwin Cannan 1904. Fifth Edition.

Smith, M. F. 1991. "Criteria for Judging Excellence." *Journal of Extension 29 (1).* See: www.joe.org

Smith. K. L. 1991. "Philosophy Diversions-Which Road?" *Journal of Extension 29(4).* See: www.joe.org

Sundquist, W. B. 2001. "A History of Agricultural and Applied Economics at the University of Minnesota, 1979-2000." Department of Agricultural and Applied Economics, University of Minnesota. See www.ageconsearch.umn.edu

Temple, J. A. & Reynolds, A. J. 2007. "Benefits and Costs of Investments in Preschool Education: Evidence from the Child-Parent Centers and Related Programs." *Economics of Education Review 26* (1).

Templin, L. 2006. "Conducting Market Research to Increase Program Demand and Financial Sustainability." Presentation at the National Association of Community Development Economic Professionals, February 15, 2006, San Antonio, Texas.

Thompson, O. E. and D. Gwynn. 1989. "Improving Extension: Views of Agricultural Deans." *Journal of Extension 27(1).* See www.joe.org

Thorstensen, H. 2009. "Extension Officials Say No Need to Panic About 4-H Programs." *Agri-News,* May 19, 2009 http://webstar. postbulletin.com/agrinews/298071549997518.bsp

Tucker, M. and T. L. Napier. 2002. "Preferred Sources and Channels of Soil and Water Conservation Information Among Farmers in Three Midwestern US Watersheds." *Agriculture Ecosystems & Environments*

Twigg, C. A. 1995. "Superficial Thinking: The Productivity Paradox." *Educom Review. 30(5).*

University Extension. 2009. *2009 ISU Extension Restructuring.* Iowa State University, Ames, Iowa, SP3514/09. http://www.extension. iastate.edu/Documents/restructuring/ExtRestructuringPlan09.pdf Accessed (May 20, 2009).

University of Minnesota Extension, 2007a. *2007 University of Minnesota Combined Research and Extension Annual Report.* submitted to Cooperative State Research, Education, and Extension Service, USDA.

University of Minnesota Extension, 2007b. "2007 Annual Master Gardener Highlight Report." http://www.mg.umn.edu/ pdfs/2007CountyReports.pdf (accessed April 10, 2009)

University of Minnesota Extension. 2007c. "Extension's Budget." St. Paul, MN. Revised 4/15/07.

University of Minnesota. No date. "Positive Youth Development among 4-H Youth Participants." Applied Youth Collaborative on Youth Development. http://www.extension.umn.edu/youth/00023.pdf (accessed April 8, 2009)

University of Minnesota Extension . 2008 "About 4-H." See: http://www.fourh.umn.edu/about.asp (accessed April 10, 2009)

University of Minnesota Extension Service. 1997. "Estimated Sources of Extension Funding, 1997-1998." St. Paul, MN 12/1/97

University of Minnesota Extension Service. 2001. "Policies and Criteria for Performance Evaluation and Promotion: of County and Cluster Academic Professionals of the University of Minnesota Extension Service." St. Paul, MN

University of Minnesota Extension Service. October 2006. *Program Business Plan Executive Summaries.* St. Paul, MN

University of Minnesota Extension Service, 2007 and 2008, Staff Directory, Online at: www.extension.umn.edu/staffdirectory/ (accessed December 3.2007 and Novermber 15,2008)

Ukaga, O. M.; M. R. Reichenbach; C. R. Blinn; D. M. Zak; W. D. Hutchinson; and N. J. Hegland. 2002. "Building Successful Campus and Field Faculty Teams." *Journal of Extension 40(2).* See: www.joe.org

U.S. Census Bureau. 2004. *Minority Links.* **See:** http://www.census.gov/pubinfo/www/hotlinks.html

U.S. Census Bureau. 2008. *The 2008 Statistical Abstract. See:* www. census.gov/compendia/statab/

USDA. 2007. The *Cooperative Extension Service Personnel Information System, Revised September 2007.* Cooperative State Research Education and Extension Service, USDA, Washington, D.C. See: http://www.csrees.usda.gov/about/ human_res/cesguide/ces_manual.pdf

USDA. 2008. *Salary Analysis of Cooperative Extension Service Positions, December 2007.* Cooperative State Research Education and Extension Service, USDA, Washington, D.C. See: http://www.csrees.usda.gov/about/human_res/pdfs/ report2007.pdf

Vlosky, R. P. and M. A. Dunn. 2009. "A Regional View of Extension Employee Perceptions of Scholarship in the Workplace." *Journal of Extension 47(1).* See: www.joe.org

Warner, P. D. and J. A. Christenson. 1984. *The Cooperative Extension Service: A National Assessment.* Westview Press,

Warner, P. D.; J. A. Christenson; D. A. Dillman; and P. Salant. 1996. "Public Perception of Extension." *Journal of Extension 34(4).* See www.joe.org

Washington, R. R. and Fowler, S. R. 2005. "Systematic Assessment of Resistance to Extension Organizational Change: Evidence from the Alabama Cooperative Extension Service." *Journal of Extension* 43(2). See: www.joe.org

Weiser, C. J. 1996. *The value of a university--Rethinking scholarship.* Oregon State University [On-line]. Available at: http://www. adec.edu/clemson/papers/weiser.html\

Weiser, C. J. and L. Houglum. 1998. "Scholarship Unbound for the 21st Century." *Journal of Extension 36(4).* See: www.joe.org

Werner, David. 2009. Assistant Dean and Chief Operating Officer, University of Minnesota Extension. Personal Correspondence.

Wheelan, C. 2002. *Naked Economics: Undressing the Dismal Science.* New York: W.W. Norton & Company.

Willis, W; S. Montgomery; and S. Blake. 2008. "Research Studies of the Expanded Food and Nutrition Education Program: 1989 to 2008." CSREES, USDA. Version 3 See: www.csrees.usda.gov/nea/food/efnep/pdf/research_studies.pdf

Willette, J. K. 2004. "Lawmakers angry with Extension." *Agri News* (March 9, 2004). See: http://webstar.postbulletin.com/agrinews/360725156209121.bsp

Wilmes, M. 2003. "Staff Named to Regional Centers." *Agri News* (Sept. 16, 2003) See: http://webstar.postbulletin.com/agrinews/74105352693460.bsp

Wise, G.; D. Retzleff; and K. Reilly. 2002. "Adapting Scholarship Reconsiders And Scholarship Accessed To Evaluate University Of Wisconsin Extension Outreach Faculty For Tenure And Promotion." *Journal of Higher Education Outreach and Engagement. 7(3).*

Wolf, S and D. Zilberman (Eds). 2001. *Knowledge Generation and Technical Changes: Institutional Innovation in Agriculture.* New York: Springer.

Index